The Craft of Governing

Patrick Weller, illustration by Kay Kane

The Craft of Governing

The contribution of Patrick Weller
to Australian political science

Edited by

Glyn Davis *and* R.A.W. Rhodes

LONDON AND NEW YORK

First published 2014 by Allen & Unwin

Published 2020 by Routledge
2 Park Square, Milton Park, Abingdon, Oxon OX14 4RN
605 Third Avenue, New York, NY 10017

Routledge is an imprint of the Taylor & Francis Group, an informa business

Copyright © Glyn Davis and R.A.W. Rhodes 2014

All rights reserved. No part of this book may be reprinted or reproduced or utilised in any form or by any electronic, mechanical, or other means, now known or hereafter invented, including photocopying and recording, or in any information storage or retrieval system, without permission in writing from the publishers.

Notice:
Product or corporate names may be trademarks or registered trademarks, and are used only for identification and explanation without intent to infringe.

Cataloguing-in-Publication details are available from the
National Library of Australia
www.trove.nla.gov.au

Index by Puddingburn
Set in 11/14 pt Berkeley Oldstyle by Midland Typesetters,
ISBN-13: 9781743319307 (pbk)

CONTENTS

A Foreword from Abroad by Peter Hennessy		vii
Part 1: Introduction		1
1	Remembering and Witnessing *Glyn Davis and R.A.W. Rhodes*	3
2	A Historian Encounters Politics: The Craft of Pat Weller *Glyn Davis and R.A.W. Rhodes*	11
Part 2: The Executive		31
3	Two Halves of a Whole: Kevin Rudd, Julia Gillard and the Politics of Prime Ministerial Vulnerability *Michelle Grattan*	33
4	Core Executives, Prime Ministers, Statecraft and Court Politics: Towards Convergence *R.A.W. Rhodes*	53
Part 3: The Public Service		73
5	Mandarins *Peter Shergold*	75

6	Pat Weller and the Machinery of Government: The Evolution of Research on Ministerial Portfolios *Evert Lindquist*	97

Part 4: **History and Biography** — 121

7	'It is not a biography . . .', it is executive practice *James Walter*	123
8	Administrative History as Biography *John Wanna*	144

Part 5: **International Organisations** — 163

9	Agents of Influence: Weller and Xu on International Organisations from a Public Policy Perspective *J.C. Sharman*	165
10	Learning a New Trick: International Civil Servants *Xu Yi-chong*	180

Part 6: **Comparative Government** — 203

11	Who rules? Democratic Versus Bureaucratic Leadership *John Kane and Haig Patapan*	205
12	Westminster Futures: Australia, Canada, New Zealand and the United Kingdom in Comparative Perspective *Robert J. Jackson*	227
13	Politics as Work: A Credo *Patrick Weller*	247

Pat Weller's Bibliography	264
Index	279

A FOREWORD FROM ABROAD

When it comes to observing the interplay of governing institutions and those who people them, there is a touch of James Bond about Pat Weller—nobody does it better. As my tribute to a formidable man and a good friend, I'd like to tap into a pair of interlocking themes which were very much a part of the intellectual compost that made us as young postwar Brits who were good at exams; the notion of an 'Establishment' and the rise of the meritocracy (i.e. people like Pat and me who benefited mightily from the ladders of opportunity which dropped down from Rab Butler's 1944 Education Act piloted through Parliament on a consensual basis by the UK World War II coalition government).

It was in the 1950s that the two themes started to fuse. In the early part of the decade, the historian A.J.P. Taylor and the political commentator Henry Fairlie revived the idea of a shadowy yet potent British Establishment which exerted an ill-defined and intangible yet real effect in public, political and cultural life. Writing at much the same time, the historical sociologist Michael Young was working on his *The Rise of the Meritocracy* which, given the surprising difficulty he encountered in finding a publisher, did not reach the shelves until 1958, and, eventually the pages of the dictionaries as a new social category-cum-concept.

First, that word, 'Establishment'. A slippery term it may be. But it's everywhere—has been now for decades. Yet its mercurial quality makes cartography near impossible, especially when it is used incontinently and imprecisely as in, 'Farage revels in shock to establishment', when UKIP enjoyed its surge in the 2013 UK local elections. To lump the Conservative, Labour and Liberal Democrat parties together as the 'establishment', instead of calling them the 'mainstream political parties', is absurd.

Some even doubt if the Establishment exists as more than a notion, a convenient piece of linguistic litter to deploy as a weapon of disdain, even denunciation, against individuals or clusters of people whom you don't care for, rather resent and wish to annoy.

Indeed, if the British Establishment does exist, part of me must be part of it. Why? I like clubs, especially the dining variety. I have a fondness for traditional institutions and, when Parliament is sitting, spend a good part of the week in the House of Lords, which many might see as the Establishment's debating chamber, canteen, broadcasting service and retirement home all folded into one.

The Establishment notion does matter because, generation upon generation, so many intelligent and not always so intelligent people have thought it does exist—though the form it takes mutates and is always and everywhere immensely stretching to capture and define. As Jeremy Paxman, who wrote a good book about it in 1990 called *Friends in High Places*, puts it: 'It is a harlot of a word, convenient, pliant, available for a thousand meaningless applications' (Paxman 1990: viii).

Yet the Brits have always had a certain idea of the Establishment as an inner track of people who fix things discreetly, unavowedly and unaccountably behind carefully painted camouflage, giving it a whiff of genteel conspiracy, perhaps even with a dash of insider trading in the influence market.

It's a concept that has stalked me for the bulk of my working life and, in return, I have stalked it, especially when I wrote about Whitehall for *The Times* in the 1970s and 1980s (when I first met Pat). In the mid-1970s, for example, the incomparable David Butler introduced me to his fabled seminar on British government and politics at Nuffield College, Oxford as, 'The gossip columnist of the British Establishment'. I was faintly irritated by this at the time—but had to admit there was something in it.

I acquired my first notion of the British Establishment by reading Anthony Sampson's second edition of *The New Anatomy of Britain* published in 1965, which I received as a sixth-form prize. In his first edition of 1962, Anthony set out to find it across a huge range of British institutions and professions. He reached an intriguing conclusion. Not only did he dismiss conspiracy theory Anthony declared that:

> My own fear is not that the 'Establishment' in Britain is too close, but that it is not close enough, that the circles are overlapping less and less, and that one half of the ring has very little contact with the other half. In particular, the hereditary Establishment of interlocking families, which still has an infectious social and political influence on the Conservative Party, banking and many industries, has lost touch with the new worlds of science, industrial management and technology, and yet tries to apply old amateur ideals into technical worlds where they won't fit. (Sampson 1965)

Anthony's thinking was very much a pre-echo of the theme Harold Wilson made his own when he became Leader of the Labour Party in 1963. Anthony was drawing, too, on that fifties revival of the Establishment notion by the powerful pens of A.J.P. Taylor and Henry Fairlie. Taylor took up the theme in what was then still called *The New Statesman and Nation* in August 1953 in a review of a new life of William Cobbett, a great denouncer of the Establishment which he called 'The Thing'. Taylor's opening paragraph remains, I think, a collector's item. 'Trotsky', he began,

> tells how, when he first visited England, Lenin took him round London and, pointing out the sights, exclaimed: 'That's *their* Westminster Abbey! That's *their* Houses of Parliament!' . . . By *them* he meant not the English, but the governing classes, the Establishment. And indeed in no other European country is the Establishment so clearly defined and so complacently secure. (Taylor 1953)

Henry Fairlie's assault on the British Establishment in his *Spectator* column was triggered by the foreign office finally admitting in September 1955 that the British diplomats, Guy Burgess and Donald Maclean, who had disappeared in May 1951 were, in fact, Soviet spies and were now living in Moscow. Fairlie convinced himself that the long, if now-broken, official silence was an example of 'the "Establishment" at work' and by 'Establishment' he meant not 'only the centres of official power—though they are certainly part of it—but rather the whole matrix of official and social relations within which power is exercised'.

Such matrices are very difficult to trace. In the mid-1980s I tried to pin at least part of the Establishment matrix down when I wrote a pamphlet for the Policy Studies Institute called *The Great and the Good: An inquiry into the British Establishment*. My cunning plan was to trace the tribe that had peopled the royal commissions and committees of inquiry since the Second World War and to pen mini-biographies of a trio of outstanding princes of greatness and goodness—John Anderson, Cyril Radcliffe and Oliver Franks, grand inquirers all.

This was a promising approach at the time but soon became less so as successive governments rather gave up on royal commissions and committees of inquiry reaching for task forces, czars, focus groups and relying on the newer think-tanks of varying quality that bloomed in the late seventies and early eighties.

The Establishment concept has been made still more elusive over the past quarter-of-a-century by the rise of a new political economy (the post-Big Bang City, hedge funds and all that) plus an electronic media explosion driven by new technologies alongside the grander newspapers not to mention the 'New Britain' 'young country again' banalities of 'New Labour' which held the field and tempted the credulous (as did something I could never grasp called the 'Third Way') for a few years after 1997.

These novel and sometimes proudly and avowedly *non*-Establishment developments intrigued me afresh last month. The first occasion was when Jonathan Hill, the leader of the House of Lords, opened the tributes to Lady Thatcher by recalling 1975 when, as Jonathan put it, 'this non-establishment figure had become leader of the establishment party'. Later in the month, while on a visit to my submariner friends at the Royal Navy's Faslane base in Scotland, a young officer, a touch nervously and apologetically, asked if I was a member of the Establishment. I replied: 'If it exists, I must be'. A couple of weeks later I was walking with a man I hugely admire, a scientist and a member of the House of Lords who has run great institutions and yet has that modesty and quietness that can go with great scientists—we were walking between his Club, the Athenaeum, and Brooks' where we were to join an ancient dining club to which we both belong that was once described as 'the Establishment at play'.

I told him about my submariner friend's question. 'I don't believe there is such a thing as "The Establishment"', he said. 'If Anthony Sampson went looking for it now he would find it completely different—in the hedge funds; in the media; the sort of people who would think that academia and the clubs are the *ancien régime*.'

My greatly admired friend set me thinking. I told him that 'If the Establishment does exist, you and I are part of it'. In fact, I reckon there is a permanent element at the core of the British Establishment—a kind of gyroscope—which embraces the grand old professions like the law and the civil service (though the latter is a tad tattered at the moment), the House of Lords (especially sections of the crossbenches where sit the former cabinet secretaries, law lords, chiefs of the defence staff and Queen's private secretaries), the Royal Society, the British Academy, the learned societies generally, the scientific and engineering institutions and the great medical colleges. The reach and clout of these institutions and tribes may fluctuate but they never truly fade let alone disappear.

While around this rooted, inner core there swirl the transient elements in the media, the financial world and the celebritocracy in constellations that vary generation upon generation. If I were planning a book on the British Establishment (which I'm not) that permanent/temporary divide would govern my approach.

That great lawyer, Cyril Radcliffe, was profoundly irritated by the Establishment notion. Writing in 1961, when the satire boom—*Beyond the Fringe* and all that—was getting going, he said: 'Let a fairy grant me my three wishes, I would gladly use them all in one prayer only, that never again should anyone using pen or typewriter be permitted to employ that inane cliché "Establishment"' (Radcliffe 1968: 175).

I fear Lord Radcliffe, up there in the Supreme Court in the sky, is doomed to disappointment. We Brits will never give up on the Establishment as a notion. It's deep within us. As a theme it's had more comebacks than the Rolling Stones. For all the angry words, the denunciations, the parodies and the conspiracy theories, we nurture it, almost cherish it. Why? Because quite apart from the fun of trying to determine who is or isn't in it in each generation, it brings fascination to the curious, a target for venting and, therefore, catharsis to the resentful and stimulus to the conspiracy theorist. The British Establishment, like that great cathedral of a British Constitution which it serves as a kind of flying buttress, is Cobbett's 'Thing'. But it's also a thing of magic, mystery and fantasy.

If I were to attempt a volume of 'Establishment studies' it would be suffused, too, by the twin theme of meritocracy. I first felt its punch not in Michael Young's pages (that came later), but in Anthony Sampson's second edition of *Anatomy*. There it was, 'meritocracy', with its attendant, fissile formula: IQ + Effort = Merit.

As a grammar schoolboy, a bit of a swot (though I tried zealously to conceal it) and, like Pat, a classic product of the 1944 Education Act, I smelled not a whiff of anything wrong with that equation. For me it was a manifesto and a self-evident truth, rather than a warning of what an unbridled pursuit of meritocracy could do.

Not until I finally read Michael Young's 1958 classic itself, with its fusion of historical sociology, satire, horizon-scanning and prediction, did I really inhale the fact that this was a warning—that Michael was foreseeing another and, once established, irreversible social and economic deprivation that would (my words; not Young's) rank alongside William Beveridge's famous 'five giants on the road to reconstruction' of his eponymous November 1942 report on social insurance—Ignorance, Idleness, Disease, Squalor and Want.

For Michael Young did see the possible rise of a society which valued intelligence above all other characteristics as a giant blemish—a society in which the intellectual haves regard the also-rans and the have-nots with disdain and without a trace of the *noblesse oblige* or compassion that had mitigated some of the worst effects of the *ancien régime* of an aristocracy based on blood and inherited wealth rather than the little grey cells. If we could rise—have risen—by our own efforts, hoisted-up by our synapses, so could they if they put their minds to it now that higher education is increasingly available; that was the meritocrats' cry.

Though I never asked him this, *The Rise of the Meritocracy* might have been Michael Young's way of projecting his 1950s thoughts about family and kinship in his other classic *Family and Kinship in East London*, (with Peter Willmott 1957) on to a national, a British scale through the medium of educational opportunity and reward. Could it be that Young, like George Orwell in his great 1941 essay, 'The Lion and the Unicorn', saw our country as 'a family with the wrong members in control'? Certainly he foresaw the wrong mix at the top in the new Establishment that would be created once the meritocracy in his fictional treatment of the post-1958 era had risen: a society lacking a sense of natural familyhood or real kinship between the meritocratic possessors and those they regarded as laggards or dullards.

A FOREWORD FROM ABROAD

Young does not draw directly on Orwell in *The Rise of the Meritocracy*. But there is one thinker/writer with a special eye for his country who suffuses his pages. For Michael Young's dystopic vision is partly built on the analysis of his great hero, the saintly economic historian, RH Tawney, in *his* classic work *Equality*, first written in 1931 and updated in 1952. Tawney believed that deep in our collective DNA as a country there was a potent, trumping molecule—a powerful, British impulse towards inequality. Tawney liked to quote Matthew Arnold on the capacity of we Brits to turn inequality into almost a religion.

One of Tawney's multiple prescriptions for a better society was ever-improving education for all—a view Michael, naturally, shared in full. But Young took a step further than Tawney in *The Rise*. Young, in the historical section of the book, with that gift for epigram he possessed, had summed up the long, grinding and never entirely complete shift from feudalism to capitalism, in these words: 'the soil grows castes; the machine makes classes' (Young 2011 [1958]: 14).

Such a society, Young declared in the speculative futurological section of *The Rise*, was 'a stratified society prepared by habit of mind to recognise a hierarchy of intelligence as soon as it was pointed out' (Young 2011 [1958]: 60).

And the 'pointing-out' in a Britain-to-come that Michael Young foresaw from the observation post of the mid to late 1950s was a trading nation and slipping former great power in the world that plumped for the unleashing of a full-throttle, unashamed meritocracy as a way of coping with global competition and reversing relative decline. It was, though Young did not put it this way, a matter of merit or die.

His argument was that economic and competitive pressures would finally force the UK to end what Young called '[t]he perpetual struggle between kinship and merit' in favour of merit. The old class system with its inefficiencies, absurdities and injustices would be swept away only to replace an aristocracy of birth with a meritocracy of talent that would, unlike the old 'ocracy' it was killing off, be both unreformable and irreversible until, that is, the riots and social disturbances of 2034 with which *The Rise* ends and during which Young's alter ego, the narrator, the social analyst of the book in whom Michael places his thoughts and words, is killed—the moral being that all seemingly triumphant 'ocracies', like all empires, light a fuse beneath themselves.

There is a fascinating book to be written, a work of special social cartography mapping meritocracy and linking it with the Establishment notion in Britain since the passage of the 1944 Education Act. I'm not a sociologist or a social scientist by trade or training, so I'm not the one to attempt it, but I hope somebody will. There are some natural cartographers of relative equality who are convinced that a good proportion of Michael Young's fears were realised.

Here, for example, is Roy Hattersley, the former deputy leader of the Labour Party, in August 2013 writing in *The Guardian* about 'A book that changed me'—Tawney's *Equality*. Some passages in *Equality* entranced me by their majestic certainty. Fifty years before meritocracy was elevated from Michael Young's satire on selfishness into a social system devoutly to be wished, Tawney dismissed equality of opportunity in two irresistible sentences. 'It is only the presence of a high degree of practical equality which can diffuse and generalise opportunities to rise. The existence of such opportunities . . . depends not only on an open road, but upon an equal start' (Hattersley 2013).

It's interesting that Roy Hattersley alights on the 1980s as the hour of the selfish version of meritocracy. In Michael Young's speculative forward look, the 1980s were key, though in his fantasy it was Croslandite democratic socialists in a future Labour government (people like Roy Hattersley) whom he foresaw as the propellants of the meritocracy or reversing economic decline school. Instead, it was a succession of Conservative governments fuelled by Mrs Thatcher's free-market economic liberalism that set out to do this.

Indeed, the very month the grammar school and Oxford educated lady became leader of the Conservative Party in February 1974, Margaret Thatcher, speaking to the Young Conservatives' Conference in Eastbourne, placed the principle of meritocracy firmly at the centre of her battle standard: 'I believe we should judge people on merit and not on background. I believe the person who is prepared to work hardest should get the greatest rewards and keep them after tax.' But how far did the meritocracy rise post-1979 when Mrs Thatcher stepped into Downing Street?

This question would surely be central to our scholarly cartographer of meritocracy and Establishment since 1945. What other ingredients might he or she inject? Here are a few thoughts:

1 The '-ocracies' that rose, which Young did not foresee (and this is not a criticism, he foresaw so much). For example, celebritocracy, the famous-for-being-famous phenomenon which has spread like a glittering rash since the late 1950s.

2   The rise of the media-ocracy is another with its attendant professions (if that is the right word) of public relations in all its varieties.
3   The rise of the consulting profession—political as well as management—with all the corrosion that has inflicted on the language of politics and government, which it would take a George Orwell to map.
4   Another rich mix would be the mingling of the Establishment notion with the idea of a rising meritocracy. The Establishment idea enjoyed a renaissance at much the same time as Michael Young was marshalling his thoughts on meritocracy, with celebrated pieces from A.J.P. Taylor in *The New Statesman and Nation* in 1953, and Henry Fairlie in the *Spectator* in 1955. 'The Establishment' is a slippery, imprecise notion. It's hinted at in that section of the *Oxford English Dictionary* definition of 'meritocracy' which spoke of 'a ruling or influential class of educated people'. But it would be fascinating to take a crack at the meritocratic rise in the grand old professions and wider.
5   Allied to the penetration of the meritocratic impulse is the thought raised about Michael Young's book by Daniel Bell in his analysis of meritocracy and equality in his fabled 1973 study of *The Coming of Post-Industrial Society*. Bell answered the question Michael Young posed by telling us that what we needed was, with a nice touch of J.S. Bach, 'a well-tempered meritocracy' which 'can be a society not of equals, but of the just' (Bell 2008 [1973]: 455).
6   Was Michael Young predicting the spread of what we would now call a 'knowledge economy'. If so, he was spot on—certainly over the past 30 years. The Work Foundation calculates that in the early 1980s 'knowledge workers' accounted for 31 per cent of the UK workforce in the early 1980s. This, they estimate, will have risen to 45 per cent by next year. Over the same period the skilled and semi-skilled proportion fell from 28 per cent to 18 per cent, and the unskilled from 16 per cent to 9 per cent. Has such an economy spawned what Ferdinand Mount, writing about Michael and *The Rise* in his fascinating book, *The New Few*, called a 'no hiding place society' in which the material criteria for success have trumped the kindlier, human ones?

Writing the history of one's own times has a special fascination and it's one Pat Weller and I share, not least the intangibles like 'meritocracy' and 'Establishment'. We would both, I think, empathise with the novelist Penelope Lively when she writes of 'the compelling matter of memory— the vapour trail without which we are undone' (Lively 2013). Long may it remain so.

Peter Hennessy

REFERENCES

Bell, D., 2008 [1973], *The Coming of Post-Industrial Society: A venture in social forecasting*, New York: Basic Books

Hattersley, R., 2013, *The Guardian*, August

Lively, P., 2013, *Ammonites and Leaping Fish: A life in time*, London: Penguin

Orwell, George, 1968 [1941], 'The Lion and the Unicorn: Socialism and the English Genius' in Sonia Orwell & Ian Angus (eds), 1968, *The Collected Essays, Journalism and Letters of George Orwell, Volume 2: My country Right or Left* (1940–1943), London: Secker & Warburg

Paxman, J., 1990, *Friends in High Places: Who runs Britain?*, London: Penguin

Lord Radcliffe, 1968, *Not in Feather Beds*, London: Hamilton

Sampson, A., 1965, *The Anatomy of Britain Today*, New York: Stein & Day

Taylor, A.J.P., 1953, book review, *The New Statesman and Nation*, August

Young, M.D. [1958] 2011, *The Rise of the Meritocracy*, New Brunswick, N.J: Transaction Publishers

PART 1

INTRODUCTION

1

REMEMBERING AND WITNESSING
Glyn Davis and R.A.W. Rhodes

What you end up remembering isn't always the same as what you have witnessed.

—Julian Barnes, *The Sense of an Ending*

Retirement and its accompanying *festschrift* provide an opportunity to reflect on a colleague's contribution over the years, and we do so in the following chapters. More than reflection, a *festschrift* is also a chance to indulge in both nostalgia and friendship. Of course, it would be inappropriate for any Australian, especially when one of us is of English extraction, to become fulsome let alone emotional. So, we remember two meetings.

Rod Rhodes first met Pat Weller at the University of Essex in the 1980s, but it was a fleeting encounter. Pat came to see Professor Anthony King, an Essex grandee, and I was the substitute. We next met at the Public Administration Committee annual conference held at York on 3–5 September 1990. Or to be more precise we met at 2:00 pm in the Deramore Arms in Heslington after the conference. I have the diary. The result was an invitation for me and my family to go to Australia, which we did in July and August 1991. I reciprocated by inviting John Wanna and Jenny Craik to the University of York for a sabbatical term. With Pat, in April 1992, they attended a workshop I organised on the 'Changing Role of the Executive in British Government'. We were to collaborate for the next twenty years.

We assembled a distinguished cast of characters, including Patrick Dunleavy, Peter Hennessy, and Philip Norton from the UK and Rudy Andeweg and Guy Peters from overseas as well as Pat and John. The Cabinet Office sent an observer. The aim was to identify key areas for future research and develop a research bid to the Economic and Social Research Council (ESRC).[1] It was a good workshop. So often at these events, discussion can be stilted but there was much bonhomie and badinage as well as intellectual debate. After one exchange in which the participants were clearly talking past one another, David Marsh made a brief yet pungent observation: 'we have just heard from the two people who have made the greatest contribution to British politics, Peter despite his complete lack of theory and Patrick despite his excess of it'. At the time, I had recently published my first paper on the British executive with Patrick Dunleavy (Dunleavy and Rhodes 1990). I did not realise that I would revisit executive studies throughout the rest of my career or, indeed, that many of these adventures would be with Pat Weller.

Glyn Davis met Pat Weller in late 1981 after driving from the University of New South Wales (UNSW) in Sydney to the Australian National University (ANU) in Canberra. I was a fourth year honours student interested in undertaking a PhD. There was a meeting arranged with a distinguished Professor at the Research School of Social Science (RSSS) at ANU, but someone suggested I also call by the Faculty of Arts.

As it turned out, Political Science in RSSS was deadly quiet. Office doors were closed, notice boards empty, the professor faintly bored by speaking to yet another potential doctoral recruit. By contrast, the Faculty was noisy and even chaotic, as students crowded the corridors and staff gathered in small knots to gossip. It was an easy choice but the chance was nearly lost when I was invited to meet senior lecturer Patrick Weller. I dutifully outlined my plan for a doctoral study of how prime ministers govern in a Westminster environment. Dr Weller smiled and said 'It's a good proposal. Indeed it's an excellent proposal, which is why I've just finished writing a book on the same topic. Got any other ideas?'

Fortunately, another project on the political independence of the Australian Broadcasting Corporation caught Pat's eye, and I was soon working in the office opposite. So, we developed a supervisor–student relationship that became a warm friendship over the decades that followed.

THE EVENTS

To talk to Pat about his impending retirement is to walk a tightrope over a deep canyon while he works the wind machine. Lacking a firm date, we had had no choice but to follow our best 'guesstimate' and we opted for his 70th birthday. We arranged a workshop entitled the 'The Craft of Governing' to which we invited his co-authors and other experts in his several fields of expertise. It was held at the Sir Samuel Griffith Centre, Nathan Campus, Griffith University, on 9 August 2013. We covered his major areas of research; prime ministers and cabinet, the public service, history and biography, international organisations, and comparative government. The book that follows is organised by these categories. The book will be presented to him on 13 September 2014, the day Pat reaches his eighth decade.

Work is important but we did not travel to Brisbane just to discuss Pat's writing. There was also the dinner. We held it in the Webb Centre on Southbank with the Brisbane River and the CBD providing a striking backdrop. There were many highlights and we can only note a few. Thérèse Rein, wife of then Australian Prime Minister Kevin Rudd and a successful international business leader in her own right, gave a charming speech about Pat Weller as a teacher and inspiration to students. Dr Kay Kane not only drew the line drawing that graces the frontispiece of this book but also painted Pat's portrait. It was presented at the dinner. Then, with much laughter, John Kane continued a tradition begun on Pat's 60th birthday party with Beatlesque tributes, leading a group named for the occasion Patrick Weller's Only Part-Time Band. On this occasion, he accompanied himself on acoustic guitar and sang a witty ditty that played much on the political biography of Kevin Rudd Pat has been writing for some years:

> We all know that in this life all good things must end
> Comes a time to put away the strife, accept what fate may send
> Well I know a feller, name of Pat Weller who's planning to retire
> Give up his labour, pack up his sabre and leave the field of fire
>
>> (Chorus)
>> Oh I'll believe it, I will believe it
>> Because I know life must go on
>> But I'll believe it, I will believe it
>> I will believe it when he's gone
>
> No more to haunt the corridors of N72
> No more to trouble Michael Powell, as he was liable to

Griffith shall free him and I can just see him strumming on a lyre
Or doing the gardening, his arteries hardening, just waiting to expire

> (Chorus)
> (Bridge)
> Oh well you know it's not gonna happen, too much left to do
> ARC grants to be winning, that walk to Katmandu

But he'll have time to take another look at prime ministerial trends
And time to finish that book, you know the tale that never ends
Of Kevin 07 and Kevin 11 and Kevin once again
The rise and fall, and fall and rise, and fall of a PM

> (Chorus)

The former guitarist of New World surpassed his own greatest hit, 'Tom-Tom Turnaround' (1971)[2], but we do not anticipate a new recording contract any time soon. The laughter at the dinner was as characteristic of the event as the appreciation expressed of Pat's research at the workshop.

SUMMARY OF CHAPTERS

Glyn Davis and Rod Rhodes open the volume with a biography of Pat Weller as political scientist and contemporary political historian. Their chapter traces Weller's unfolding academic career, focusing on his key publications and projects. The chapter closes with a discussion of the intellectual themes running through his work, notably historical imagination, Realpolitik as his emploted explanatory framework, and the importance of comparative and international studies.

Part 2 of the book focuses on the role and study of the executive in Westminster systems of government. Michelle Grattan's chapter pays homage to Weller's work on prime ministers, noting its pioneering nature and continuing relevance. Then, she explores the recent tumult surrounding the governments of Kevin Rudd and Julia Gillard, suggesting each had skills the other needed. While Rudd and Gillard were not the only Australian prime ministers forced from the position by their own party, their particular experiences offer useful lessons into the workings of executive government. She concludes Rudd and Gillard were both victims of each other and of themselves.

Rod Rhodes discusses the several approaches to studying executive government. He observes that Pat Weller has made a major contribution to Australian prime ministerial and cabinet studies, filling key gaps. He then builds on Weller's contribution by exploring ways to extend the study of executive government. He argues there has been a convergence around the idea of 'court politics', and discusses the strengths and weaknesses of this focus.

Part 3 of the book turns to the study of the public service. Peter Shergold draws on his experience as a former head of the Department of Prime Minister and Cabinet for the Australian Government between 2003 and 2008. He presents a lively analysis of senior public servants—the 'mandarins' of popular parlance. He explores the role mandarins play in the craft of democratic governance. Throughout the chapter, he argues that the potency of Weller's work comes from its interdisciplinary character, where insights from political science, administrative studies and history are mobilised, and his extensive interviewing of the key players. While Shergold agrees with Weller's observation that, while the power of senior public servants is in decline in Australia, nonetheless they remain crucial to effective government.

Evert Lindquist provides a detailed treatment of how prime ministers have managed the machinery of government in Australia and across different Westminster jurisdictions. The chapter reviews key research in the field, situates Weller's work and identifies areas for further study. He argues that a characteristic of Pat's work is the dialectic between '*practitioner logic*, which he has always taken seriously and always tried to ascertain and convey to others; and *academic logic*, which sought to chronicle, measure, and explain decisions at varying levels of analysis.' As a result Lindquist suggests, Pat should be understood as a 'pracademic'.

Part 4 of the book focuses on Pat's historical and biographical writing. Jim Walter's chapter highlights the importance of several types of biography in Weller's research; prosopography, institutional biography as well as more conventional political biographies. All share a characteristic. They do not simply tell a chronological life story but seek to answer questions about how government works; these works pay 'exemplary attention to what political actors actually do'.

John Wanna's chapter discusses Pat's work on Australian administrative history. He reviews the state of the art in administrative history in Australia before locating Pat's work in this broader field. Weller's administrative histories focus on two core political institutions; the Commonwealth's Department of Prime Minister and Cabinet and the Queensland Premier's Department. Although the subject matter is organisational structures and institutional resources, Weller never forgets that politics cannot be removed from the interplay of people, institutions and events. His administrative histories are always part of this broader struggle in which people make history.

Part 5 of the book focuses on Pat's work on international organisations. Jason Sharman reviews the books on the World Trade Organization, the World Bank and other international institutions, arguing Pat's main contribution is to transplant insights from the study of domestic public policy to international organisations. Sharman places this work in the broader International Relations literature. He discusses the prospects for 'International Public Policy' or 'Global Public Policy' as a subfield that applies the theory and methods of domestic studies of public bureaucracies to the institutions and processes of global governance.

Xu Yi-chong, Weller's co-author in the study of international organisations, points out that the existing literature on international organisations substantially ignores the work and influence of international civil servants. We do not know what they do, how they do it and with what consequences. Her work with Pat addresses these gaps in our knowledge. Xu examines different approaches to understanding the work and place of international civil servants. She identifies and discusses some of the specific influences on their behaviour: organisational structure, mission and culture, career structures, skills, and legitimacy.

Part 6 of the volume discusses Pat's work in the subfield of comparative government. John Kane and Haig Patapan, two long-time colleagues of Pat in the Centre for Governance and Public Policy, Griffith University, discuss the intersecting themes of leadership and administration. They examine the nature of leadership in, and by, public bureaucracies. They ask what challenges bureaucratic leadership presents to democratic elected leadership. After presenting a brief history of the topic, Kane and Patapan focus on the way democratic leaders have taken up the challenge of righting the balance of authority and control between democratic and bureaucratic leaders. They explore the unintended consequences of managerialist reforms. They conclude that the tension between bureaucratic and democratic authority is perennial. It may be more or less well managed but can never be definitively resolved.

Bob Jackson analyses the 'Westminster futures' of Australia, Canada, New Zealand, and the United Kingdom, taking Pat's work on *Comparing Westminster* as his launching pad. Jackson discusses the internal and external challenges to governments in Australia, Canada, New Zealand,

and the United Kingdom. The internal challenges include: the limits on central government authority and control, the declining importance of party majorities, quirks of each electoral system, and decentralisation and federalism. The external challenges include: evolving technology, changing international norms and dynamics, and the tendency for many problems to have both a domestic and international dimension, especially around security. Jackson concludes the chapter by discussing the capacity of Westminster systems to meet these challenges.

In the final chapter, Pat discusses significant influences on his work, most notably: Lindsay (1933); Loveday and Martin (1966); Heclo and Wildavsky (1974); and Caro (1982). He then turns to the question of how we understand politics and defends the proposition that 'Politics is not, and cannot be, a natural science, because the core of our subject is the uncertainty and contingency that pervades political life'. Despite the 'unscientific' nature of the subject, research still matters. If we write clearly, we can make sense of an issue, inform, persuade, debate and provoke. Yet we are at best part of a process of knowledge creep, since 'decisions are not ours to make'. As Dirty Harry said, 'a man's got to know his limitations'. Political scientists are no exception; 'no one, absolutely no one, could have anticipated the combination of *Tampa* and 11 September'.

We opened with a quote from the elegiac musings of Julian Barnes on memory and death. We have all witnessed different events and the same events differently. In this book, we remember our stories about Pat with all the frailties of memory. None of us know what, if anything, in the work discussed here will interest future generations. We hope, but we cannot expect. Amid such uncertainty, though, we have witnessed a craftsman at work, and all our work is the better for studying his skill and discussing his insights.

ACKNOWLEDGEMENTS

A venture that involves both a workshop and an edited collection inevitably incurs many debts. Angela MacDonald organised the workshop and the dinner with unflagging skill and enthusiasm ably assisted by Tracee McPate (Griffith) and Toni Andon (Melbourne). The workshop was funded by: the Vice Chancellor of Griffith University, Ian O'Connor; the Pro Vice Chancellor of Business at Griffith, Michael Powell; the Deputy Dean of the Australian and New Zealand School of Government (ANZSOG), Peter Allen; and the Director of the Centre for Governance and Public Policy (CGPP), Haig Patapan. It would not have happened but for their support. An unintended consequence of the workshop was the opportunity for Vice Chancellor Ian O'Connor to show off the innovative, 6-star green-rated Sir Samuel Griffith Centre building at the heart of the Nathan campus. We thank him for suggesting we use the building. When the idea of the workshop was first mooted, it was still under construction. It provided a splendid setting.

Patrick Gallagher, the Chairman of Allen & Unwin, was a staunch supporter from the outset, no doubt as recompense for the many thrashings he gave his namesake on the golf course. Kylie Westaway took efficient care of the day-to-day business. We are grateful for their support.

Our task as editors was helped greatly by the careful work of Dr Gwilym Croucher, who coordinated the many versions of chapters and produced elegant summaries of key themes. We appreciated also the copy editing work of Helen Koehne, and the noteworthy promptness of our contributors. Last, we thank Pat's past and present colleagues for their encouragement, support, advice and criticism. We know that convention dictates that responsibility for the final product lies with us. On this occasion, we are happy to share it widely.

NOTES

1   The Proceedings of the Conference were submitted to ESRC under the title *Changing Role of the Executive in British Government* (July 1992) with a report to the Research Programmes Board of the ESRC entitled *The Changing Nature of the British Executive: A summary report.*
2   See <http://en.wikipedia.org/wiki/New_World_(band)>.

REFERENCES

Barnes, Julian, 2011, *The Sense of an Ending*, London: Cape
Caro, Robert A., 1982, *The Years of Lyndon Johnson: The path to power*, New York: Alfred A. Knopf
Dunleavy, P. & Rhodes, R.A.W., 1990, 'Core Executive Studies in Britain', *Public Administration*, vol. 68, no. 1, pp. 3–28
Heclo, H. & Wildavsky, A., 1981 [1974], *The Private Government of Public Money*, 2nd edn, London: Macmillan
Lindsay, Philip, 1933, *King Richard III: A chronicle*, London: Ivor Nicholson & Watson
Loveday, Peter & Martin, Allan, 1966, *Parliament Factions and Parties: The first thirty years of responsible government in New South Wales, 1856–1889*, Melbourne: Melbourne University Press

2

A HISTORIAN ENCOUNTERS POLITICS: THE CRAFT OF PAT WELLER[1]

Glyn Davis and R.A.W. Rhodes

I rediscovered what writers have always known (and have told us again and again): books always speak of other books, and every story tells a story that has already been told.

—Umberto Eco, *Postscript to The Name of the Rose*

We have a simple aim; to provide a brief intellectual biography of Patrick Moray Weller (from now on Pat), political scientist and contemporary historian. We do not provide a life history but describe his unfolding academic career. Along the way, we discuss key works before, finally, identifying the intellectual themes that run through his many projects. We tell our story of his story, and this book speaks of his books.

EARLY DAYS

Born amid tumultuous events, educated at ancient schools and universities in the heart of England, it was no surprise that history fascinated the young Pat Weller. The turn to politics was less predictable. It led him to use the historical imagination to think about how institutions work; to focus on the intersection of politics, policy and institutions. It led to the craft of Pat Weller.

On 13 September 1944, as the Western Allies fought their way into France in the sixth year of a world war, Pat Weller was born into a medical family. His parents met at Great Ormond Street Hospital, where Stanley (Sam) was a doctor and Irene a nurse. Sam was the son of English missionaries in China, Irene the daughter of a cleric. They served through the London Blitz and married in August 1941.

Sam Weller joined the Black Watch regiment as a doctor. He would serve with the regiment at El Alamein, in Sicily, and in Normandy, and be wounded twice in action. After her first son, Robin, was born in March 1943, Irene stayed with her parents in the coastal town of Sidmouth in Devon, where her father held a parish. Patrick Moray was born in nearby Exeter soon after. It would be late 1946 before Sam Weller was demobbed, and the family did not move into its own home in South London until 1950. Two daughters completed the family.

Pat recalls a 'very English' upbringing—the kindergarten divided children for games into groups labelled Oxford and Cambridge. At a local prep school, he was in the top form for over two years, preparing for the scholarship exam for public school. Here Pat first encountered the study of history through a book on Richard III, written ironically by an Australian author (Lindsay 1933). Nearly 60 years later he could still recall the argument and powerful closing images of the book—Richard the capable administrator and popular young king, Henry VII, by contrast, 'a usurper, murderer and tyrant'. When he won a school prize at the age of twelve, and was offered a choice of books, Pat immediately asked for another historical study: Clements Markham's *Richard III: His Life and Character* (1906). The master looked askance at the suggestion and gave him a book by Arthur Ransome. A portrait of Richard III has hung above Pat's desk for the past 50 years.

The romance of history now held Pat's full attention. In his early teenage years, Pat sought out both formal studies of English history and a wide array of historical novels, from stories of empire to books about Russia and the United States. Aged thirteen, he won a scholarship to King's School Canterbury, a school then approaching its 1350th anniversary, and pursued history through to A levels and university entrance. Pat enjoyed the school, studying in the precincts of Canterbury Cathedral, walking past the tomb of the Black Prince, and playing rugby union badly as he prepared for the Cambridge entrance exams.

But time and chance intervened. Cambridge held all its entrance exams in December. Oxford split them into three groups. As insurance, in case he failed to get a place at Cambridge, Pat looked at the Oxford January options. He noticed the Stapledon scholarships offered at Exeter College. They were named after the founder of the college, Walter Stapledon, bishop of Exeter, and were open to students born or educated in the West Country counties. Because of the war, his mother had been living in Devon when Pat was born, and he was eligible to apply. He did not initially get a place at Cambridge, so he worked over Christmas for the Oxford exams. In the event, Pat was offered a place at Jesus College the day he was expected to go to Oxford. He decided to go anyway, sat the papers and met with Exeter Rector and Professor of Government Sir Kenneth Wheare (a former Rhodes Scholar from the University of Melbourne). With a place at Cambridge already guaranteed, Pat went into the interview relaxed and assured. He emerged with a Stapledon Exhibition in history at Exeter College, which he accepted. Sir Kenneth would become the first Australian appointed as Vice-Chancellor at Oxford, while Pat was an undergraduate.

Looking back, Pat could see that Oxford aligned well with his intellectual concerns. Though arriving at Exeter by happy accident, he understood retrospectively that the history syllabus at 'Cambridge is much more socio-economic and Oxford is much more political, which suits me down to the ground because that's what I was interested in'. He arrived in 1963, soon after turning nineteen. Exeter, founded in 1314, was a middle-ranking college in the Oxford hierarchy.

History teaching at Oxford followed a long-established pattern. In the first term, the 500 or so history students studied the same course, with preliminary exams after just eight weeks of study. Provided they passed, students had to write four compulsory papers: three on English history, and one on political thought. They then had to select another five from a series of choices on European and constitutional history. Going to lectures was optional in those days. Everyone relied on reading books. The key learning proceeded through the tutorial system—weekly meetings with tutors, writing up to twelve essays during the eight-week term. Essays were read to the tutor and discussed, usually with just one or two students present. In Pat's experience, the incentive to attend lectures was modest. A poor lecturer could find his 500 students quickly reduced to less than ten students attending regularly. Occasionally Pat would go to lectures with less than five students in the audience. Yet writing weekly essays and discussing them with tutors provided him with solid writing and analytical capacity.

At Oxford, Pat read history exclusively and took no courses in present-day political science, even though it would later become his disciplinary identity. Nonetheless, Pat learnt some politics from his lecturers and guest speakers. A few lecturers proved mesmerising. Pat can still imitate Isaiah Berlin on Machiavelli, the heavy Russian accent ploughing through the long list of historical understandings of this key Renaissance thinker, and can recall the power of E.H. Carr's *What is History?* (1961).

Though Pat never studied politics, his interest in it was constant. A year earlier Britain had held its collective breath as the USA and Russia confronted each other over Cuba. Then, in his first term, President John Kennedy was assassinated. Everyone could remember where they were when they heard the news. The next day, in a moment organised by word of mouth alone, hundreds turned up in the Radcliffe Square, stood silent for two minutes and dispersed with not a word spoken. At the national level, the long-term Conservative government was tottering, undermined by sex scandals and divisions. An outburst of satire on stage and television mercilessly excoriated political behaviour. 'Beyond the Fringe' and 'That Was the Week that Was' were bitter and funny, and broke with the conformist tedium of the 1950s. At the local level, Pat had his first experience of election rigging, the willing pawn in the ambitions of a colleague to be elected president of the Oxford Union Liberal club. He also joined the Oxford Union, where he would listen to the debates by revolutionaries including Tariq Ali, future Tory grandees such as Douglas Hogg, and Jonathan Aitkin, or visiting speakers including Malcolm X.

At Oxford, there were no examinations or assessments after the first eight weeks of the first year until the end of third year. The final examinations lasted a week, with two exams a day. The finals were an exhausting end to studying at Oxford, a test of physical stamina as well as learning. For those seeking a first-class degree, there was a further exam required. On the advice of his tutor, Pat chose not to sit it. When he returned to Oxford, eight weeks after the final exam for his viva, Pat learned he had secured a Bachelor of Arts with second-class honours. His viva procedures suggested he was being considered for a first. Had he sat that extra paper, his result might have been different. Nonetheless, Pat was happy with his degree classification.

Once again, fate rather than planning dictated the next moves. His degree complete, Pat did not think about further study. Indeed, at this point he had not considered a university career. School teaching was his preference, and he had places at Bristol and Oxford to begin a Dip. Ed. But staying at university for a further year to secure a diploma was not an enticing prospect. During university vacations, Pat had enjoyed travel in the United States and Europe, and decided to spend some more time abroad. One Saturday in London, he set out to explore his prospects. As he enjoyed retelling the story in later years, Australia House was open while Canada House was closed. So, he signed up as a ten pound migrant bound for Australia, with a promise to spend at least two years in his new home. It was a big step with no compelling logic beyond the freedom of youth and a curiosity about the rest of the world. The one point he did check was that he would not be eligible for the national service draft, recently introduced by the Liberal government.

On 30 July 1966, the day that England won the World Cup, Pat Weller graduated from Oxford, and three months later he caught a plane to Sydney, arriving the day Galilee won the Caulfield Cup. He quickly found temporary work as a judge's associate, standing in for a student who was completing his law exams, and sought a teaching job. When the opportunity arrived, it required a move to Albury, and a grammar school was where Pat began teaching in early 1967. He had no teaching qualifications, but to hold a degree was sufficient for Albury Grammar at the time. It proved an unsatisfying assignment, and soon Pat began looking for a new role. He applied for a lectureship in History at the University of Tasmania and, although unsuccessful, was offered a tutorship. By August 1967, Pat had packed his growing library into an old car, said farewell to Albury, and was heading south.

Now based in Hobart, Pat became an historian again. He was tutoring ten hours a week in European history and twentieth-century Australian history. The University of Tasmania was small and friendly, often with only a few students in each class. Many were mature aged—when Pat came to teach a third-year class of three students on World War II, he found himself the only person in the room who had not fought in the conflict.

With his appointment to the University of Tasmania came the first opportunity to do research. Professor Gordon Rimmer, head of the history department, wrote institutional histories and would contribute many articles to the *Australian Dictionary of Biography* on pioneering

Tasmanian figures. Yet he judged Tasmanian history too narrow, and encouraged Pat to look more broadly for research topics. To get him started, Rimmer recommended Pat read a recent study by Peter Loveday and Allan Martin (1966) on parliament, factions and parties in New South Wales. The book created a lively argument about the emergence of the first political parties in the original Australian colony. It is now recognised as the standard work on the topic, an important contribution to explaining why transitory factions were supplanted by more enduring political organisations with programs and internal rules. Pat found the work fascinating, and the Reader in History, Michael Rose, suggested he meet Allan Martin, a fellow historian now based at La Trobe University.

When Pat visited La Trobe, Martin was tied up in meetings. So, Pat met with Peter Loveday instead. Peter trained in history and philosophy at the University of Sydney and, from 1968, was Senior Fellow in Political Science at the Australian National University (ANU). Loveday explained the method underpinning the book on factions and parties and suggested Pat reproduce the study for Tasmania, by counting votes in the Tasmanian lower house, and recording the results on computer punch cards.

The suggestion would lead to Pat's first solo piece of research, with his first articles published in 1971 in *Labor History*, and the *Papers and Proceedings of the Tasmanian Historical Research Association*. Though the subject concerned politicians, the approach was informed by history. It set a direction that would become a defining characteristic of Pat's career.

After a year in Hobart, Professor Rimmer took Pat aside to talk about career options.

'Do you want to be an academic?' he asked.

'Yeah.'

'Then go to the ANU and do a PhD fulltime.'

Peter Loveday agreed to be supervisor, with political scientist Don Aitkin as second supervisor, and the ANU provided a scholarship. There was some tussle between the history and the political science programs about the most appropriate location, but in February 1969 Pat began his thesis in political science at the Research School of Social Science (RSSS). He would submit his doctoral thesis exactly three years later, a political historian who had never taken an undergraduate course in the American science of politics. Whether this omission is a strength or weakness is a moot point.

Pat's time in Canberra was shared with a young family. In late 1967, Pat attended the annual University of Tasmania game between the men's rugby team and the women's hockey side. There he met Bronwyn Stevens, a Victorian completing her arts degree at the University. She was playing in the game while Pat carried the drinks. They married the following year, and shared two sons, born nine years apart. Bron Stevens would pursue her own career as a political scientist, teaching and writing on Australian politics and international relations at several institutions, most recently at the University of the Sunshine Coast. Though usually working on their own, at times Bron and Pat published together, either on large institutional histories or when an item of household discussion suggested a quick commentary.

STARTING OUT

On graduating from the ANU in early 1972, Pat had accepted a teaching position at the Riverina College of Advanced Education in Wagga Wagga, but was keen to return to Canberra. Meantime, Gough Whitlam had tired of scholars wanting to consult the Australian Labor Party (ALP) caucus minutes held in his office and asked Professor Robert Parker at the ANU if he could appoint an editor to oversee their publication. Pat's background in political party history made him the ideal candidate. In early 1973, he returned to RSSS, and began the challenging task of bringing order and coherence to records of Labor Party parliamentary meetings dating back to Federation.

Though access to Labor caucus minutes was straightforward, it required two years to track down all the federal executive records, some held in private hands since the Labor Party split acrimoniously in 1955.[2] Pat and his research assistant, Beverley Lloyd, slowly pieced together an almost complete set of documents. The three-volume *Caucus Minutes* would be published by Melbourne University Press in 1975, and remains a key resource for historians interested in early Labor history. The federal executive minutes were published three years later (Weller and Lloyd 1978).

With the caucus minutes' project nearly completed, Pat considered his next research assignment. At first, he proposed to work on political parties again, but Peter Loveday and others saw diminishing returns from further work. They suggested Pat 'think on', so he returned to a question he had been mulling over for some time: how does national government make decisions? Although a much-studied topic in other countries, and promoted by visiting scholars to the ANU such as David Butler

(1973), the workings of the cabinet and the senior public service had attracted only limited academic attention in Australia.[3] This focus on the intersection of politics, public policy and the institutions of government, on the Realpolitik of life at the top, became a lifelong interest and a second defining characteristic of Pat's work.[4]

Not everyone saw merit in pursuing the subject. Professor of Political Science, and former Serjeant-at-Arms of the federal Parliament, Gordon Reid warned that no information would be available: 'you won't get past the front door, so it's pointless', was his verdict. Pat was willing to try.

He found allies among younger scholars, in particular Geoff Hawker and R.F.I. (Bob) Smith, who had graduated from ANU in the late 1960s with doctorates in political science. They approached political leaders and public servants—and found themselves pushing on an open door. Senior players wanted to explain their understanding of the system, and to share information. In a small city such as Canberra, it was easy to turn personal connections into structured interviews. During the 1974 election campaign, when Pat and Geoff talked about caretaker conventions with Sir Geoffrey Yeend, later Secretary of the Prime Minister's Department, their view that it was possible to produce an informed analysis of public administration in the Commonwealth government was confirmed.

Appointed to a five-year research position in political science at RSSS from 1974, Pat focused on central government institutions. He published both alone and with several collaborators, opening new topics of study. With James Cutt, for example, Pat examined the first study of federal financial agencies. His research included conversations with Sir Frederick Wheeler, the legendary Treasury Secretary once described as 'a master of guerrilla warfare in the bureaucracy'.[5] Weller and Cutt (1976) not only described the Treasury's confidence in its judgement, but showed the tenuous nature of administrative power. They reported senior ministers' frustrations with the Treasury. Indeed, Prime Minister Malcolm Fraser was in the middle of an epic battle with the Treasury about spending cuts, while Treasury refused to provide an adequate analysis of policy options. There was such a breakdown of trust that the prime minister decided, just as Pat's book was about to be published, to split the Treasury Department and create a separate Department of Finance to manage the annual budget process. Sir Frederick protested vigorously, but to no effect.

Sometimes described as public administration, and sometimes as public policy, this focus on the intersection of politics, policy and institutions became an enduring theme in Pat's work. With ANU colleagues Bob Smith and Geoffrey Hawker, Pat would publish many articles and edited books on public servants, interest groups and decision-making. Work with the Coombs Royal Commission into Commonwealth administration provided first-hand insight into government, as did a year on secondment to the Public Service Board as Director of Research in 1978–79.

Pat's work grew closer to international academic debates on public policy. Dick Neustadt (1960) was a long-standing and admitted influence. Now Pat added Graeme Allison (1974) and Hugh Heclo and Aaron Wildavsky (1981) to his list of luminaries to read, with Peter Self (1972) and Richard Crossman (1975) from the UK. Pat was keen to adapt their studies to the Australian context, willing to learn rather than reinventing the wheel.

With their appointments in RSSS drawing to conclusion, the informal team of political scientists exploring public policy dispersed. Bob Smith would become a public servant, serving in senior roles in Victoria and Queensland. Geoff Hawker moved to the Canberra College of Advanced Education, and later to Macquarie University. A timely vacancy allowed Pat to stay closer to home. A senior lectureship in the Department of Political Science in the Faculties at ANU saw Pat lecture first-year classes in Australian politics.

THE DOYEN OF EXECUTIVE STUDIES

As Pat moved into a conventional teaching and research position, his interests shifted to the political and the present-day. With eminent journalist Michelle Grattan, he published *Can Ministers Cope?* (1981). It was the first study of Australian cabinet ministers, using both in-depth interviews and access to private papers. They examined the complex calculations ministers make between political imperatives and good policy. Many interview subjects recognised the relentless demands of a role for which there is little training, with ministers becoming political casualties following minor mistakes.

The book was reviewed widely, and triggered much media interest. Pat found himself on radio, the start of what would become many years of regular commentary on the events of the day. His reflections would always remain carefully free of partisanship, if also politely sceptical about the claims made by government and opposition. As Pat observed on many occasions, political rhetoric may offer grand ideas but the Realpolitik of governing is more practical.

The study of ministers led, inevitably, to prime ministers. It was a topic Pat tackled in two books. *First Among Equals* was a comparative study of prime ministers in Westminster systems, and was the first of several comparative books; a third characteristic of Pat's body of work. It was the first comparative study of Westminster prime ministers, seeking to trace continuities and differences in the role of first ministers.

His biography of Malcolm Fraser (Weller 1989) followed. Pat once again used extensive interviews and primary documents to explore in unprecedented detail how one prime minister used the office. He drew inspiration from the first volume of Robert Caro's 1982 biography of Lyndon Johnson, and from the case study method of Allison (1974). Access to Fraser's cabinet records ensured claims made through interviews could be tested closely against the record. The historian in Pat Weller knew how to organise and make sense of a vast array of data, while the political scientist used the information to interrogate arguments about power at the centre of government.

The task required deft handling of contentious issues. The sacking of the Whitlam government in 1975, when Malcolm Fraser used Coalition numbers to block supply in the Senate, remained a dividing line in Australian politics. Though Fraser was no longer prime minister when Pat first met with him, the dismissal still loomed large.

'Why do you want to write about me?' asked Fraser.

'The public image of you is a very dominant prime minister', started Pat, 'but everyone I talk to stresses how much you consulted.'

Fraser was not impressed.

'Just because I consulted does not mean I didn't dominate, you know.'

And Fraser moved the conversation straight to the topic on Pat's mind.

'Should the Governor-General have done it?' he asked.

'Well I'm interested in the prime minister, so this really pre-dates your time in office. But since you ask—no, he should've waited until the money ran out.'

'Yes he should have, and he should have done so earlier', snapped back Fraser.

With that matter settled, Fraser proved a willing and gracious subject. His opening lines provided the argument for the book that followed—a prime minister who could dominate through consultation, until exhaustion led to agreement. He authorised access to cabinet documents and arranged for Pat to speak with senior officials. There was no attempt to impose conditions or vet the text.

The book is less a biography and more 'a study of the way in which Malcolm Fraser acted as prime minister'. It focuses on a prime minister in action and on 'the exercise of power and influence within the Australian political system' (Weller 1989: xi–xvii). It seeks to understand the way Australia is governed, and reaches for conclusions on the difficulties of political leadership. The portrait is not the Fraser of popular, public imagination—determined, intolerant, powerful, and trampling over all in his way. Rather, we see a man whose power resided in consultation and his ability to persuade, manipulate and, on occasion, direct as necessary. We learn much about Fraser, and even more about the occupation of prime minister.

Pat returned to the study of the core executive and its constituent parts repeatedly over the years, often working in tandem with Rod Rhodes (see Chapter 4 below). His interest in the people at the centre of government would not diminish. On Australia, there were edited volumes on the development of the work of prime ministers (Weller 1992), and research monographs on departmental secretaries (Weller 2001), ministers (Tiernan and Weller 2010), and cabinet government (Weller 2007). There were institutional histories of Queensland's Department of Premier and Cabinet (Weller et al. 2010); and the Commonwealth Department of the Prime Minister and Cabinet (Weller et al. 2011). There were also edited comparative books on the hollowing out of the executive (Weller et al. 1997); the world of top officials (Rhodes and Weller 2001); and Westminster systems in the Pacific (with Patapan and Wanna 2005); and a research monograph on the evolution of Westminster systems (with Rhodes and Wanna 2009).[6] This body of work on the core executive is unrivalled in the study of Australian government.

It is not feasible to talk about each book in any detail, but there are some highlights that cannot pass unnoticed. For example, he wrote a short book, *Don't Tell the Prime Minister* (Weller 2002), about the children overboard scandal. The government alleged that refugees had deliberately thrown their children overboard to gain access to the Australian mainland. He wrote the book in just six weeks using evidence from a parliamentary committee. What is the significance of this book? It remains the only Weller book to make any best-seller lists.

Also, we have not mentioned his many articles, but one is of particular importance. Pat's article for the international journal *Public Administration* is a skilful and probably definitive dissection of the meaning of 'cabinet government' (Weller 2003). Simply put, Pat is the doyen of executive studies in Australia.

INSTITUTION BUILDING

In the 1990s, Pat's career embraced a new field—public administration, a term that encompasses both public policy-making and the new public management. These changes reflected a change in location and colleagues. In 1984, Pat accepted the role of Foundation Professor of Politics and Public Policy at Griffith University on the southern outskirts of Brisbane. His task was to establish a new school to train administrators. Pat proved a capable, enthusiastic and successful institution builder. He could recruit his own team, including several who became long-term collaborators, including recent doctoral graduates John Wanna and Glyn Davis and, a little later, Ciaran O'Faircheallaigh from Papua New Guinea. British political scientist Rod Rhodes would become a frequent visitor to the new School of Politics and Public Policy. His influence was soon apparent, at first in the study of policy networks and governance, and later for interpretive theory and ethnographic fieldwork.

Under Pat's leadership, the Griffith team set itself an ambitious task: to offer a distinctive Australian voice on public policy. In effect, the team sought to meld Pat's earlier work on central government with new American and British perspectives on how nations and sub-national governments organise for collective action. The result was two widely cited textbooks: *Public Policy in Australia* (Davis et al. 1988), and *Public Sector Management in Australia* (O'Faircheallaigh et al. 1992). Both books attracted critics and competitors, but became standard texts through multiple editions and regular updates.

A single remarkable Commonwealth grant helped shape the new Griffith enterprise—$240,000 secured from the Commonwealth to create the Centre for Australian Public Sector Management (CAPSM). Pat would become CAPSM director in 1988 and hold the role for sixteen consecutive years, overseeing a program of seminars, national conferences and edited books. As author and editor he would contribute to books on corporate management (Davis et al. 1989); public service reform (Davis et al. 1993); royal commissions (Weller 1994); institutional capacity

(Weller et al. 2000) and the notion of citizens as customers (Weller and Davis 2001).

As the academic entrepreneur engaging with government, Pat also chanced his arm in a public sector leadership role. He served as Chair of the Queensland Corrective Services Commission from 1994 to 1996. Prisons are often controversial, and Pat was asked to chair an organisation grappling with one of the great governmental dilemmas—whether to continue running prisons, or to contract out to private providers the responsibilities of incarceration and rehabilitation. Always the academic, Pat insisted on data, and encouraged an evidence-based approach within the agency. He was happy to pose awkward questions; for example, are prisoners customers, clients or subjects? He published his reflections on corrective services (Weller 1997). When Queensland required further prison facilities, he led a detailed and professional procurement process to settle the mix of public and private among new prisons. He insisted a new prison be designed around the policy aims of the Commission, so staff experience could inform the plans. The new facility proved unusually secure, with a reduced rate of recidivism among those who spent time behind bars. These results suggest the design successfully incorporated the benefits of policy learning. The Queensland Corrective Services Commission proved a fascinating excursion into a new world, and a chance to explore ideas about public administration in a specific and difficult environment.

Pat has also been university manager and entrepreneur. In nearly 30 years at Griffith, he has performed many roles, including Head of Department, Centre Director, Dean, and Acting Deputy Vice-Chancellor (Research). For the political science profession he has served as editor of the principal Australian journal, *Politics* (now the *Australian Journal of Political Science*), and as president of the Australasian (now Australian) Political Studies Association (APSA). Pat has supervised many successful doctoral candidates, and mentored countless more early career colleagues. His track record in winning competitive grants is formidable, with thirteen Australian Research Council (ARC) grants between 1986 and 2011. He is a senior member of the Australian political science fraternity, and his contribution was recognised in his election as a Fellow of the Academy of Social Sciences and the award of Officer of the Order of Australia. Perhaps above all else, the greatest accolade came in 2012 when the Australian Research Council announced the results of the second evaluation of *Excellence in Research for Australia* (ERA), which applied to research undertaken between 1 January 2005 and 31 December 2010. Political science at Griffith University was awarded a 5—the highest possible grade and second only to ANU (see also Sharman and Weller 2009). It was the crowning glory of this institution-builder's career.

IN HIS POMP

In his pomp, Pat could move in whatever direction interested him. Bored after decades spent studying Australian government, jaundiced by an extended period of ill health, it is scarcely a surprise he sought to move into new fields. Enter Xu Yi-chong and a surge of enthusiasm about international agencies.

After spending some time as a visiting scholar, Xu eventually joined Griffith University as a research professor. She and Pat shared an interest in the question of the 'art of governing', but internationally, not just domestic. They saw an opportunity to extend skills mastered in national studies, and arranged to spend time researching inside first the World Trade Organization (WTO) and later the World Bank.

The results were soon in print; a book-length study of international civil servants working in the secretariat of the General Agreement on Tariffs and Trade at the WTO (Weller and Xu 2004); and an analysis of the workings of the World Bank (Weller and Xu 2009). This international theme continues with a new project, comparing six international organisations: the World Intellectual Property Organization, the World Health Organization, the Food and Agriculture Organization, the IMF, WTO and the World Bank. These agencies are under challenge as emergent international leaders such as China, Russia and Brazil seek to shape and change the architecture of cooperation they have inherited. The future for specialist global agencies established immediately after 1945 is suddenly less clear. Once again, the project adopts Pat's tried and trusted methods. It focuses on the intersection of politics, policy and institutions, and builds up the analysis through extensive fieldwork interviews that ask respondents to explain their roles and routines. The historian in Pat must enjoy watching chaotic international forces intersect with the precise and rule-bound world of dedicated agencies, as they struggle to hold together a policy consensus.

As he approaches his 70th birthday, Pat continues to develop his three strands of intellectual interest. In addition to his comparison project of the six organisations, there is a biography of former Prime Minister Kevin

Rudd nearing completion, based on extensive interviews and access to government documents. Pat is also working on a comparative study of prime ministers in Australia, Britain, Canada and New Zealand, funded by the ARC.

MAKING SENSE OF IT ALL

The subject matter may change, but Pat Weller is still the historian looking at politics. There are recurring, evolving themes in his work: the historical imagination, Realpolitik, and comparative and international studies. We have briefly documented each one.

In explaining his career, Pat stresses contingency—the accidents of birth in Exeter giving access to Oxford, the chance to travel to Australia, even the sudden decision to apply for a university job in Tasmania to escape teaching in an unhappy country school. All might have worked out differently. Where he did have firm plans, such as becoming a historian, life intervened by providing alternative opportunities. Thus, the shift to political science was made possible by coincidence, with early mentors recommending such subjects as parties, ministers, prime ministers and civil servants.

Yet not all was happy accident. His mentors worked in established intellectual traditions. Australian political science comprises at least three long-standing traditions: modernist empiricism as exemplified by American political science; the British humanities tradition as exemplified by Oxbridge history and philosophy; and the public intellectual tradition of civic engagement (Rhodes 2009: 2–8). With his background in Oxford history, Pat was bound to meet like-minded colleagues in Australia. He transplanted himself to fertile soil. The Canadian High Commission may have been closed, and the Canadian political science may also not have been open to his intellectual gifts given its proximity to a dominant American academy.

The historian in Pat has remained strong and active but not unchanged. His interest in primary evidence, enthusiasm for testing ideas against the experience of practitioners, and a polite scepticism about any theory not grounded in empiricism remains strong. The Oxford tradition of historical study provided Pat with methods he has applied consistently through his academic work. He describes himself as someone who talks with people. He builds trust with his public service and political interviewees. As a result, they allow him to be part of the discussion inside government.

Working through the files, he then compares his interviews and informal conversations with the record. As this evidence mounts, he develops an account of the phenomenon under investigation. 'I'm an inductive political scientist', is how Pat describes his approach.

Laughingly, he will, on occasion, call himself an interpretive or constructivist historian, aware that facts are not given but created by historians in the stories they tell. He remembers the historiographical debates of his youth and occasionally speaks about the work of such idealist philosophers of history as R.G. Collingwood (1946) and Michael Oakeshott (2004), if only to remind an overenthusiastic co-author that his current enthusiasms are not new. His inductive approach also has deeper roots. At the heart of Pat's approach is a Faustian world in which rulers are ephemeral, temporal and survive on borrowed time until the dark forces get them. We are back with Richard III and telling 'sad stories of the death of Kings'.[7] In one sense, this Faustian world is a theory of power. We hasten to add that Pat does not espouse any of the models of power common in political science. There is no learned discourse on elitism, pluralism or Marxism. Rather, we have the metaphor of an historian to capture the elusiveness and contingency of power. He talks of ministers and prime ministers situated in contexts that they struggle to understand as they decide what to do. Truly, they 'sail a boundless and bottomless sea; there is neither harbor for shelter nor floor for anchorage, neither starting point nor appointed destination. The enterprise is to keep afloat on an even keel' (Oakeshott 1962). He has been known to talk of political leaders as 'situated agents' (Bevir and Rhodes 2006: chapter 1), but only in moments of weakness that quickly pass!

Pat may be sceptical of theory, but its benighted presence informs his work; these Faustian ideas are his theory. They provide 'the "meaning" of the story by identifying the *kind of story* that has been told'. This form of explanation is called 'emplotment' and it guides the collection and marshalling of facts. The contemporary historian is a storyteller who constructs a story from facts that, in their raw state, make no sense at all. All narratives have 'an irreducible and inexpungible element of interpretation' (White 1973: 7, 1978: 51). Pat tells a good Faustian story.

A second refrain also cannot be dismissed as contingency—the unremitting energy and engagement expressed in a work ethic that would daunt lesser mortals. There is a slight problem—the word 'work'. The alternative expression 'vocation' is often reserved for priests and doctors. This doctor and nurse's son may not have followed the family profession, but he has a vocation all the same. There may not be a divine call to scholarship, but it commands an unswerving commitment. Indeed, that commitment comes to define the person. It is not a job for pay but is part of one's self-definition; part of who you are. Pat's life story demonstrates a passionate belief in the importance of scholarship, and a wish to contribute to a larger conversation about ideas. The sheer volume of Pat's publications since 1971 attests to that belief. It explains his reluctance to accept the role of mere grandee.

His scholarship is not confined to the written word. Pat enjoys a deserved reputation as a teacher, with a particular liking for large classes. In early 2013, the Chancellor of Griffith University, lawyer Leneen Forde, decided to sit in on a first-year subject. She chose Pat's course on Australian politics, and dutifully attended each class. Her verdict was glowing— engaging content, superb delivery and an apparent effortlessness that masks a lifetime of study and practice. The written and spoken words come together with the historical imagination to give us the ancient craft of the Storyteller: 'Stories have to be told or they die, and when they die, we can't remember who we are or why we're here' (Kidd 2003).

NOTES

1. We would like to thank Pat Weller for patiently supplying information and book references; and Cain Roberts for his patient and skilful transcript of the conversation with Pat. We are also grateful to the participants at the workshop on 'The Craft of Governing', Sir Samuel Griffith Centre, Nathan Campus, Griffith University, 9 August 2013 for their comments on the first draft.
2. Arthur Calwell, leader of the Australian Labor Party (ALP) from 1960 to 1967, observed, 'I have witnessed three disastrous splits in the Australian Labor Party during the past fifty-six years . . . The first split occurred in 1916 over conscription in World War I; the second in 1931 over the Premiers' Plan for economic recovery in the Great Depression; and the third in 1955 over alleged communist infiltration of the trade union movement. The last was the worst of the three . . .' (Calwell 1972: 188).
3. The only example of any note was Encel (1962) on cabinet government. See Rhodes and Wanna 2009.
4. The dictionary definition Realpolitik talks of: 'Governmental policies based on hard, practical considerations rather than on moral or idealistic concerns. *Realpolitik* is German for "the politics of reality" and is often applied to the policies of governments that consider only their own interests in dealing with others'. See: *The American Heritage New Dictionary of Cultural Literacy*, 3rd edn, New York: Houghton Mifflin Company, 2005.

5   See <http://oa.anu.edu.au/obituary/wheeler-sir-frederick-henry-1567>, accessed 5 July 2013.
6   We have not been comprehensive because we are highlighting key themes and trends in Pat's career, mainly in his books. There were also significant comparative articles. See, for example, Davis et al. 1999; and Bevir et al. 2003a and 2003b.
7   This quote from *Richard III* was the epigram for Weller et al. (1997: vi).

REFERENCES

Allison, G., 1974, *Essence of Decision*, Boston: Little, Brown

Bevir, M., Rhodes, R.A.W. & Weller, P., 2003a, 'Traditions and Comparative Governance: Interpreting the changing role of the public sector in comparative and historical perspectives', *Public Administration*, vol. 81, no. 1, pp. 1–17

—— 2003b, 'Comparative Governance: Prospects and lessons', *Public Administration*, vol. 81, no. 1, pp. 191–210

Bevir, M. & Rhodes, R.A.W., 2006, *Governance Stories*, Abingdon, Oxon: Routledge

Butler, D., 1973, *The Canberra Model*, New York: St Martin's Press

Calwell, Arthur, 1972, *Be Just and Fear Not*, Melbourne: Lloyd O'Neil

Caro, Robert A., 1982, *The Years of Lyndon Johnson: The path to power*, New York: Alfred A. Knopf

Carr, E.H., 1961, *What is History?*, Cambridge: Cambridge University Press

Collingwood, R.G.S., 1946, *The Idea of History*, T. Knox (ed.), Oxford: Clarendon Press

Crossman, R.H.S., 1975, *The Diaries of a Cabinet Minister, Volume 1, Minister of Housing*, London: Jonathan Cape

Davis, G., et al., 1988, *Public Policy in Australia*, Sydney: Allen & Unwin

Davis, G., Lewis, C. & Weller, P. (eds), 1989, *Corporate Management in Australian Government: Reconciling accountability and efficiency*, Melbourne: Macmillan Education for the Centre for Australian Public Sector Management

Davis, G., Forster, J. & Weller, P. (eds), 1993, *Reforming the Public Service: Lessons from recent experience*, Melbourne: Macmillan Education for the Centre for Australian Public Sector Management

Davis, G., Weller, P., Eggins, S. & Craswell, E., 1999, 'What Drives Machinery of Government Change? Australia, Canada and the United Kingdom, 1950–1997', *Public Administration*, vol. 77, no. 1, pp. 7–50

Eco, Umberto, 1984, *Postscript to the Name of the Rose*, New York: Harcourt

Encel, S., 1962, *Cabinet Government in Australia*, Melbourne: Melbourne University Press

Heclo, H. & Wildavsky, A., 1981, *The Private Government of Public Money*, 2nd edn, London: Macmillan

Kidd, Sue Monk, 2003, *The Secret Life of Bees*, new edn, London: Headline Publishing

Lindsay, Philip, 1933, *King Richard III: A chronicle*, London: Ivor Nicholson & Watson Ltd

Loveday, Peter & Martin, Allan, 1966, *Parliament Factions and Parties: The first thirty years of responsible government in New South Wales, 1856–1889*, Melbourne: Melbourne University Press

Markham, Clements, 1906, *Richard III: His life and character*, London: Smith, Elder & Co.

Neustadt, Richard E., 1991 [1960], *Presidential Power and the Modern Presidents: The politics of leadership from Roosevelt to Reagan*, rev. edn, New York: The Free Press

Oakeshott, M., 1962, *Rationalism in Politics and Other Essays*, London: Methuen

—— 2004, *What is History and Other Essays*, Exeter: Imprint Academic

O'Faircheallaigh, C., Wanna, J. & Weller, P., 1992, *Public Sector Management in Australia: New challenges, new directions*, South Yarra: Macmillan

Patapan, H., Wanna, J. & Weller, P. (eds), 2005, *Westminster Legacies: Democracy and responsible government in Asia, Australasia and the Pacific*, Sydney: UNSW Press

Rhodes, R.A.W., 2009, 'In Search of Australian Political Science', in R.A.W. Rhodes (ed.), *The Australian Study of Politics*, Houndmills, Basingstoke: Palgrave-Macmillan, pp. 1–15

Rhodes, R.A.W. & Wanna J., 2009, 'The Core Executive', in R.A.W. Rhodes (ed.), *The Australian Study of Politics*, Houndmills, Basingstoke: Palgrave-Macmillan, pp. 119–30

Rhodes, R.A.W., Wanna, J. & Weller, P., 2009, *Comparing Westminster*, Oxford: Oxford University Press

Rhodes, R.A.W. & Weller, P. (eds), 2001, *The Changing World of Top Officials: Mandarins or valets?*, Buckingham: Open University Press

Self, P., 1972, *Administrative Theories and Politics*, London: Allen & Unwin

Sharman, J.C. & Weller, P., 2009, 'Where is the quality? Political science scholarship in Australia', *Australian Journal of Political Science*, vol. 44, no. 4, pp. 597–612

Tiernan, A. & Weller, P., 2010, *Learning to Be a Minister: Heroic expectations, practical realities*, Melbourne: Melbourne University Press

Weller, P. (ed.), 1975, *Caucus Minutes 1901–1949: Minutes of the Meetings of the Federal Parliamentary Labor Party. Volume 1, 1901–1917. Volume 2, 1917–1931. Volume 3, 1932–1949*, Melbourne: Melbourne University Press

Weller, P. & Cutt, J., 1976, *Treasury Control in Australia: A study in bureaucratic politics*, Sydney: I. Novak

Weller, P. & Lloyd, B. (eds), 1978, *Federal Executive Minutes, 1916–1955*, Melbourne: Melbourne University Press

Weller, P. & Gratton, M., 1981, *Can Ministers Cope? Australian Federal Ministers at work*, Melbourne: Hutchinson

Weller, P., 1989, *Malcolm Fraser PM: A study in prime ministerial power*, Melbourne: Penguin

Weller, P. (ed.), 1992, *Menzies to Keating: The development of the Australian prime ministership*, London: Hurst

Weller, P. (ed.), 1994, *Royal Commissions and the Making of Public Policy*, Melbourne: Macmillan Education for the Centre for Australian Public Sector Management

Weller, P., Bakvis, H. & Rhodes, R.A.W. (eds), 1997, *The Hollow Crown: Countervailing trends in core executives*, London: Macmillan

Weller, P., 1997, 'Are Prisoners Clients?' *Australian Journal of Public Administration*, vol. 56, no. 1, pp. 125–7

—— 1999, *Dodging Raindrops: John Button—A Labour Life*, Sydney: Allen & Unwin

Weller, P., Keating, M. & Wanna, J. (eds), 2000, *Institutions on the Edge? Capacities for governance*, Sydney: Allen & Unwin

Weller, P., 2001, *Australia's Mandarins: The frank or the fearless?*, Sydney: Allen & Unwin

Weller, P. & Davis, G. (eds), 2001, *Are You Being Served? State, citizens and governance*, Sydney: Allen & Unwin

Weller, P., 2002, *Don't Tell the Prime Minister*, Melbourne: Scribe Books

—— 2003, 'Cabinet Government: An elusive ideal?' *Public Administration*, vol. 81, no. 4, pp. 701–22

Weller, P. & Xu, Yi-chong, 2004, *The Governance of World Trade: International civil servants in the GATT/WTO*, Cheltenham: Edward Elgar

Weller, P., 2007, *Cabinet Government in Australia, 1901–2006*, Sydney: UNSW Press

Weller, P., & Xu, Yi-chong, 2009, *Inside the World Bank: Exploding the myth of a monolithic bank*, Houndmills, Basingstoke: Palgrave Macmillan

Weller, P. et al., 2010, *The Engine Room of Government: The Queensland Premier's Department 1859–2001*, St Lucia: University of Queensland Press

Weller, P., Scott, J. & Stevens, B., 2011, *From Postbox to Powerhouse. A centenary history of the Department of Prime Minister and Cabinet*, Sydney: Allen & Unwin

White, H., 1973, *Metahistory*, Baltimore: Johns Hopkins University Press

—— 1978, *Tropics of Discourse*, Baltimore: Johns Hopkins University Press

PART 2

THE EXECUTIVE

3

TWO HALVES OF A WHOLE: KEVIN RUDD, JULIA GILLARD AND THE POLITICS OF PRIME MINISTERIAL VULNERABILITY
Michelle Grattan

> *Australian prime ministers . . . sit at the centre of the political maelstrom, blown by forces they cannot entirely control, and calculate how best to use their limited capacities and resources.*
>
> —Patrick Weller, Menzies to Keating

A well-worn political science debate has been over whether we now have 'prime ministerial' government rather than cabinet government, an emerging 'presidential system' rather than a traditional Westminster one. The extraordinary experiences of the Rudd–Gillard Labor governments, which lasted less than six years but saw not only the overthrow of two prime ministers but the resurrection of the first in a counter coup, tell us more about the limits of prime ministerial power than the opportunities for its extension. They also highlight the degree to which personal disposition, and the ability to manage relationships and recognise mutual interdependencies, are vital not just to the success of a prime minister, but to his or her survival. The story of these leaders, which started with such promise, became an unexpected and remarkable one of vulnerability, a saga of individual and mutual destruction. It is also a narrative of political 'pairing', of which we see many in politics. These often end badly, but usually with fewer spectacular twists than in this case.

For Labor, the 2007–13 period raised fundamental questions about its culture and ways of doing things. It squandered a good deal of the opportunity presented by its 2007 victory; internal disloyalty almost certainly cost it majority government at the 2010 election; by 2013 it made the choice to reward destabilisation in a desperate attempt to save some of its 'furniture'. These were years in which a political party cannibalised itself.

Rudd and Gillard are not the only Australian prime ministers to be forced out of leadership by their own parties, although Rudd was the first to meet that fate in an initial term. On the Labor side, the electorally successful Bob Hawke was brought down by Paul Keating in 1991; Liberal prime minister John Gorton left the job after a tied vote in his party room. The timeframes of the Gillard and Rudd coups were different from that against Hawke, who had been in office for close to nine years. But the motive was similar in the 1991, 2010 and 2013 coups. In each case, the party was trying to shield itself against, or minimise the size of, electoral defeat.

Pat Weller's work on prime ministers was ground breaking. It has been correctly noted that *First Among Equals* (1985) 'was a pioneering analysis of prime ministers in the Westminster world' (Strangio et al. 2013: 9). In that study Weller devoted a chapter to 'Incumbency and Vulnerability'. His observations have a prescient ring when we consider the experiences of Kevin Rudd and Julia Gillard:

> Vulnerable prime ministers must pay constant attention to the backbench, and to public image. If their party fears they may lose the next election, it may take preventive action . . . They can ill-afford to sack popular senior ministers, who might act as the centre of an internal party opposition. Rumour can be a deadly device as party opponents try to destabilise the situation and cast doubt on their leaders' ability.

Also:

> If a vulnerable prime minister is doing badly, it creates the conditions for constant plotting and intrigue; while the uncertainty lasts, all the prime minister's attention will be directed toward survival—governing must wait. On the other hand, vulnerability does create answerability. The prime minister must listen to the party, must heed the views of influential colleagues and must keep an open door. However dominant personally, he or she can not afford to ignore the power-base. (Weller 1985: 70–1)

Weller's observation several years on, in a collection he edited dealing with prime ministers, is especially relevant to the events of recent years: 'Those who are elected by opinion polls may find their position undermined when the polls show declining support' (Weller 1992: 211).

Nearly two decades later, Mark Evans argued that the 'Rudd debacle' showed that 'sustainable prime ministerial power rests on the incumbent's recognition that their powerbase is determined by a broad set of resource dependencies' needed to 'govern effectively and legitimately'. He points to four: 'the core executive territory, media relations, the citizenry and the Prime Minister's party itself' (Aulich and Evans 2010: 262).

In her 2013 scathing critique of Rudd, former Labor minister Nicola Roxon gave a list of 'housekeeping tips' for a future Labor government and prime minister. Particularly apposite for a prime minister are these: keep the focus on the high level, spend time and energy on what really matters; delegate; welcome debate; be polite and be persuasive; have the diary in good shape; choose good staff; and 'accept you are not always right, and cannot always fix everything' (Roxon 2013). Ignoring or flouting some or all of these rules will increase a prime minister's vulnerability.

The relationship between leader and party can be seen as a classic grand bargain. Leaders are invested by their colleagues and, if the party has won an election, by the voters, with authority, power, and status. In return, leaders are expected to deliver results—primarily, but not only, to win elections, which is the most important single measure for the party, and to govern effectively, which is the voters' first measure. The two measures of success are, of course, linked.

From a party's point of view, choosing a leader is almost inevitably a gamble. A candidate's strengths (for example, popularity or 'selling' skills) can seem obvious. Vulnerabilities tend to emerge when the pressure of the prime ministership comes on. In the hothouse of power, strengths can morph into weaknesses (attention to detail transforms into failing to see the wider picture) or disappear (the good communicator suddenly can't talk to the electorate). The media cycle that makes the news as much as reports it feeds on and contributes to a prime minister's vulnerability: it boosts a leader who is on the way up, and tears at one on the way down.

Political capital is easier to spend than to acquire. In probably most instances, including those of both Rudd and Gillard, a prime minister arrives in office with a store that erodes through poor performance or simply the effluxion of time. Or it might be deliberately spent (as John Howard did in 1998 when he put forward his GST policy). Sometimes a leader manages to regenerate the capital. This clearly happened with Robert Menzies and Howard; Menzies nearly lost the 1961 election and then bounced back in 1963; Howard was returned with a minority of votes in 1998 but went on to win well in 2001 and 2004. Rudd's return to the leadership in 2013 signified he had renewed his capital in the eyes of caucus colleagues—or just that he had more capital than Gillard. Looked at another way, a majority of caucus admitted that Rudd had been cut down while he still had something in the bank (measured by the polls); he was brought back to spend it for the collective good.

In opposition, these days a leader who is seen to fail, on an electoral or even a policy front, faces the danger of quick removal. On the Liberal side, neither Brendan Nelson nor Malcolm Turnbull was allowed by his party to face an election. Nelson was regarded as ineffective; Turnbull as unacceptable on climate policy and non-consultative in style. Nelson was always potentially vulnerable because Turnbull was waiting in the wings; Turnbull became vulnerable despite there being no obvious preferred alternative.

Given the seriousness of ditching a leader while in office, a prime minister would expect to have greater security, even taking into account the lack of patience in modern politics. Labor in 2010–13 belied this expectation. But while parties have been extremely reluctant to force out prime ministers, until recently, this doesn't mean there haven't been leadership rumblings. Howard's future was contemplated when he was headed for defeat in 2007; Malcolm Fraser and Andrew Peacock faced off. Even Menzies (who had to quit the prime ministership in 1941 after losing party support) encountered internal muttering in the early 1960s, as did Harold Holt later that decade.

Kevin Rudd arrived in office with the authority of a strong election win, high personal popularity, and the ability (not enjoyed by any Labor prime minister since the first, Chris Watson) to choose his own ministry. It is true that there were reservations about him in sections of the party, and the union movement was no fan, but if anyone had seriously predicted in November 2007 that Rudd would be removed before he faced another election, the proposition would have seemed ridiculous. Indeed, to most of his colleagues it appeared improbable up until the coup itself, on the night of 23 June 2010.

Although Rudd had never served in government before he became prime minister, he had experience of government, working previously for Queensland Labor premier Wayne Goss, both in Goss's office and as Director-General of the Cabinet Office. Some of the seeds of Rudd's later problems were obvious to observers there, especially his controlling and demanding personality. One approach that he picked up and was determined to transfer to his own administration was having a kitchen cabinet. At the federal level this was called the Strategic Priorities and Budget Committee; it comprised Rudd, Deputy Prime Minister Gillard, Treasurer Wayne Swan, and Finance Minister Lindsay Tanner. This group was demonstrably needed during the Global Financial Crisis (GFC), when frequent meetings and flexibility were essential. But its wider domination, driven partly by Rudd wishing to avoid leaks from the full cabinet, created resentment among other ministers and meant that at the top of the government, political advice was narrower than was desirable.

Rudd brought an agenda and considerable self-confidence to his management of the office. Throughout his political career he had pushed his way forward. Elected to parliament in 1998, with a background in the diplomatic service as well as his Queensland experience, he had managed by 2001 to supplant the Labor opposition's foreign affairs spokesman Laurie Brereton to become shadow foreign minister. But his eyes were always on the top job. When Simon Crean's leadership became terminal in 2003, Rudd's name was mentioned, but he did not have the numbers to run. He put his hand up in early 2005 when Mark Latham collapsed politically, but he had to pull it down again for lack of support; Kim Beazley obtained uncontested the opposition leadership (which he had previously held from 1996 to 2001).

Through 2006, Rudd had worked assiduously in the caucus and the Labor organisation to secure enough backing to replace Beazley. Successfully carrying the opposition attack on the AWB wheat bribery scandal raised his profile. He had also cultivated a popular image with his regular appearance with Liberal frontbencher Joe Hockey on a breakfast TV show. There was a recurring pattern in Rudd's behaviour in federal politics: he targeted a job he sought and its occupant's point of vulnerability. Beazley's weakness was that he was regarded as only an 'on balance' proposition to win the 2007 election, when Labor wanted maximum insurance. Though Beazley was a much liked figure in the party, he was seen to lack toughness and inclined to unforced errors. Despite his internal campaign, Rudd was short of support. He needed an alliance with Gillard, who was from the left. After that was forged, Rudd launched the challenge and beat Beazley 49–39 in December 2006.

The timing was good for Rudd and for Labor. Howard had acquired a reputation for invincibility, but his electoral position was softening. The man who in the 1980s once famously said (prematurely, as it turned out) that the times would suit him found himself unsuited to the times in 2007. An electorate increasingly bombarded by the 24-hour media cycle was looking for something and someone new. Howard was out of sync with rising issues—especially climate change, where he was forced to make an unconvincing late entry to the debate about the desirability of an emissions trading scheme (ETS). The fresh-faced Rudd appeared an unthreatening alternative (a younger version of Howard, some said). Rudd carried appeal across the political divide; he brought the prospect of change, of a responsible sort.

Albeit from the right, Rudd lacked a firm factional base. Although he had identified with the ALP even while at school (attending Young Labor meetings), some colleagues did not see him as being of the Labor party. His appeal to the Labor movers and shakers as a potential leader had been his general popularity. The fact that Rudd was not deeply embedded in Labor meant he had no loyal core of supporters, which would weaken his position when trouble came. Both his ascension in 2006 and his dispatch in 2010 were, from the party's point of view, the ultimate 'transactional' events; so indeed was his 2013 resurrection.

Rudd's modus operandi was based on keeping decision-making at close quarters. In opposition, he seized the power to choose his own frontbench (rather than just allocate the portfolios). Recent Labor leaders had been able to influence who was on the frontbench, but this was a huge change of party culture. In government, the caucus ratified the new system with only four dissenting voices. Caucus chairman Daryl Melham accused Rudd of centralising power and encouraging subservience.

Rudd in government started strongly, symbolically and in activity. On his first day in office he began the process for Australia to ratify the Kyoto protocol. When parliament commenced in early 2008 he made his initial priority the apology to indigenous Australians. His commencement was not as frenetic as the Whitlam two-man cabinet of the early 1970s, but the pace was quick, and behind the scenes Rudd was driving his staff and the bureaucracy. When there were complaints about the load on public servants he was tellingly unrepentant: 'I understand that there has been some criticism around the edges that some public servants are finding the hours a bit much. Well, I suppose I've simply got news for the public service—there'll be more' (Marr 2013: 117).

Just as he could be insensitive to the ordinary needs and feelings of those around him, Rudd lacked emotional intelligence when it came to the Labor party. This showed in small things—for example, Labor people were surprised and appalled when he missed the funeral of party icon John Button, but was seen the same day visiting actor Cate Blanchett with a gift for her new baby. Excuses about other commitments preventing him from flying to Melbourne cut little ice. Another explanation for some of Rudd's 'tin ear' behaviour was that he did not care much about the niceties.

Certainly he was dismissive of colleagues for whose conduct he had little time, or whom he believed had turned against him. His alienation of key Labor players deprived him of vital support, and he did not take steps to repair broken fences. His dressing down of Victorian-right power-broker David Feeney in a discussion about entitlements ensured Feeney's enmity; he was one of those who plotted to bring Rudd down. Similarly, and more dangerously, Rudd froze out key NSW-right figure Mark Arbib, who had helped his rise to the leadership, which was a strategically bad call. As pressure mounted on Rudd's leadership in mid-2010, Bruce Hawker, a confidant and political adviser who had just been brought into the Prime Minister's Office, tried unsuccessfully several times to arrange a meeting between Rudd and Arbib to 'clear the air around the exclusion of key strategists from Kevin's advisory team' (Hawker 2013: 8).

Rudd's poor management of government was a critical negative. Gillard told her biographer Jacqueline Kent in 2013:

> The events in May and June 2010 had their own momentum. The media said at the time [the impetus to topple Kevin Rudd] was all to do with opinion polls, but it wasn't. It was about a

plan of capacity for the future. We were all desperately concerned about where we were as a government and political party, and distressed. We knew we had to do something, things were getting more and more chaotic. (Kent 2013: 11)

Rudd's disorganisation had contributed to Labor's declining electoral fortunes, measured in the polls. He was better at ideas and planning than executing. He tried to do too much; he also lacked the ability to keep his eye on all the various balls in the air (or make sure that others were watching those that he could not). He displayed signs of obsessive behaviour, as when he insisted in early 2010 on visiting a large number of hospitals. He was preoccupied with health policy at the time, but this did not require such extensive personal tours.

In *The Stalking of Julia Gillard*, Kerry-Anne Walsh quotes from the recollections of a senior Rudd government policy and political adviser who listed the flaws in Rudd's governing style as the radical centralisation of decision-making to Rudd himself, even though he would not make decisions; his bad handling of cabinet, ignoring or wasting the skills of ministers and officials; trying to do too many things, and too quickly; neglect of policy in favour of political and media considerations; and a culture of blame and retribution that stifled honest advice and undermined decision-making (Walsh 2013: 196–7).

Much has been said about the youth and inexperience of the Prime Minister's Office under Rudd. While the criticism is valid, the main responsibility must rest with Rudd himself. An effective, organised prime minister makes sure they have an office that operates well, and also that their own work and life habits are conducive to the demands of the role. Rudd himself later acknowledged that he did not get enough sleep; clearly he had a problem with time management, notoriously running late and keeping people waiting. Ministers, officials and staffers had to travel aboard his VIP plane to get face time with him. Speech writer James Button recorded: 'Rudd even summoned an adviser halfway around the world to consult him on a domestic issue. But on the flight home Rudd was distracted and the meeting never took place' (Button 2012: 65).

After being deposed, Rudd was aware that his own faults and mistakes had influenced his colleagues. During his February 2012 challenge he conceded he had got some things wrong, but was still inclined to defiance. 'I'm the first to admit that I wasn't some perfect creation of public administration. But, guess what, I don't think that would be the reflection of any Australian prime minister in their first term if we have a proper perspective on history'. When he was again prime minister in 2013, he heavily stressed his new consultative style, with a (limited) concession about past faults. 'If I have learnt one thing from my previous period as prime minister, and I've learned quite a lot . . . [it] is the absolute importance of proper, orderly consultation with cabinet colleagues on any major decision . . . We can all say "it's too busy, there's a global financial crisis going on, sorry colleagues, don't have time, we've got to save the banks from falling". These all seem pretty good justifications at the time, but frankly, decision-making is always much better when it can be done collegiately'.

Critics scoffed, saying the leopard would not change its spots. On the evidence of his second prime ministership, which lasted less than three months, they were fundamentally right. In the 2013 campaign, Rudd fell into old habits: he and his trusted group tried to keep tight control, which caused some friction with campaign headquarters, and there were signs of the chaotic style.

Although some colleagues, including Gillard, argued that it was his way of running the government that was the major factor in the coup against Rudd, the polling was equally likely the killer. It was certainly used as the poleaxe, shown around by key players to others whose support was being sought to bring Rudd down. The climate issue, that had helped him to power, was a crucial factor in eroding his public standing. First, Rudd could not deliver the ETS he had made so much of, because he could not get parliamentary support. Arguably, he might have obtained this backing in 2009 if he had not gone in so hard against then opposition leader Turnbull, who wanted to do a deal with the government. Rudd saw his opponent's vulnerability as a weakness to be exploited. He was unable to see that by undermining Turnbull he would also undermine his own opportunity to land a core promise. Second, Rudd refused to chance his arm by calling a double dissolution on the ETS—colleagues were critical, though it is a fine judgement as to whether that would have been a wise course. Third, when he and senior ministers in 2010 decided, in the face of the Senate's obstructionism, to delay the ETS, a decision that was leaked prematurely, he did not properly explain why. The leader who had once communicated so well could not put the setback into context for the public. Sean Kelly, the press secretary who briefed him before the news conference announcing the postponement, gave one explanation: 'He was burning with rage, not just over the leak but, I suspect, over his own decision. He sincerely believed in carbon pricing and was furious at himself and his colleagues for putting politics over principle. He was a man divided' (Kelly 2013).

It can be argued that Rudd had difficult forces lined up against him when the climate issue went so badly wrong. But a measure of a prime minister is how they handle adverse circumstances. Rudd did not have enough skill to do so, and then, as the polls deteriorated, he had no protection in the form of goodwill among colleagues.

If Rudd had been a less controlling character, more personally secure at his core, less afraid to admit fallibility, he might have been offered (and been more receptive to) greater feedback from ministerial colleagues and the caucus, which can be a good sounding board for a leader. But critical colleagues were sullen and excluded from the inner circle, and the caucus under Rudd was quiescent (though there was questioning about the hospital visits).

Towards the end, complaints about Rudd's style from cabinet ministers were finding their way into the media. But, while Gillard tried to deal with the situation, most ministers did little. Some have put the inexplicable failure of ministers to chide or confront the prime minister down to his power to hire and fire. If so, this surely shows an acute underestimation of their own potential strength. There was no way Rudd could have sacked a whole bunch of cabinet ministers. Whether, however, tough representations would have changed an ingrained style is another matter.

Even taking all these factors into account, the swift execution was extraordinary, with some senior ministers caught unawares on the night of the coup, and many in the caucus ignorant of what was happening. The coup was planned and driven by a handful of factional chiefs, mostly unknown to the public. Also extraordinary was that there was so little resistance within caucus that, by the next morning, Rudd was persuaded to abandon his initial inclination to make a fight of it. In the end his power had become a facade that was easy to knock down, because it had no sandbagging to defend it. Roxon summed up Rudd's political execution in crude terms: 'Removing Kevin was an act of political bastardry, for sure. But this act of political bastardry was made possible only because Kevin had been such a bastard himself to so many people'. She admitted the dismissal was never legitimised to the public. 'If Kevin had been an employee, he would have won his unfair dismissal case. Not because there wasn't cause to dismiss him, but because we didn't explain the reasons properly to him, let alone to the voting public' (Roxon 2013).

Like Rudd, Gillard had the patina of a winner on the way to the top job. As deputy prime minister she was popular, a feisty performer on the floor of parliament, and seen as a competent administrator despite some problems with the GFC schools building program. Inside the government, she was regarded as much more competent at turning around the paperwork than Rudd; colleagues went to her to get things done when she was acting prime minister.

Gillard was the logical successor, the prime minister-in-waiting. Yet people tended to believe her when in 2010 she said repeatedly she was not lining up for a crack at Rudd's leadership. The public understand that some politicians are political assassins, but many people would not have put Gillard in this category (she had been up to her eyeballs, during the later stages, in Beazley's removal, but this was not widely known or, at least, remembered). So there was real shock when it was found she had knifed Rudd. This gave her a vulnerability that would subsequently combine with other factors to weaken her.

In retrospect, Gillard and her colleagues believed they had erred in not fully explaining their actions as a response to Rudd's behaviour, but whether they would have been any better off by doing so is open to question; even after ministers trenchantly attacked him in early 2012, he retained high public popularity. There was also the risk of a dispute. For example, Rudd supporters such as Chris Bowen did not share the harsher descriptions of him. Whether or not Gillard could have done better with another tactic, her explanation that 'a good government was losing its way' was unconvincing. In addition, she arrived in the leadership inadequately prepared for the election she soon called.

Despite the problems, including her own muddled campaign, with her declaration at one point that people would now see the 'real Julia', Gillard may well have won a majority of seats at that election if it had not been for the damaging Rudd-inspired leaks. These leaks suggested, among other things, that she had not been supportive of paid parental leave and had questioned a big pension rise. They were devastating for the new prime minister who was trying to find her feet and weave a narrative between past and future. One could argue that the handful of seats that made the difference between minority and majority government was the key to many (though not all) of the problems that subsequently unfolded for Gillard. These included her formal alliance with the Greens, and the speed and form of her action on climate change. Having promised 'no carbon tax under the government I lead' and a consensus-building process, the carbon scheme she brought in, at the insistence of the Greens, had a 'tax' for its first three years. She later said she should not have accepted the description 'tax', but it is unlikely her rejection of the terminology would have made any difference.

Bringing down Rudd, combined with the broken carbon tax promise, left Gillard highly vulnerable on the grounds of trust; she became an easy target for an opposition leader as tough as Tony Abbott, whom she and Labor generally consistently underestimated.

Gillard's acknowledged strength was as a negotiator. After the coup against Rudd, she and Wayne Swan landed a deal on the mining tax; Rudd had been unable to complete this. In the wake of the election, she rounded up the necessary crossbench support to underpin her minority government, outmanoeuvring Abbott (though she started with an advantage—the relevant independents had issues with the conservatives). But she had weaknesses in terms of policy substance, and also did not adequately look ahead to the consequences of deals (or was not too concerned). The settlement with the miners led to a flawed tax. In putting together crossbench support she could have stopped short of a formal alliance with the Greens. They had no practical choice but to support Labor on supply and confidence with their one vote in the lower house. Also, she promised independent Andrew Wilkie an outcome on gambling that she could not deliver. In each case, the immediacy and urgency of the politics drove the deals, but Gillard paid a price later.

As prime minister, Gillard was like a mountain climber who never got her foothold. Given her situation, it was going to take a great deal of political skill for her to resist the inevitable, recurring Rudd attacks. Rudd (foreign minister between September 2010 and February 2012) was determined to regain the prime ministership, which he believed had been stolen from him. He would rely on his popularity in the polls as his main weapon, combined with a destabilisation campaign based on those polls. For guaranteed survival, Gillard needed, if not higher personal popularity than Rudd, to establish Labor as comfortably ahead in the polls on a sustained basis. This she could not do. Indeed, in the Nielsen poll, Labor was never in front on a two-party basis between the elections of 2010 and 2013.

The Gillard government had some substantial achievements, including the carbon price, the beginning of a national disability insurance scheme, and a means test on the expensive health insurance rebate (which had been initially put forward by the Rudd government but failed in the

Senate). It passed much legislation; on the relatively few occasions when it could not get crossbench support it avoided defeat by the expedient of not going ahead with the measure in question. But it could not translate its achievements into political coinage, just as Rudd could not reap political benefit from his substantial achievement of keeping Australia out of recession during the GFC. In his case, bad implementation and disputes about whether too much money was being spent offset (in political terms) the economic positives; with Gillard, focus on distracting negatives overwhelmed the political debate.

We can't know how much better Gillard would have done, even with the hung parliament, if Rudd had disappeared after the 2010 election. Somewhat better, undoubtedly, although she would still have had considerable weaknesses. In three years, there were two leadership challenges before the final one that ended Gillard's prime ministership. The first was in early 2012 when Rudd, manoeuvred by the Gillard forces into going early, had minimal support. The second was the 'faux' challenge of March 2013 when, lacking numbers, he declined to stand.

The Rudd threat and the challenges triggered some of the ministerial shuffling which then played back into the leadership issue. Reshuffles are always dangerous for embattled leaders. By demoting left winger Kim Carr to the outer ministry in December 2011 because of his perceived support for Rudd, Gillard cemented his hostility. Her two-stage demotion of Robert McClelland, who began as attorney-general, ensured another bitter critic. He did immense damage to Gillard by airing obliquely in Parliament an old scandal from her days as an industrial lawyer, which centred on allegations against her then boyfriend and legal advice she had given. Her failure to promote Joel Fitzgibbon to the ministry (who, under Rudd, had been forced to quit the defence portfolio in controversial circumstances) turned him into a vociferous detractor. Bizarrely, Fitzgibbon was able to run interference on Gillard from the position of chief government whip. The whip is classically supposed to protect the prime minister's back. But the fragility of her situation meant she could do nothing about him.

Her position was destabilised inadvertently when, at the start of 2013, two cabinet ministers, Nicola Roxon and Chris Evans (who was Senate leader) announced long-held plans to retire at the election. This came immediately after Gillard had taken the novel step of announcing the election date many months ahead of time, a move she hoped would increase stability, but instead started the longest election campaign in memory. The announcements by Evans and Roxon could easily be viewed as senior figures deserting. On quite a different plane, several senior and respected frontbenchers resigned their portfolios (either under pressure or by choice) after the March 2013 leadership debacle, reinforcing the impression of shambles. This was disruptive and allowed some to become even more active in the Rudd cause.

The Labor poll results were kept down by multiple factors: the trust problem; scandals involving Labor backbencher Craig Thomson and Peter Slipper (a Coalition defector whom Labor recruited as Speaker, to improve its numbers); difficulties with particular issues, including the misjudgement of bringing forward controversial media reforms in the last days of the term; the Rudd presence; and constant negative media coverage, especially in the Murdoch press. The hung parliament gave the impression of instability—despite lasting the distance and operating satisfactorily, it always had the possibility of collapse.

In politics, as in the animal world, weakness attracts the crows. Australia's first female prime minister would have inevitably received some sexist attacks, but if she had been popular (as she was as deputy and briefly after she took over) and Labor had been doing well, this would have been of minimal account. As it was, gender became a weapon used by some of her critics (epitomised by 'Ditch the Witch' and similar placards at an anti–carbon price rally). Gillard initially had not wanted to play up her sex, although Labor used the gender card against Abbott, of whom women were suspicious on account of his views on abortion and the like. Eventually Gillard made a spectacular strike in the gender wars. Her dramatic 2012 speech in Parliament accusing Abbott of 'misogyny' will be among her most remembered political moments, but more generally her fight back against sexism could be cast by opponents as playing the victim and became a further vulnerability. Gillard was correct when, on the night she lost the prime ministership, she said of the effect of gender on her political situation: 'It doesn't explain everything, it doesn't explain nothing, it explains some things'.

A prime minister needs to be able to connect with both colleagues and the public. Rudd was bad at the first; Gillard failed at the second. 'Gillard was not a natural storyteller,' Kent writes. 'She was a solver of problems, an answerer of questions' (Kent 2013: 89).

Faced with her inability to move the polls, Gillard decided on denial. Interviewed by Kent shortly before she was replaced, she said:

> One of the things I say to [colleagues who are nervous about opinion polls] is that out in the big wide world, voters don't worry about them when it comes to the crunch. The questions they have for all politicians . . . are: Do you have a sense of purpose, and what are you in politics for? . . . And if for any political party the most popular person is leader simply because they are the most popular, well . . . I have always believed that chasing popularity is the death of purpose. (Kent 2013: 123)

Her analysis was flawed. For one thing the polls, which were consistent, reflected where the electorate's thinking was at, not some temporary flight of voters' fancy, and the Labor party knew this. For another, a successful prime minister needs both purpose and popularity. A prime minister should not have to be popular all the time—a party should have the strength of nerve to live with unpopularity in hard periods, such as the one Rudd went through in 2010. An effective leader will retain enough goodwill for this to happen. But a leader cannot afford to be popular none of the time. If the prime minister is so disliked (or despaired of) that they haven't any prospect of winning an election, all the 'purpose' in the world will count for nothing.

After she was replaced, Gillard saw it as caucus succumbing; she obviously thought it was a moment of caucus weakness rather than strength. 'I understand that at the caucus meeting today, the pressure finally got too great for many of my colleagues', she said in her statement to the media on the night of her loss. Later she wrote that the decision to change leaders was not done on the basis of embracing new policy or because caucus now believed Rudd had the greater talent for governing. 'Caucus's verdict of 2010 on that was not being revoked. It was only done—indeed expressly done—on the basis that Labor might do better at the election. Labor unambiguously sent a very clear message that it cared about nothing other than the prospects of survival of its members of parliament at the polls' (Gillard 2013).

Gillard is right: the caucus's decision to turn to Rudd was a cold-blooded calculation about which of the two leaders would lose fewer seats. But it is hard to argue that this was anything other than rational. After the 2013 election Bob Carr, who had been recruited into the Parliament in 2012 by Gillard to be foreign minister, but switched to vote for Rudd, explained his decision by saying that the polls had shown Labor was threatened with being reduced to a vote from which it would be very hard to recover. 'There's a big difference between [getting] 33% of the vote and getting 27%' or lower. The balance of opinion within the party after the election was that Rudd had put a floor under the vote that was significantly higher than where it would have been under Gillard, and so Labor had a better base from which to rebuild. ALP national secretary George Wright said publicly after the election that in the second quarter of 2013, Labor polling showed the party was looking at being reduced to as few as 30 House of Representatives seats (it won 55).

Caucus acted knowing that there would be much collateral damage (six ministers quit the frontbench immediately, regardless of what Rudd wanted them to do) and that the opposition had all the earlier negative character references Rudd's colleagues had given.

Like Gillard in 2010, Rudd in 2013 struggled for a narrative about the change, although this time everyone knew the story lay squarely with the polls. Rudd's slogan 'a new way' was unconvincing, not least because the party had returned to an old way. Labor's tangled situation was vividly highlighted when Rudd's former press secretary Lachlan Harris appeared on the ABC's 7.30 program. Asked how Rudd would begin to counter the material the Coalition had to use against him, Harris declared: 'I think he has to effectively say that a vote for Kevin Rudd is a vote against all that Labor party instability you saw over the last three years. He has to position himself effectively as the person who's taking on Abbott and taking on Labor instability.' This was the instability of which Rudd and his followers had been a major cause.

The caucus's decision meant Rudd was invested with virtually untrammelled authority (challenged only marginally during the campaign weeks themselves by campaign director Wright). An unfettered presidential style had been Rudd's vulnerability in 2010, yet in 2013, Labor strategists said unabashedly the campaign would be a 'presidential' one. For a few weeks Rudd would be invulnerable. As Wright explained later, having changed leaders in such circumstances, Labor had to emphasise Rudd and his strengths and 'work the party strategy into making the most of these'. Rudd had 'earned the right . . . to campaign to his strategy'.

Before the formal campaign for the September election, Rudd changed ALP rules and core policy, including promising to bring forward the start of the ETS and announcing a draconian asylum-seeker policy that would send all boat arrivals offshore and never allow them to settle in Australia.

On the Labor rules, his moves had major implications for future Labor prime ministers. He had already conceded in 2012 that he had been wrong to take away caucus's ability to elect the frontbench; it was no surprise he proposed this be returned. More dramatic was his move to prevent any future aspirant doing what he had just done to Gillard, and she to him in 2010. He put forward a new method of choosing the leader, with the party rank-and-file membership having a 50 per cent say. A prime minister could only be moved against with the support of 75 per cent of the caucus. His original idea was to put the 75 per cent threshold in for a spill against an opposition leader, but this was lowered to 60 per cent in face of complaints that it was too high. The caucus ratified the democratisation, which was greeted with enthusiasm by the party at large. A minority of critics went unheeded, although the national conference is the ultimate arbiter and the threshold limits may be questioned or challenged when the conference next meets.

The reform to give the party rank and file a voice in choosing the leader reflects methods used in various other countries. That it came to Labor when it did was totally due to Rudd's circumstances and history. If there had not been the coup against him, it is unlikely he would have proposed the change. Having been reinstated, he had two imperatives. He wanted to send the message to voters that if they elected him, they would get him for the full term. He was also making sure that, in the event he pulled off an unlikely victory—not ruled out in his own mind at that stage—he would never again be internally vulnerable. Giving the rank and file a half say in choosing the leader was as big a single reform as any in modern Labor's history. It helped sustain the party in the early days after the 2013 defeat. The man whose weakness was that he failed to adequately share and delegate power brought the party a major step forward in power-sharing. The autocrat left a democratic legacy.

After handing itself to Rudd a second time, the party's angst was later evident. Campaigning for the post-election leadership, Bill Shorten told a Labor meeting: 'The era of the messiah is over. No more messiahs!' Yet the nature of politics is that parties will always look for, and be vulnerable to, 'messiahs'—those who are magnets for votes.

One feature of prime ministerial government is that of 'pairing', and the nature of that pairing can be crucial for how leaders operate and the nature of their political ends. The pairing, in which the second person is often but not always deputy, can be complementary or competitive, or both, or the former can transform into the latter. The obvious British example of competitive pairing was Tony Blair and Gordon Brown. James Walter has described the 'increasingly destructive tango' between the two as 'a battle between fiercely intelligent men, with giant egos, each driven by a distinctive sort of narcissism' (Strangio et al. 2013: 39). In the Australian context, Gough Whitlam and his deputy Lance Barnard formed a complementary pair, in which Barnard completely supported and helped his leader, and was never seen as a threat or a potential successor. On the Liberal side, John Howard and Peter Costello were in a competitive relationship that was never ultimately tested because Costello did not challenge; the competition from time to time was damaging, but the complementarity was more significant. A parallel relationship between Bob Hawke and Paul Keating delivered much economic reform for the country but progressively deteriorated, ending in Keating prevailing over Hawke.

How a competitive, or potentially competitive, pairing works out can be a function of time, the skill of the number-one player to manage the relationship, and the determination and ability of the second partner to ascend to number-one position. Costello's inability to wrest the leadership from Howard was largely because he lacked the numbers for the challenge. He did not attract a critical mass of support because he was not seen as likely to be the better vote winner. The balance in the Hawke–Keating pairing tipped after Labor members of parliament judged Hawke was vulnerable to the Coalition.

Despite Rudd always having had an eye to Gillard's likely ambition, in 2010 the competitive nature of their relationship was less developed and overt than in these other examples. It was mentioned from time to time—in opposition when leadership numbers were being compared, and in the months before the coup when Rudd was under attack and Gillard was repeatedly asked about her ambitions. But more often Gillard was seen as a longer term successor—in the next term, as criticism of Rudd mounted. And unlike what usually happens when there is a competitive pairing, she did not background journalists against her leader. Indeed, she later made a point of challenging any journalist who had heard her speak against Rudd privately to say so, freeing them of confidentiality obligations. Even in these circumstances journalists would usually be unwilling to reveal conversations, but presumably she felt secure that there was nothing anyone could produce.

Although Rudd supporters believed that Gillard was actively plotting against him in the run up to the coup, it seems more likely that she was loyal until a very late stage. Indeed, in her discussion with Rudd on the night of the coup, she was willing to accede to his request for a few months to try to get his act together. When she relayed this plan to her backers, they rejected it totally and she was forced to renege.

While Gillard's removal of Rudd occurred before their relationship had, in any public sense, moved into a full-blown competitive phase, it surely would have progressed to that if he had survived into another term. His weaknesses would have become more obvious, as would her strengths.

After the 2013 election, Hawker (who had been at Rudd's side as his main adviser during the election campaign) reflected on the conflict and complementarity in the Rudd–Gillard pairing. Labor's 2007–13 story would always be framed by the relationship between them, he wrote. It came to be characterised as one of 'deep and abiding antipathy'. But in the early years they were a team. He was the 'big-picture Leader', not a factional player, and sceptical of the unions' power in the party. She was 'the deal-making poster child of the Labor party', able to 'negotiate outcomes that supported Rudd's political ambitions'.

> The public respected him and the Party loved her. He could woo the electorate and she could pull the caucus in behind him. They were the yin and the yang of the Labor Party. Together they were indomitable, but apart they were vulnerable: he to the faction leaders and she to public opinion. (Hawker 2013: xi–xiii)

Looked at that way, this pair of Labor prime ministers can be viewed as two halves of a whole. Neither had a sufficient skill set to do the job effectively, at least not in the circumstances they faced. They needed each other.

Rudd fell, most dramatically, to those who felt wronged and excluded, and who believed he was leading the government to hell in a hand basket. More deeply, he was a prisoner of his own personality. It is hard to believe that if he had wrought a miracle in 2013, he would have lived up to his promise of a new way of doing things. Gillard's fate was determined when she said yes instead of no to those who sought to overthrow Rudd. She arrived in the job undercooked. If, instead of acquiring it via a coup, there had been a smoother transition when she had gained greater experience, her prime ministership might have run quite differently.

The tipping point for Labor and these leaders was early to mid-2010. When trouble mounted in the form of Rudd's leadership style, issues starting to run out of control and falling polls, the pair and the party needed to find solutions that preserved the partnership, at least into a successful election outcome and a next term. As it was, Rudd and Gillard were victims of each other and of themselves; the Labor party, by allowing and promoting their wrecking behaviour, fell victim to them both.

ACKNOWLEDGEMENTS

Thanks to Rod Rhodes for suggesting I explore 'pairing'; to Anne Tiernan for comments on the draft, and to Gabrielle Hooton, Pera Wells and Matt Dawson for help with research.

REFERENCES

Aulich, C. & Evans, M. (eds), 2010, *The Rudd Government: Australian Commonwealth Administration 2007–2010*, Canberra: ANU E Press

Button, J., 2012, *Speechless: A year in my father's business*, Melbourne: Melbourne University Publishing

Gillard, J., 2013, 'Julia Gillard Writes on Power, Purpose and Labor's Future', *Guardian Australia*, 14 September 2013

Hawker, B., 2013, *The Rudd Rebellion: The campaign to save Labor*, Melbourne: Melbourne University Publishing

Kelly, S., 2013, 'Labor Abandons Policy at its Peril', *Sydney Morning Herald*, 31 October 2013

Kent, J., 2013, *Take Your Best Shot: The prime ministership of Julia Gillard*, Melbourne: Penguin

Marr, D., 2013, *Rudd v Abbott: Two classic Quarterly Essays*, Collingwood: Black Inc.

Roxon, N., 2013, *John Button Memorial Lecture 2013*, 16 October 2013

Strangio, P., 't Hart, P. & Walter, J. (eds), 2013, *Understanding Prime-Ministerial Performance: Comparative perspectives*, Oxford: Oxford University Press

Walsh, K.A., 2013, *The Stalking of Julia Gillard: How the media and Team Rudd contrived to bring down the prime minister*, Sydney: Allen & Unwin

Weller, P., 1985, *First Among Equals: Prime ministers in Westminster systems*, Sydney: George Allen & Unwin

Weller, P. (ed.), 1992, *Menzies to Keating: The development of the Australian prime ministership*, Melbourne: Melbourne University Press

4

CORE EXECUTIVES, PRIME MINISTERS, STATECRAFT AND COURT POLITICS: TOWARDS CONVERGENCE[1]

R.A.W. Rhodes

Rhodes and Wanna (2009) concluded that the study of the Australian core executive placed description over theory, commentary over fieldwork, and teaching over research. Pat Weller agrees with this assessment. He notes that the academic literature provides 'slim pickings for a reader who wants to know how the executive system of government works in Australia' (Weller 2005: 37). Weller's work is the exception. He has repaired many of the gaps in our knowledge and become the doyen of prime ministerial and cabinet studies in Australia.

This chapter acknowledges his contribution by building on it and exploring ways forward in the study of executive government. I discuss recent developments in executive studies, mainly in Australia and Britain; argue that there is a convergence on the idea of court politics; and discuss the advantages of a focus on court politics. No doubt fulfilling Pat's worst fears, I focus on theory, but there is a link—the idea of Realpolitik. The shared concept of our otherwise different approaches is the analysis of court politics. We both analyse a Faustian world in which rulers are ephemeral, temporal and survive on borrowed time until the dark forces get them (see Davis and Rhodes, this volume, Chapter 2).

APPROACHES TO THE STUDY OF EXECUTIVE GOVERNMENT[2]

I discuss five developments in executive studies since 2000: the core executive; the 'prime ministerial predominance' thesis; the 'statecraft' thesis; the 'New Political History'; and interpretive ethnography. I argue that these contributions converge on the study of court or high politics, which holds out the prospect of reinvigorating executive studies.

Core executive studies

Dunleavy and Rhodes (1990) proposed the concept of the core executive. It was developed and refined in Rhodes (1995); Elgie (1997); Smith (1999); and Marsh, Richards and Smith (2001) over the next decade. The idea recognises that the institutions of the executive are not limited to the prime minister and cabinet, but also include ministers in their departments. It includes 'all those organizations and procedures which coordinate central government policies, and act as final arbiters between different parts of the government machine'. Thus, the core executive comprises 'the complex web of institutions, networks and practices surrounding the prime minister, cabinet, cabinet committees and their official counterparts, less formalised ministerial "clubs" or meetings, bilateral negotiations and interdepartmental committees' (Rhodes 1995: 12). Twenty years on, as Elgie (2011: 64) notes, the 'core executive' is well established in the political science literature. It is widely deployed in the study of British central government, in European countries and Australia (for example, Davis 1997).

Core executive studies challenged mainstream analyses of the British executive, which were 'positional'—assuming power inhered to key positions (the prime minister, the cabinet) and their incumbents. It posed a focus on resource dependence and asked such questions as: 'Who does what?' and 'Who has what resources?' In contrast, under core executive assumptions, power is fluid; it is not fixed by, and does not accrue to, a particular position. It varies according to the relative power of other actors and to prevailing circumstances. Power relations vary because all core executive actors have some resources, but no one consistently commands all the resources necessary to achieve their goals. So, they exchange such resources as, for example, money, legislative authority or expertise. These exchanges take the form of games in which actors manoeuvre for advantage. Resource dependence thus characterises relationships within the core executive. Elgie (2011: 64) claims that the ideas of the core executive and resource dependence have become the 'new orthodoxy' in executive studies, but there are significant variants, most notably prime ministerial predominance.

Prime ministerial predominance

This thesis is associated with the work of Richard Heffernan and Mark Bennister. For Heffernan (2003: 348) the proposition that power is relational and based on dependency is 'only partially accurate. Power is relational between actors but it is also locational. It is dependent on where actors are to be found within the core executive, and whether they are at the centre or the periphery of key core executive networks'. He agrees the core executive is segmented, but disputes that power is as fragmented and dispersed as Rhodes and others have suggested. An inherently unequal distribution of resources affords leaders unique advantages, creating the potential for prime ministerial predominance.

Since power-dependence characterises core executive relationships, it follows that attention should focus on the distribution and dispersal of resources and shifting patterns of dependence between multiple actors. Prime ministers command many 'institutional resources', including patronage, prestige, authority, political centrality and policy reach, knowledge, information and expertise, Crown Prerogative (for example, to delegate powers and responsibilities to ministers and departments) and control of the agenda (Heffernan 2003: 356–7). They also have 'personal resources' such as reputation, skill and ability; association with actual or anticipated political success; public popularity; and high standing in the party (Heffernan 2003: 351, 2005: 16). It follows that the more resources a prime minister has, or can accumulate, the greater their potential for predominance. But ministers also have access to many resources that are not available to the prime minister, including 'a professional, permanent and knowledgeable staff, expert knowledge and relevant policy networks, time, information and, not least, an annual budget' (Heffernan 2005: 614).

So, the unit of analysis in core executive studies cannot be solely the prime minister, nor can it be just the cabinet; power is more widely dispersed. Prime ministers remain key actors who, because of their access to institutional and personal resources and their position at the centre of key networks (Heffernan 2003; 2005), have the *potential* to exercise significant power. The experiences of Tony Blair, John Howard and Kevin Rudd, who at key points in time were regarded as 'predominant' prime ministers, remind us that unpredictable forces shape, constrain and sometimes undermine leaders' ability to get their own way. So, we must examine the relations between leaders and their colleagues in cabinet, the party room, and other 'followers' on whom they also depend.

Indeed, both Bennister (2007: 328) and Heffernan (2005: 607) agree the core executive approach need not necessarily abandon the idea of a strong executive government; the two approaches are not mutually exclusive. Even Heffernan's (2003: 350) initial version of the argument had many qualifications. He suggests the prime ministerial authority is 'contingent and contextual'. Prime ministers have the 'potential' to be predominant, 'but only when personal resources are married with institutional power resources, and when the prime minister is able to use both wisely and well'. The prime minister's personal resources are 'never guaranteed. They come and go, are acquired and squandered, are won and lost' (Heffernan 2003: 356). Moreover, 'there is . . . a vast and sprawling system of networks, committees and taskforces where most work is undertaken' (Bennister 2007: 335). Later versions of the prime ministerial dominance argument introduce more significant qualifications:

> Prime ministers can be sure-footed or clumsy, be associated with policy success or failure, have a low or a high party standing, a solid or a weak parliamentary reputation, become electorally popular or unpopular. He or she can preside over a happy or unhappy parliamentary party and can face weak or powerful intra-party rivals. Prime ministers can be lucky or unlucky and face strong or weak inter-party opponents. Often, an underperforming economy, or some other such record of policy failure, can prove the instrument of the prime minister's downfall. (Heffernan 2005: 616–17)

Proponents of the core executive approach never abandoned the idea of strong executive government. Rather, they opened the debate about the power of the prime minister to the limits imposed by contingency and context, and identified the variety of core executive practices. For example, Elgie (1997) identifies six patterns of core executive practices in prime ministerial and semi-presidential systems ranging from, for example, monocratic government where prime ministers predominate, to ministerial government where the political heads of major departments decide policy, to bureaucratic government where non-elected officials in government departments and agencies decide policy (see also Rhodes 2006).

The advantage of this formulation is that it gets away from bald assertions about the fixed nature of executive politics. While one pattern of executive politics may operate at any one time, there can still be fluidity as one pattern is succeeded by another. Take for example, the rapid decline in public support for Kevin Rudd that followed his decision to abandon his commitment to an emissions trading scheme. This policy change created an opportunity for those angered by Rudd's domineering leadership style to harness discontent among ministers and the Labor caucus. Allegiances, including those of Rudd's former supporters, shifted to his deputy, Julia Gillard. Overnight, Rudd was ousted in a party-room challenge that, lacking support, he didn't contest.

Unintended consequences and the effect of one damn thing after another, concentrates the mind on contingencies and on the question of which pattern of executive politics prevails. When, how, and why did it change? Focusing solely on the power of prime minister and cabinet is limiting, whereas these questions open the possibility of explaining similarities and differences in the court politics of the core executive (Elgie 1997: 23 and citations). Indeed, 'predominance can . . . ebb and flow' (Bennister 2007: 340). Few would have difficulty accepting that the prime minister is the 'principal node of key core executive networks' (Heffernan 2005: 613; and see Burch and Holliday 1996).

So, I read the later Heffernan (2005) and Bennister and Heffernan (2011) as an important set of qualifications to the prime ministerial dominance argument. It is significant that they wrote their first version during the heyday of the Blair 'presidency', while their qualifications reflect his later decline. In his most recent article, in reply to Dowding (2013), Heffernan (2013: 642, 643) emphasises that the prime ministers can have 'more or less political capital' and their 'power waxes and wanes'. These qualifications bridge the gap between their approach and proponents of the core executive approach. By downplaying prime ministerial predominance, Heffernan (2005: 616–17) opens the way for a convergence on the notion of court politics.

Statecraft

The ideas of high politics and statecraft crept into political science most notably in the work of James Bulpitt.[3] For Bulpitt (1995: 518), 'The court is . . . the formal Chief Executive, plus his/her political friends and advisers'. Members of the court, the political elite, have an 'operating code', which is 'less than a philosophy of government and yet more than a specific collection of policies. It refers to the accepted rules of "statecraft" as employed over time by political elites' (Bulpitt 1983: 68, n. 23). The statecraft of the court comprises a set of governing objectives (or 'beliefs'); a governing code (or 'practices'); and a set of political support mechanisms, for example, for party management (Bulpitt 1995: 519). 'Statecraft is about the relationship between ideas and political practice. It is about short-term politicking or tactical manoeuvring' (Buller 1999: 695). It is about gaining and keeping office, creating an image of governing competence, and creating government autonomy over high politics. It is another exercise in Realpolitik.

The approach rests on three assumptions. First, Bulpitt (1995: 517) assumes that the court will 'behave in a unitary (united) fashion'. Second, he assumes the court possesses a 'relative autonomy' from structural factors (Bulpitt 1995: 518). Finally, he assumes the court is rational, that it will 'develop strategies which will enable them to attempt to pursue consistently their own interests' (Bulpitt 1995: 519).

Bulpitt is well served by several followers, most notably Jonathan Bradbury, James Buller and Toby James, as they claim him for the new institutionalism and the realist school of political philosophy. The criticisms that follow apply to the statecraft thesis, not just to Bulpitt.

First, a persistent criticism of the statecraft thesis 'has been its indifference to empirical refutation' and, indeed, to methods more generally (see Buller 1999: 704). Bulpitt (1983: 239) concedes the point; 'the supporting data for many of these arguments is much less than perfect'. As Buller (1999: 704) notes, 'acquiring knowledge about governing codes is a task beset with analytical problems'. I suggest below that the 'New Political History' addresses these matters more satisfactorily.

Second, Buller (1999: 699–705) argues that Bulpitt neglects ontological and epistemological questions. This observation is undoubtedly accurate, and the muddles that ensue can be clearly seen in Bulpitt's three assumptions about the court, none of which are necessary, and all betray a lingering modernist-empiricism in his thought. Indeed, Bulpitt (1995: 517) considered all his assumptions to be 'operating assumptions, something to guide the analysis until it becomes unsatisfactory'. He qualified the first assumption straight away, calling the question of who is the principal actor 'a very real problem' (Bulpitt 1995: 518). For the analysis of court politics, it is less important to ask when the court is united than to ask when there are factions, and with what consequences. Bevir (2010: 443) concluded that Bulpitt was unusual in combining modernist empiricism with Tory historiography. I suggest it will be more profitable to employ the notion of 'situated agency' and ask what traditions shape the court's beliefs and practices (that is, its statecraft).

Buller seeks to resolve many of these issues by appealing to critical realism. This creates a new set of problems, mainly because critical realism and Bulpitt's work are uneasy bedfellows. As Bevir (2010: 445) suggests, Bulpitt's work owes a 'debt to a Tory Tradition . . . in particular . . . historians such as Lewis Namier and Jack Plumb'. Bulpitt treats 'their portrait of the eighteenth century court as an ideal type applicable to the whole of British history' (Bevir 2010: 445). This 'Tory moment' is the source of Bulpitt's notions of court and country and high and low politics. There is also a clear overlap with the work of the latter-day Tory historian Maurice Cowling; they share a concern with the political elite, high politics and Realpolitik.

Bulpitt's modernist empiricism has led commentators to assimilate him to the new institutionalism and critical realism (Buller 1999: 705–19), but as Bevir (2010: 446) notes 'that is only half the story'. Bulpitt was ambivalent about the ideas of institutions and structure when they were used to explain elite actors' behaviour. Rather, he leaves the definition of structure 'to the designated principal actors' because 'they will be able to choose which structural features preoccupy them and in what sequence they will be tackled' (Bulpitt 1995: 518). This constructivist view of structure fits uneasily with the claim by critical realists of 'necessity' and 'emergent properties'; it simply does not admit structures that have 'causal powers' (Buller 1999: 706).

At this point we can see the overlap between Buller's views on structure and Heffernan's analysis of prime ministerial predominance. Heffernan (2005: 610) argues that the exchange of resources occurs 'under the structures imposed by the political system'. He makes the strong claim that 'institutional *imperatives decide* the arrangement of relations between, say, the executive, the legislature and the judiciary'. These imperatives also *determine* intra-executive, legislative and judicial configurations' (emphasis added). Both Buller and Heffernan reify and overstate the effect of 'structure'. Instead, I suggest below that we focus on traditions, beliefs and practices. Most discussions of 'structure', when looked at critically, dissolve into 'traditions' and 'practices', and if they do not, they have not been looked at critically enough (Bevir and Rhodes 2006b and 2006c).

The New Political History

Although there is no defining statement, no manifesto, Craig (2010) draws together the strands and provides a helpful conspectus of the main contributors. In the New Political History, the focus is the study of high politics and low politics. The founder of this school of history is Maurice Cowling.

For Cowling, the high politics approach meant studying the intentions and actions of a political leadership network that consisted of 'fifty or sixty politicians in conscious tension with one another whose accepted authority constituted political leadership'. High politics was 'a matter of rhetoric and manoeuvre' by statesmen (Cowling 1971: 3–4). He explores the tension between 'situational necessity and the intentions of politicians' using the letters, diaries and public speeches of this network of elite leaders. His people behave 'situationally', but Cowling never deploys such reified notions as institution or class. Such 'structures' are defined by the elite; they choose which ones they will pay attention to. Instead he asks, 'What influences played upon, what intentions were maintained, what prevision was possible and what success was achieved by the leading actors on the political stage' (Cowling 1967: 322). In short, Cowling analyses the Realpolitik of the governing elite. His approach is characterised by 'relativistic individualism' (Ghosh 1993: 276 n. 76) and an emphasis on historical contingency.

As Williamson (2010: 131, 141) observes, Cowling's 'most noted and notorious contribution to political history' was high politics and his insistence that political leaders had 'relative autonomy, with substantial independence in taking decisions'. The new political historians are Cowling's heirs, but their interests are not confined to high politics, rather they extend to such topics as electoral politics and labour history (see Lawrence and Taylor 1997). This shift to low politics means that elite actors are no longer privileged. Rather, the intention is to focus the spotlight on the manifold stories of multifarious government actors. It directs us to the local and the overlooked. Nonetheless, as Pederson suggests, there is an intellectual convergence between students of high politics and low politics, although 'Maurice Cowling would surely have not been in sympathy' with these theoretical trends (Pederson 2002: 40–2; see also Williamson 2010: 140). In both cases, there has been a move away from structural and class-based explanations of politics to politics as 'an enclosed rule bound game' and to the 'intellectual setting' of that game. So, there is a convergence around the study of political leaders, political culture and political ideas.

A fine present-day example of high politics for political scientists is historian Philip Williamson's biography of Stanley Baldwin. Williamson (1999: 12–18) argues two approaches are necessary to understand major politicians. First, there is the interpretive study of high politics; 'the narrative is not of one politician nor even of one party, but rather of the whole system of political leadership'. So, the biographer must place individuals in 'the full multi-party and multi-policy contexts'. Second, there is biography, where it is necessary to go beyond chronological narrative to examine 'the nature and practice of political leadership'. This approach explores, 'the remorseless situational and tactical pressures, the chronic uncertainties, and the short horizons which afflict all political leadership'; and it looks for 'the qualities that really distinguish and explain a politician's effectiveness'. This focus on the patterns in high politics and the practices of political leaders leads to the study of statecraft.

Baldwin's reputation suffered 'enduring denigration' as the prime minister who betrayed the nation, putting party before country by delaying rearmament and appeasing Hitler (see Williamson 2004 for rebuttal). Yet he was one of the most successful interwar politicians. He was leader of the opposition, *de facto* prime minister as Lord President of the Council in the coalition, and prime minister in his own right. In total, he was at the forefront of British politics for some fourteen years. Williamson explores the foundations of Baldwin's success by analysing his use of political rhetoric in his speeches and other public political and non-political presentations. He suggests that 'politicians are what they speak and publish', so he uses the speeches to show how Baldwin persuaded his audiences, shaped opinion and created political allegiance. Baldwin was the first politician to master public broadcasting, but he also used photographs and the cinema to present himself attractively. Williamson adds these presentational skills to Baldwin's skills at ministerial coordination, his political judgement, party management and reputation in parliament to explain his standing between the wars. But, and crucially, the bedrock to this reputation lay in his detachment; his non-political persona; his probity; and his ability to address the anxieties of the ordinary citizen in a way that harnessed them to the Conservative cause. He eased the process of social reconciliation after the Depression; socialised the Labour Party to parliamentary ways and government; and created modern 'One Nation' Conservatism, capturing the political centre and restoring popular respect for politicians.

Williamson's craft lies in his analysis of Baldwin's personal papers, speeches, publications and film appearances. Like Cowling, he shows we can explore the beliefs and practices of the governing elite by studying their letters, diaries and speeches (Williamson 2010: 119–20; and see Cowling 1967: 311–40 for his discussion of sources). The 'New Political History' demonstrates the importance of their methods for political scientists. Thus, Kavanagh argues that 'the contribution of history, as the systematic study of the past, to political science has been more as a body of knowledge than as a set of methods' (Kavanagh 1991: 480). He identifies several uses of history in political science: for example, history as a database, as a way to test theories, and as a source of lessons (Kavanagh 1991: 483). In effect, he reduces historians to collectors of facts for political scientists. It is scarcely a surprise that historians do not agree. Lawrence and Taylor (1997: 15–16) are only two of the dissenting voices. They reject the historian's role of 'furnishing anecdotal material and suggestive counter evidence for the [models of] political scientists'. Rather they argue 'the proper task of the historian should be to render theory problematic . . . because many theories simply do not time-travel very well'. Archival research using the private papers and speeches of elite actors is an essential tool for uncovering the beliefs and practices of the governing elite and understanding their actions. Cowling and Williamson exemplify the skills that political scientists could use in the service of their own questions and concepts. And political scientists need the help. For example, I noted earlier the persistent criticism of the statecraft thesis that it neglects evidence and methods. The historians of high politics surmount these problems and take us inside the black box. In short, to turn Kavanagh on his head, history is less a body of knowledge and more a set of methods; tools we can use to explore beliefs and practices in context.

Interpretive ethnography

Political anthropology is a minority sport in political science, and until recently there was little work (Aronoff and Kubik 2013: 19). Although over the past decade there has been a surge in comparative politics, little changed in the study of Australian and British government.

By long association, participant observation has been a defining characteristic of ethnography. Phrases such as deep immersion or unstructured soaking abound whether looking at a congressional district, a government department or a tribe in Africa. Ethnography is a broad and theoretically eclectic church. Interpretive ethnography is one prominent strand and its high priest is Clifford Geertz. The idea of meaning lies at its heart. It seeks to understand the webs of significance that people spin for themselves. It provides 'thick description' in which the researcher writes his or her construction of the subject's construction of what the subject is doing (adapted from Geertz 1993: 9). So, the task is to unpack the disparate and contingent beliefs and practices of individuals through which they construct their world; to identify the recurrent patterns of actions and related beliefs. And if thick descriptions are a 'rather uneasy combination of involvement and detachment', they are 'still the best method we have for exploring the complexities of human cultures' (Fox 2004: 4). In short, what works is best, so we are *bricoleurs* or Jacks-of-all-trades, gathering material when, where and how we can (Levi-Strauss 1966: 16–17).

There are several examples of such ethnographic research on British government. They include Heclo and Wildavsky (1981 [1974]) on the Treasury and public expenditure; Burns (1977) on the BBC; Crewe (2005) on the House of Lords; Faucher-King (2005) on party conferences; and Rhodes (2011) on British government departments. One brief example must suffice.

Rhodes (2011) seeks to understand the ways in which the political and administrative elites of British central government departments made sense of their worlds. It provides 'thick descriptions' through an analysis of their beliefs and everyday practices. Rhodes shadowed two ministers, three permanent secretaries and their private offices for some 420 hours, with a further 67 hours of interviews. The fieldwork covered three ministries: the Department of Trade and Industry (DTI), the Department for Education and Skills (DfES), and the Department for Environment, Food & Rural Affairs (DEFRA). Following the established practice of latter-day ethnographers, he undertook 'yo-yo fieldwork', repeatedly going in and out of the field (Wulff 2002: 117). He also went to more than one fieldwork site because he was 'studying through'; that is, following events through the 'webs and relations between actors, institutions and discourses across time and space' (Shore and Wright 1997: 14).

In short, the book tells a story about departmental courts that practise willed ordinariness using elaborate protocols and rituals. It suggests that distinctions between policy and management, politician and civil servant, become meaningless when confronted by the imperative to cope and survive. It describes the world of 'political-administrators', who are dependent on one another to carry out their respective roles, each role one side of the same coin. Every rude surprise demonstrates their mutual dependence. This portrait of a storytelling political-administrative elite, with beliefs and practices rooted in the Westminster model that uses protocols and rituals to limit rude surprises, is not the conventional portrait.

In the space available it is possible to give only one brief example to illustrate the general argument and approach. Each department had its own tradition or departmental philosophy that acted as the storehouse of many stories. It was a form of folk psychology. It provided the everyday theory and shared languages for storytelling. It was the collective memory of the department; a retelling of yesterday to make sense of today.

Senior civil servants used stories not only to gain and pass on information and to inspire involvement, but also as the repository of the organisation's institutional memory. As Boje (1991: 106) suggests 'stories are to the storytelling system what precedent cases are to the judicial system'. Most, if not all, civil servants accepted that the art of storytelling was an integral part of their work. Such phrases as: 'Have we got our story straight?', 'Are we telling a consistent story?', and 'What is our story?' abound. Civil servants and ministers learn and filter current events through the stories they hear and tell one another.

Storytelling had three characteristics: a language game, a performing game and a management game. The language game identified and constructed the storyline, answering the questions of what and happened and why. The performing game told the story to a wider audience, inside and outside the department. Officials tested the facts and rehearsed the storyline in official meetings to see how their colleagues responded. They had to adapt the story to suit the minister, and both ministers and officials had to judge how the story would play publicly. They then performed that agreed story on a public stage to the media, Parliament and the public. Finally, there was the management game, which involved implementing any policy changes and, perhaps even more important, getting on with 'business as usual' as quickly as possible. So, storytelling is not an example of academic whimsy. It is an integral part of the everyday practice of civil servants. Stories explain past practice and events, and justify recommendations for the future.

What lessons can we learn from interpretive ethnography? First, and most obvious, observation is another essential method for the political scientists' toolkit, one currently conspicuous mainly for its absence. As

Agar (1996: 27) comments: 'no understanding of a world is valid without representation of those members' voices'. Thick descriptions provide those members' voices. Observation may be the defining method in ethnography, but there are many other tools: for example, focus groups, oral histories, and informal conversations. Using multiple methods enhances the reliability of the evidence; for example, observation is an essential complement to interviews, enabling the observer to compare what is said with what is done.

Second, given the perennial excuse that the pervasive secrecy of Australian and British government limits access and, therefore, the opportunities for observation, Rhodes (2011) and the several other studies noted here demonstrate that such fieldwork is possible.

Third, observation offers the prospect of moments of epiphany. Rhodes did not set out to explore storytelling. It emerged during the fieldwork encounters and is a clear demonstration of how ethnography opens new windows for analysis. Fieldwork can deliver serendipity and surprise.

Finally, the approach helps to analyse the symbolic dimensions of political action. Most political behaviour has a strong symbolic dimension. Symbols do not simply 'represent' or reflect political 'reality', they actively constitute that reality. By drawing out the negotiated, symbolic and ritual elements of political life, ethnographic analysis draws attention to deeper principles of organisation that are not visible to empiricist or positivist approaches.

AND SO TO COURT POLITICS

Court politics have existed throughout the ages (see Campbell 2010) but in its current reincarnation the idea marries the core executive to the analysis of prime ministerial predominance and to the study of statecraft. It is a shift of *topos* from institutions and positions to individuals and the practices of court politics. It focuses on the beliefs and practices of core executive actors. Practices are actions that display a stable pattern; they are what a group of people do. So, a government department or a core executive network or the court is a set of embedded practices. We interpret these actions by ascribing beliefs to them. Practices presuppose apt beliefs, and beliefs do not make sense without the practices to which they refer.

Beliefs and practices are passed on through inherited departmental traditions. At the heart of this analysis of tradition is the notion of *situated agency*; of individuals using local reasoning consciously and subconsciously to reflect on and modify their contingent heritage. So, analysis shifts to people's beliefs and practices, the traditions in which they are located, and the games interdependent people play to resolve dilemmas (Bevir and Rhodes 2003; 2006a). This shift to the practices of the court captures the intense rivalry between, for example, Tony Blair and Gordon Brown, or Kevin Rudd and Julia Gillard. It also rejects any notion of dominance by any one actor or set of actors.

Court politics exists as journalists' reportage, in the autobiographies, biographies, diaries and memoirs of politicians.[4] The nearest usage to that employed here is that of Savoie (2008: 16–17). He defines the court as 'the prime minister and a small group of carefully selected courtiers'. It also covers the 'shift from formal decision-making processes in cabinet . . . to informal processes involving only a handful of actors'. This conception is too narrow. I accept there is often an inner sanctum, but participants in high politics are rarely so few. I prefer Cowling's more expansive definition, allied to Burch and Holliday's (1996) notion that the centre is a set of networks. These networks are still exclusive. The number of participants is still limited. But, as well as the core network or inner circle, I can also talk of circles of influence (Hennessy 2000: 493–500); a term that accords with political folklore and practice.

The court is a key part of the organisational glue holding the centre together. It coordinates the policy process by filtering and packaging proposals. It contains and manages conflicts between ministerial barons. It acts as the keeper of the government's narrative. It acts as the gatekeeper and broker for internal and external networks. The notion also directs our attention to the analysis of rival courts in departments and in other levels of government. Baronial politics live inside and outside the heart of government.

It also has something interesting to say about the problems of effective government. For Walter (2010: 9–10), 'court politics' implies small, closed-group decision-making. He is concerned about the potential for dysfunction—poor decision-making, an inability and unwillingness to engage in 'rigorous reality-testing' and other pathologies—if this mode of decision-making should become routine. Rhodes (2011: 275–6) reports a siege mentality, which fosters a short-term focus, stereotyping, and inward-looking processes of decision-making during a political crisis. However, it is a mistake to focus only on the pathologies of small-group decision-making. We should ask about the pros and cons of court politics.

Thus, Savoie (2008: 232) argues that the court helps prime ministers 'to get things done, to see results, and to manage the news and the media better than when formal cabinet processes are respected'. It dispenses with the formalities of government, such as records and minutes and other formal processes. However, on the downside, Savoie (2008: 230, 339) argues that the key adverse consequences are centralisation and the collapse of accountability: 'the centre has slowly but surely been made deliberately stronger'; and 'the chain of accountability . . . has broken down at every level'.

There are also more prosaic but no less important consequences. For example, Pollitt (2007: 173) gives his recipe for losing institutional memory: rotate staff rapidly, change the IT system frequently, restructure every two years, reward management over other skills, and adopt each new management fad. Savoie agrees: 'senior civil servants no longer have the experience, the knowledge, or the institutional memory to speak truth to power' (Savoie 2008: 25; see also Rhodes 2011: 293–5). We need to tease out both the intended and unintended consequences of court politics.

CONCLUSIONS

My use of the term 'court politics' has five advantages.

First, the term not only 'blurs genres' (Geertz 1983: 19) between political science, history and anthropology, but also leads to a convergence of approaches in political science. It builds bridges within and between disciplines, expanding the available approaches to the study of executive government in political science. It brings together previously separate approaches such as the core executive and prime ministerial predominance; for example, Bennister (2007: 337) cites with approval Bevir and Rhodes (2006a) on court politics.

Second, allied to an interpretive approach, it provides the ontological and epistemological foundations missing from earlier uses of the term high politics by, for example, Bulpitt and Cowling. As Craig (2010: 470–4) argues, there is a clear affinity between Cowling's historiography and interpretive ethnography in political science.

Third, the approach provides the organising concepts for a systematic analysis of elite actors. I suggest that court politics is more than a metaphor because the notions of beliefs, practices, traditions and dilemmas are effective tools for unpacking the statecraft of elite actors and their networks. It marries the analysis of individual actors, such as the prime minister, to the broader context of the court and its traditions.

Fourth, I have shown that the toolkit of political science must include the skills of the historian, biographer and ethnographer. Documentary evidence in its many forms is the bedrock for the analysis of court politics. It is not good enough to plead that governmental secrecy precludes observation because nowadays there are too many examples of ethnographic fieldwork on governing elites. The study of court politics will enlarge the toolkit of political scientists.

Finally, court politics can address matters of practical import. A key question is whether court politics support or undermine the search for effectiveness. Under what circumstances are court politics an effective form of executive governance? Though briefly, I have shown that the approach is not just an exercise in intellectual curiosity, but one that raises important questions about effectiveness and accountability.

Of course, the study of court politics poses practical challenges. Observation is time-consuming. We have to wait for documentary material to become available from families and friends as well as official sources. Perhaps we are too concerned to comment on the present-day; private and official documents for the Thatcher era are only now becoming available. Perhaps we underestimate just how much is out there. The volume of 'private information' reported in the work of biographers like Anthony Seldon and journalists like Andrew Rawnsley is impressive, and will bear secondary analysis such as mapping the membership of the Blair and Brown courts. If we are dedicated *bricoleurs*, we need to mine all publicly available information, irrespective of discipline or profession. It behoves us to try because court politics matters to all of us as citizens.

Court politics are ubiquitous and to focus on its games is an exercise in Realpolitik. It may well be true that the games of court politics have been more often described than analysed, more often judged than unpacked. However, we can move beyond the metaphor to study the beliefs, practices, and traditions of governing elites. This chapter seeks to marry my concern with theory to Pat's concern with Realpolitik. My aim is to show that the historical and ethnographic study of high politics will open what Pat and I agree is a Faustian world:

> Most nights are slow in the politics business but once in a while you get a fast one, a blast of wild treachery and weirdness that not

even the hard boys can handle. It is an evil trade, on most days, and nobody smart will defend it. (Thompson 2009: 679)

Tony Blair, Gordon Brown, Kevin Rudd and Julia Gillard are all familiar with blasts of wild treachery, as were the Manchu Court, Imperial Rome, and the English court during the Wars of the Roses. It is the stock of fiction, whether the faction of *The White Queen* or the fantasy of *The Game of Thrones*. Prime ministers live in shark-infested networks. We can watch from the safety of the side-lines. It is not our business to defend. It is our business to report and analyse who does what to whom, when, where, how and why, not because we are prurient but because court politics matters for effective and accountable government.

NOTES

1. I would like to thank Glyn Davis (Melbourne), Paul 't Hart (Utrecht), Bob Smith (Ackland Smith Consulting), Anne Tiernan (Griffith), the participants at the 63rd PSA Annual Conference, City Hall, Cardiff, 25–27 March 2013, and the participants at the workshop on 'The Craft of Governing', Griffith University, 9 August 2013, for their comments and advice on an earlier version of this chapter.
2. For earlier surveys see Rhodes (2006) and Rhodes and Wanna (2009). These chapters looked backwards to the twentieth century. In the 2000s, there is evidence of a reinvigorated field in Australia. See Bennister (2012); Dowding and Lewis (2012); Strangio et al. (2013); and Rhodes and Tiernan (2014).
3. As well as the references in the body of the text, see Dennis Kavanagh's obituary in *The Independent*, 25 May 1999; and the special issue of *Government & Politics*, vol. 45, no. 3, 2010.
4. On the reportage, autobiographies, biographies, memoirs and diaries relevant to court politics, there are too many items for a complete listing here. Recent examples for Australia include Blewett (1999) and Watson (2002). Recent examples for the UK include Blunkett (2006); Rawnsley (2001, 2010); Seldon (2004); Seldon et al. (2007); and Seldon and Lodge (2010).

REFERENCES

Agar, M., 1996, *The Professional Stranger*, 2nd edn, San Diego: Academic Press

Aronoff, M.J. & Kubik, J., 2013, *Anthropology and Political Science: A convergent approach*, New York and Oxford: Berghahn Books

Bennister, M., 2007, 'Tony Blair and John Howard: Comparative predominance and institution stretch in the UK and Australia', *The British Journal of Politics and International Relations*, vol. 9, no. 3, pp. 327–45

—— 2012, *Prime Ministers in Power: Blair and Howard compared*, Houndmills, Basingstoke: Palgrave

Bennister, M. & Heffernan, R., 2011, 'Cameron as Prime Minister: The intra-executive politics of Britain's coalition government', *Parliamentary Affairs*, vol. 65, no. 4, pp. 778–801

Bevir, M., 2010, 'Interpreting Territory and Power', *Government and Opposition*, vol. 45, no. 3, pp. 436–56

Bevir, M. & Rhodes, R.A.W., 2003, *Interpreting British Governance*, London: Routledge

—— 2006a, *Governance Stories*, London: Routledge

—— 2006b, 'Interpretive Approaches to British Government and Politics', *British Politics*, vol. 1, no. 1, pp. 1–29

—— 2006c, 'Disaggregating Structures as an Agenda for Critical Realism: A reply to McAnulla', *British Politics*, vol. 1, no. 3, pp. 397–403

Blewett, N., 1999, *A Cabinet Diary: A personal record of the first Keating government*, Kent Town, South Australia: Wakefield Press

Blunkett, David, 2006, *The Blunkett Tapes: My life in the bear pit*, London: Bloomsbury

Boje, D., 1991, 'The Storytelling Organization: A story of story performance in an office-supply firm', *Administrative Science Quarterly*, vol. 36, no. 1, pp. 106–26

Buller, J., 1999, 'A Critical Appraisal of the Statecraft Interpretation', *Public Administration*, vol. 77, no. 4, pp. 691–712

Bulpitt, J., 1983, *Territory and Power in the United Kingdom: An interpretation*, Manchester: Manchester University Press

—— 1995, 'Historical Politics: Macro, in-time, governing regime analysis', in J. Lovenduski & J. Stanyer (eds), *Contemporary Political Studies 1995, Volume II*, Belfast: Political Studies Association, pp. 510–20

Burch, M. & Holliday, I., 1996, *The British Cabinet System*, Englewood Hemel Hempstead: Prentice Hall/Harvester Wheatsheaf

Burns, T., 1977, *The BBC: Public institution and private world*, London: Macmillan

Campbell, J., 2010, *Pistols at Dawn: Two hundred years of political rivalry from Pitt & Fox to Blair & Brown*, London: Vintage

Cowling, M., 1967, *1867 Disraeli, Gladstone and Revolution: The Passing of the Second Reform Bill*, Cambridge: Cambridge University Press

—— 1971, *The Impact of Labour 1920–1924*, Cambridge: Cambridge University Press

Craig, D., 2010, '"High Politics" and the "New Political History"', *The Historical Journal*, vol. 53, no. 2, pp. 453–75

Crewe, E., 2005, *Lords of Parliament: Manners, rituals and politics*, Manchester: Manchester University Press

Davis, G., 1997, 'The Core Executive', in B. Galligan, I. McAllister & J. Ravenhill (eds), *New Developments in Australian Politics*, Melbourne: Macmillan, pp. 85–101

Dowding, Keith, 2013, 'The Prime Ministerialization of the British Prime Minister', *Parliamentary Affairs*, vol. 66, no. 3, pp. 617–35

Dowding, Keith & Lewis, Chris (eds), 2012, *Ministerial Careers and Accountability in the Australian Commonwealth Government*, Canberra: ANU E Press

Dunleavy, P. & Rhodes, R.A.W., 1990, 'Core Executive Studies in Britain', *Public Administration*, vol. 68, no. 1, pp. 3–28

Elgie, R., 1997, 'Models of Executive Politics: A framework for the study of executive power relations in parliamentary and semi-presidential regimes', *Political Studies*, vol. 45, no. 2, pp. 217–31

—— 2011, 'Core Executive Studies Two Decades On', *Public Administration*, vol. 89, no. 1, pp. 64–77

Faucher-King, Florence, 2005, *Changing Parties: An anthropology of British political conferences*, Houndmills, Basingstoke: Palgrave-Macmillan

Fox, K., 2004, *Watching the English: The hidden rules of English behaviour*, London: Hodder & Stoughton

Geertz, C., 1983, 'Blurred Genres: The Refiguration of Social Thought', in C. Geertz, *Local Knowledge: Further essays in interpretive anthropology*, New York: Basic Books, pp. 19–35

—— 1993 [1973], *The Interpretation of Cultures*, London: Fontana, pp. 3–30

Ghosh, P., 1993, 'Towards the Verdict of History: Mr Cowling's doctrine', in M. Bentley (ed.), *Public and Private Doctrine: Essays in British history presented to Maurice Cowling*, Cambridge: Cambridge University Press, pp. 273–321

Heclo, H. & Wildavsky, A., 1981 [1974], *The Private Government of Public Money*, 2nd edn, London: Macmillan

Heffernan, R., 2003, 'Prime Ministerial Predominance? Core executive politics in the UK', *British Journal of Politics and International Relations*, vol. 5, no. 3, pp. 347–72

—— 2005, 'Exploring and Explaining the British Prime Minister', *The British Journal of Politics and International Relations*, vol. 7, no. 4, pp. 605–20

—— 2013, 'There's No Need for the "-isation": The prime minister is merely prime ministerial', *Parliamentary Affairs*, vol. 66, no. 3, pp. 636–45

Hennessy, P., 2000, *The Prime Ministers*, London: Allen Lane, The Penguin Press

Kavanagh, D., 1991, 'Why Political Science Needs History', *Political Studies*, vol. 39, no. 3, pp. 479–95

Lawrence, J. & Taylor, M., 1997, 'Introduction: Electoral sociology and the historians', in J. Lawrence & M. Taylor (eds), *Party, State and Society: Electoral behaviour in Britain since 1820*, Aldershot: Scolar Press, pp. 1–26

Levi-Strauss, C., 1966, *The Savage Mind*, London: Weidenfeld & Nicolson

Marsh, D., Richards, D. & Smith, M.J., 2001, *Changing Patterns of Governance in the United Kingdom*, Houndmills, Basingstoke: Palgrave

Pederson, S., 2002, 'What is Political History Now?', in D. Cannadine (ed.), 2002, *What is History Now?*, Houndmills, Basingstoke: Palgrave Macmillan, pp. 36–56

Pollitt, C., 2007, *Time, Policy, Management: Governing with the past*, Oxford: Oxford University Press

Rawnsley, A., 2001, *Servants of the People: The inside story of New Labour*, rev. edn, London: Penguin Books

—— 2010, *The End of the Party: The rise and fall of New Labour*, London: Viking

Rhodes, R.A.W., 1995, 'From Prime Ministerial Power to Core Executive', in R.A.W. Rhodes & P. Dunleavy (eds), *Prime Minister, Cabinet and Core Executive*, London: Macmillan, pp. 11–37

—— 2006. 'Executive Government in Parliamentary Systems', in R.A.W. Rhodes, S. Binder & B. Rockman (eds), *The Oxford Handbook of Political Institutions*, Oxford: Oxford University Press, pp. 324–45

—— 2011, *Everyday Life in British Government*, Oxford: Oxford University Press

—— & Tiernan, Anne, 2014. *Lessons of Governing: A profile of prime ministers' chiefs of staff*, Melbourne: Melbourne University Academic Press

—— & Wanna, J., 2009, 'The Core Executive', in R.A.W. Rhodes (ed.), *The Australian Study of Politics*, Houndmills, Basingstoke: Palgrave-Macmillan, pp. 119–30

Savoie, D., 1999, *Governing from the Centre*, Toronto: Toronto University Press

—— 2008, *Court Government and the Collapse of Accountability in Canada and the United Kingdom*, Toronto: Toronto University Press

Seldon, A., 2004, *Blair*, London: Free Press

—— with Peter Snowden & Daniel Collings, 2007, *Blair Unbound*, London: Simon & Schuster

—— & Lodge, G., 2010, 2011, *Brown at 10*, London: Biteback Publishing

Shore, C. & Wright, S. (eds), 1997, *The Anthropology of Policy: Critical perspectives on governance and power*, London: Routledge

Smith, M.J., 1999, *The Core Executive in Britain*, London: Palgrave Macmillan

Strangio, Paul, 't Hart, Paul & Walter, James (eds), 2013, *Prime Ministerial Leadership: Power, party and performance in Westminster systems*, Oxford University Press

Thompson, Hunter S., 2009, *The Gonzo Papers Anthology*, Basingstoke and Oxford: Pan Macmillan

Walter, J., 2010, 'Elite Decision Processes: The "court politics" debate', paper presented at the Australian Political Studies Association Annual Conference, University of Melbourne, 27–29 September

Watson, D., 2002, *Recollections of a Bleeding Heart: A portrait of Paul Keating PM*, New York: Knopf

Weller, P., 2005, 'Investigating Power at the Centre of Government: Surveying research on the Australian Executive', *Australian Journal of Public Administration*, vol. 64, no. 1, pp. 35–40

Williamson, P., 1999, *Stanley Baldwin*, Cambridge: Cambridge University Press

—— 2004, 'Baldwin's Reputation: Politics and history, 1937–1967', *Historical Journal*, vol. 47, no. 1, pp. 127–68

—— 2010, 'Maurice Cowling and Modern British Political History', in R. Crowcroft, S.J.D. Green & R. Whiting (eds), *Philosophy, Politics and Religion in British Democracy: Maurice Cowling and Conservatism*, London: I.B. Tauris, pp. 108–52

Wulff, H., 2002, 'Yo-Yo Fieldwork: Mobility and time in multi-local study of dance in Ireland', *Anthropological Journal of European Cultures*, vol. 11, pp. 117–36

PART 3

THE PUBLIC SERVICE

5

MANDARINS
Peter Shergold

In early 1974, at the height of Britain's worst peacetime crisis, on the eve of an all-out miners' strike, the nation's top mandarin, Sir William Armstrong, was preparing for the end of the world. According to the great Whitehall historian Peter Hennessy, Sir William's 'influence was quite extraordinary for a civil servant' (Hennessy 1989: 219). Assertive and articulate, he always gave frank and fearless advice to the Prime Minister Edward Heath. Now he was ready to do so again.

On 31 January, whilst attending a seminar, he took the prime minister's principal private secretary aside for a discussion. It was, to say the least, an unusual meeting. Sir William 'stripped off his clothes and lay on the floor, chain-smoking and expostulating wildly about the collapse of democracy and the end of the world' (Wheen 2010: 60–1). The next day, at a regular meeting of permanent secretaries, he advised them to return home and prepare for Armageddon. After a long silence, the head of the Treasury, Sir Douglas Allen, gently led him away: 'the most powerful man in Whitehall had gone off his rocker' (Wheen 2010: 60–1). The prime minister, when informed that his head of the civil service had been locked up, responded that he had thought he 'was acting oddly the last time I saw him' (Leake 2008).[1]

When Prime Minister John Howard asked me to become Sir William's equivalent in Australia some 30 years later. I paused to reflect on Sir William's fate. Might I go the same way? The world of mandarins is generally hidden from public gaze but, as I had seen first-hand, the pressures and responsibilities they face are sometimes as great as those faced by the ministers they serve. Their story deserves to be told. Patrick Weller has done so, for more than a quarter of a century.

ENCOUNTERS WITH WELLER

I am delighted to contribute to the *festschrift* honouring Weller's extraordinary achievement. My interest is to assess the role of mandarins in the craft of democratic governance. As suggested above, my commentary will have a personal tone. I will seek to throw a veneer of academic respectability across my essay, but at heart it will still reflect my own experience. How can it be otherwise when I have been one of the many mandarins whom Weller has interviewed at length and whose comments have subsequently been quoted, scrutinised and analysed forensically.[2] Think of my chapter, if you will, as 'subject bites back'.

The term 'mandarin' has a rich etymological history, which I cherish. It is a word, borrowed from the Malay by the Portuguese during their colonial presence in the Malacca Sultanate. It has its roots in the Sanskrit verb, 'to think'. The word was employed by the Portuguese to describe the Chinese high officials with whom they had contact. They found that the mandarins they met were not just civil servants but scholars, immersed in reading, literature and Confucian learning. They were an educated elite. In Vietnam, where the mandarin system was adopted and adapted, those who retired from the royal court were expected to return to their hometown to teach in local schools. It was a distinguished and honourable profession.

Yet in truth I have always found it hard to think of myself as a mandarin. In large measure that is because, in contemporary use, the term has a pejorative connotation. It is usually a label imposed upon one by others. Earlier this year, when Google alerted me that the UK *Independent* had published an article on the 'mandarinate', I was able to guess—entirely correctly—that the author would reveal an obsessive dislike of the nation's top civil servants for ruthlessly looking after their own interests (Garrett 2013). That, in the public mind, is what today's mandarins do.

I have learnt to live with such characterisations. As Secretary of the Department of the Prime Minister and Cabinet (PM&C) I found myself routinely billed as the nation's 'top mandarin'. A diminutive colleague, who had upset a Senator of a minor party, earned the even more unfortunate sobriquet of 'Cumquat' for being perceived as a small, bitter mandarin. When I left the Australian public service (APS), *Crikey* anticipated, with woeful historical understanding of Chinese hierarchy, that it would necessitate 'Shuffling the chairs of the Mandarin emperors' (Kerr 2006). Even today I am sometimes referred to in the press as the 'former Howard mandarin': the three words, taken together, serve to forewarn unwary readers that my ideas should be treated with caution. In a wonderful juxtaposition of stereotypical images, on my retirement from the APS to establish the Centre for Social Impact at the University of New South Wales, the ABC Radio National transcript description read 'Mandarin Shuns Millionaires' Professional Afterlife', noting that I had 'opted to don the tweed jacket of academia' and live in relative penury (ABC 2008).[3]

Look up the definition of mandarin—I used the online Merriam Webster dictionary—and you will find that it is no longer a term employed to describe the superior grades of public officials in the Chinese Empire. Rather, in modern idiom, it is a synonym for a functionary or pedantic official, generally elderly, frequently traditionalist, often reactionary and given to ornate complexity of language. The mandarin, today, is usually appointed in the public imagination to head Dickens's Office of Circumlocution.

When used in a book title—think Simone de Beauvoir's *The Mandarins* or Noam Chomsky's *American Power and the New Mandarins*—the term is redolent with satirical derision and barely concealed contempt. That's why Patrick Weller's book, *Australia's Mandarins*, published in 2001, might have surprised readers. It has a far more sympathetic tone although its subtitle, lurking behind the academic colon, is *The frank and the fearless?* The question mark makes it clear that Weller intends to ask critical questions of public-sector leadership. Of course, Australia's mandarins are omnipresent in Weller's oeuvre of public administration. Rather like Polonius (the ageing and officious counsellor to the king in *Hamlet*), senior public servants appear occasionally in Weller's writings downstage under the spotlight; more usually, they lurk discreetly in the wings; and on occasion stand, intrusive but unseen, behind the arras of decision-making—loitering, perchance, like a tedious old fool, unprepared for a brutal end. For Weller, mandarins are only occasionally the subject of his scrutiny but always they serve as discreet informers to his insights on the craft of governing.

Weller's deserved reputation comes not just from the interdisciplinary skill that he brings as a political scientist, historian and expert on public-sector management, but from a methodological approach more usually associated with ethnography. For four decades he has lived alongside the mandarin class but remained apart from them—a witness to their travails, an acute observer of their traits, and a teller of their tales.

Weller reads what secretaries and director-generals write. He scrutinises their speeches. Notebook at hand, tape recorder at his elbow, he holds strategic conversations with them, always recognising the inherent danger that 'interviewing departmental secretaries is interviewing winners' (Weller 2001a: 17). He is aware of the pithy wisdom of the goodtime girl Mandy Rice-Davies when, during the UK's Profumo Affair in 1963, she proclaimed accusingly of Lord Astor that 'he would [say that,] wouldn't he?' when he denied having sex with her.[4] I have learned from personal experience that a gently raised eyebrow suggests that Weller is not entirely convinced either of my memory or judgement: I would argue that the public service had maintained its apolitical non-partisanship, wouldn't I?

It is this combination of cautious empathy and quiet doubt that allows Weller to examine critically the way in which public service leaders view their role. He brings to that task the benefit of his detailed understanding of other Westminster traditions and conventions. He assesses their performance against the standards and values they set for themselves. He seeks to interpret their actions and motivation. It was only because of Weller's insight that I properly recognised the manner in which my own speeches and public essays were intended to refract, transmit and recalibrate the governance role of public servants. They were 'public rhetorical leadership'. The speeches, which I had written intending to illuminate and inspire, were deemed to be 'important data . . . candid statements, expressions of self-interest or exercises in myth making' (Rhodes, Wanna and Weller 2008: 462; see also Grube 2011).

Weller tests, too, the mandarins' public pronouncements. My heart sank when, in *Cabinet Government in Australia*, Weller started a chapter with my avowedly 'arresting proposition' that only in this country have the traditions of cabinet government been maintained. It skipped a quiet beat of relief when, after careful and astute comparative analysis, Weller concluded that I was almost correct—although, it must be admitted, in ways that I had not fully comprehended (Weller 2007: 268, 278–80).

On occasion Weller has engaged as a participant in public policy. More often he has acted as a consultant to federal and state governments and the Commonwealth parliament, serving as a member of reviews, committees and advisory groups. Yet, in the most profound sense, he has always been involved with, but stood apart from, the institutional structures of governance.

His judgements are careful and considered, even when political events test the limits of his righteous indignation. I have no doubt, for example, that his account of the 2001 'Children Overboard Affair' was driven by deep concern about the exercise of 'plausible deniability' among ministers, their political and media advisers, senior defence personnel and public servants. Yet in spite of this, *Don't Tell the Prime Minister* provides one of the most succinct, readable and carefully balanced appraisals of the manner in which mandarins have to exercise apolitical responsiveness. For that reason, his conclusion that on this occasion 'the urge to serve overpowered the need to be critical', is more persuasive (Weller 2002: 69).

Weller is insightful in his assessment of motivation and behaviour among Australia's mandarins. Yet the modus operandi of so much of his intellectual endeavour, interviewing senior public servants and capturing their voice, is strengthened by the critical admiration he reveals for those whom he studies. Weller's Law, he notes regretfully, is not named after himself, but it does capture well the respect that he brings to his analysis of the relationship between the observer and the observed: 'nothing is impossible for the person who does not have to do it' (Weller 2001a: 239). He understands, in short, that the high-pressure life of a contemporary mandarin is not easy.[5] They might even, like Sir William, suffer the indignity of a nervous breakdown. That is, perhaps, why his assessments are not only academically rigorous, but also determinedly fair and critical, yet sympathetic.

THE CHALLENGES FACING THE PUBLIC SERVICE

In 1996, when I was public service commissioner, I was invited to Hanoi to attend a meeting of the Eastern Regional Organization for Public Administration. On a peaceful Sunday morning I hired a bicycle and rode to the Temple of Literature, built in 1070. Entering the main gate I carefully avoided the central pathway (reserved in past times for the monarch) and took, instead, the less travelled path to the left, intended for the royal court's administrative mandarins. In the third courtyard I came to the carvings that had encouraged my visit. Stelae, standing like tombstones, depicted the names and birthplaces of 1307 graduates of

82 triennial royal exams held between 1442 and 1779. I had a photograph taken of me paying homage. Typically—for I was a mandarin never properly trained in the more routine tasks of clerical administration—I seem to have mislaid it.

I discovered that Vietnam's mandarins, like their Chinese counterparts, were of nine ranks. In China, at least, the classes were separated by the hat-pins they sported. Those at the bottom wore coral; above them more senior officials showed off a hierarchy of sapphire, lapis lazuli, white jade, gold and silver. Weller, it must be said, reserves most of his comments only for those mandarins of the highest level, the secretaries and director-generals. In China they were the mandarins distinguished by a pin of flashing ruby. The ruby elite of the Australian public services' senior executive class are the focus of my remarks.

Sadly, according to Weller, their best days are in the past. Their power, if not their star, is in decline. Forget the glorious past dynasties of China and Vietnam; think, instead, of Australia, New Zealand, the United Kingdom and Canada in the 1940s and 1950s. These decades, Weller asserts, represented 'the era of the mandarins' (Weller 2001a: 2). In the Australian public service they were epitomised by the 'seven dwarfs', men of short stature but immense influence: Nugget Coombs, John Crawford, Henry Bland, Alan Brown, Richard Randall, Frederick Sheddon and Roland Wilson. Other eminences—Arthur Tange, Alan Westerman, John Bunting and Fred Wheeler—followed.

These men wielded great authority.

AUSTRALIA'S MODERN MANDARINS

In 2004, I gave the Sir Roland Wilson Oration and, doing my preparatory homework, came to appreciate more fully the extraordinary dominance that he exerted over the treasurers whom he served. The administrative world in which Wilson plied his trade was not nearly as constrained as it was for me. Power was far less trammelled.

Weller, always a master of context, explains succinctly the reasons for diminished power in *The Mandarins*. 'In 1950', he notes, 'officials were almost the only stream of advice', with ministers relying almost entirely on APS secretaries for their assistance (Weller 2001a: 2). The mandarins were distinguished from most of their colleagues by the breadth of their education and intellect; the secrecy and confidentiality of their actions were assured; their position was permanent; their advice and actions were unbounded by the panoply of administrative law; and the media were less intrusive. Their dominance and ascendancy were rarely challenged.

In preparing my oration, I came to a similar but more critical conclusion. Perhaps I was driven by a personal frustration that I and my colleagues were often perceived to be lesser lights, scarcely fit to stand in the shoes of the old 'imperial bureaucracy'.[6] I entitled my oration 'Once was Camelot in Canberra'. It was turned into an article which asked whether public servants had become mere 'Lackies, Careerists, Political Stooges?' (Shergold 2004). The alternative choice offered by Rhodes and Weller was Mandarins or Valets (Rhodes and Weller 2001)

My argument was that the so-called golden age of the mandarin immortals was, in reality, often marked by intense territorial warfare, the exercise of monopoly power, weak collegiality and—by contemporary standards—a lack of public accountability. My piece, you will have discerned, had a certain polemical intensity. However, my purpose was absolutely not, as John Nethercote later suggested, to run a 'campaign to exalt recent luminaries', including myself (Nethercote 2012; Wanna, Vincent and Podger 2012; Shergold 2008). Rather it was intended to interpret the changing environment within which mandarins operate. I sought to explain and evaluate perceptions of their declining power.

Weller, writing three years earlier, had as usual put the arguments far better (Weller 2001a). He brought critical objectivity to his assessment but came to a similar if more nuanced conclusion. Mandarin power, he posited, has been progressively reduced as media scrutiny has increased, administrative regulation heightened and sources of political authority widened. It is this sense of historical perspective that provides the benchmark to the questions that Weller asks of Australia's mandarins: just how responsive should they be to their political masters; is their embrace of managerial professionalism beneficial; how has their influence been weakened or corrupted by the introduction of ministerial political advisers; is the career service being eroded; and—the question I am still asked most frequently, usually rhetorically—has the public service been politicised?

These are the questions I intend to address. They frame Weller's account of Australia's mandarins. I am keen, however, to embrace the broad diversity of Weller's research and not just confine my commentary to the book of the title. I will structure my remarks around what I consider the four key roles of modern mandarins: advisers to government;

implementers of government decisions; facilitators of collaborative program design and delivery; and finally but importantly, colleagues.

Advisers to the government
I want to examine Weller's long interest in whether the policy counsel provided by mandarins has been weakened by the change in their working environment. Mandarins must wield a degree of independence (in providing advice and implementing policy), but must also serve, with equal commitment, successive elected governments. It's a question of balance. Some mandarins have been 'highly critical of the excessive shifts in the 1990s and early 2000s . . . towards responsiveness and away from those values that emphasise independence' (Podger 2013: 79). Others, such as myself, continue to believe that the advice we provided in confidence remained professional, impartial and—as necessary—robust.

In Canberra, this large question is often narrowed to a debate on the changes introduced to secretaries: dispensing with the term 'permanent head' in 1984; the introduction of fixed-term contracts in 1994; and the subsequent confirmation that contracts could be terminated when they had lost the confidence of government. Partly as a consequence, the term of a departmental secretary is likely to be shorter than in the past, and more at risk; compared to elsewhere in the Westminster world, they now 'retain their positions at the pleasure of the Prime Minister' (Rhodes, Wanna & Weller 2009: 173). Does that make mandarins more cautious or respective to political direction? Does it cause them to be fearful and compliant? Critics, particularly in academia and the media, believe so. In contrast, I have argued that the ability to provide frank and fearless advice is more a matter of personal conviction and courage than contract and remuneration. Weller remains unpersuaded. How can one of us convince the other?

Mandarins are themselves divided. Andrew Podger, for example, remains persuaded that secretaries' behaviour is likely to be weakened by the fact that their employment conditions have become more similar to those of a private sector CEO. I disagree. Indeed, there has been a very public debate between past and present public service commissioners (Shergold 2007; Podger 2007a, 2007b; Briggs 2007).

In my defence, I call the expert witness, James Button. Button worked in PM&C in 2009–10, after I had left. He found that senior public servants were always explicit about the need to maintain the independence of their advice. It was a badge of pride. He watched the deputy secretary 'carefully mark out the limits of the Department's advice—"That's for you to decide, not us"—when the PM's adviser began discovering the politics of an issue'. Neutrality, he concluded, remained a cornerstone of faith, infused across the public service hierarchy. At least within the APS, mandarin power continued to reign supreme. Button could not 'overstate the velvety power of the word "Secretary" . . . the title spoke of the unchanging position to which [the] ultimate loyalty [of public servants] was owed' (Button 2012: 115).[7]

Certainly I am convinced that modern employment conditions have not constrained the power of the mandarins nearly as much as the other changes in the mandarins' working environment. The provision of policy advice is now subject to far more scrutiny than in the past. Senate Estimate Committees were introduced from the early 1970s. Almost alone among my colleagues, I rather enjoyed being subject to questioning. I found the attempts by opposition Senators to extract sensitive information to be almost a form of parliamentary theatre. I don't want to exaggerate the drama. To the casual observer, just as little happens most of the time as in a fourteenth-century Japanese Noh play. There's always the chance, however, of an unexpected revelation. For that reason, perhaps, the questioning of mandarins on their administrative performance is now routinely broadcast on Foxtel's A-PAC channel.

This enhanced parliamentary scrutiny has been complemented by administrative review. Since 1982, Commonwealth documents have been open to the rigors of the *Freedom of Information (FOI) Act 1982*, the provisions of which were strengthened in 2009 and 2010. FOI is a good thing. It clearly enhances the transparency of policy advice, administrative decision-making and government service delivery. It enables citizens to challenge the manner in which they are treated. The question is whether it can also constrain the content, form and mode of presenting advice. Certainly many mandarins of the past strongly opposed the introduction of the FOI Act for such reasons. Perhaps they foresaw how difficult it would become to maintain confidentiality under pressure from an expansive judiciary.

The recent review of the FOI Act by a former mandarin, Allan Hawke, found that such concerns still remained, even 30 years on. Some respondents argue that the exemption of deliberative processes from scrutiny fails adequately to protect the wider range of written briefing papers that public servants prepare. They worry that 'the possibility of public disclosure limits the capacity of officials to provide comprehensive advice to ministers' (Hawke 2013: 48).[8]

I know how they feel. I was surprised to discover that the 'conclusive certificates' I had relied upon to protect some documents (incorporating policy advice on the 1998 waterfront dispute) from the FOI Act were not adjudged conclusive when the matter was taken from the Administrative Appeals Tribunal to the Full Federal Court. Indeed, the long-running case of *Shergold v. Tanner* has become a significant footnote to textbooks on Australia's administrative law (see, for example, Groves and Lee 2007: 296). As the conscientious student soon discovers, in most legal regards the mandarin lost convincingly.

It is not just the FOI Act that makes things harder. There exists a panoply of administrative review mechanisms, including since 1976 the investigative powers of a Commonwealth Ombudsman (enhanced by the *Public Interest Disclosure Act 2013*). These mechanisms mean that the actions of mandarins have never been more open to scrutiny. Yet the public, and more particularly the media, still think too much advice is provided behind closed doors. In contrast, public service mandarins wonder if the confidentiality of their counsel may be weakened by too great an openness and, consequently, that the tone of their advice may become more cautious and circumspect and (by some definitions) 'political'.

Partly, too, the question of the mandarins' ability to influence ministers relates to the role now played by political advisers. 'Staffers' were first introduced at a state level by Premier Don Dunstan in South Australia, and at the federal level by Prime Minister Gough Whitlam. The Commonwealth's *Members of Parliament (Staff) Act 1984* created a class of advisers employed outside the public service. The ability of this group to influence ministerial direction, or at least to act as gatekeepers to the ministers they serve, is often perceived as weakening the authority of mandarins and pressuring them to be more responsive to political direction.

I'm not so sure, and have broken ranks with many of my erstwhile colleagues who complain that they now find themselves undermined by 'the boy scouts in the minister's office'. They don't like being second-guessed by advisers who are still 'wet behind the ears'. I empathise. Yet in my heart I think the policy advice of mandarins should be challenged.

Weller has an each-way bet, suggesting that it 'is difficult to argue that contests for ideas are necessarily harmful to government' (Weller 2001a:

101). I suspect that many mandarins, serving or retired, would view this position as too pusillanimous in its implied criticism of advisers, although elsewhere, Weller condemns staffers as 'the black hole of government' (Weller 2002: 70). In contrast, I perceive Weller's conclusion as too weak a statement of the benefits of countervailing ideas. I see ministerial advisers as a vital part of political life, with the power to instigate policy, to comment upon it and, on occasion, to veto it. Their contribution can add real value to discussion of options. Indeed, the presence of advisers allows mandarins to be robustly non-partisan in their advice, knowing that those in the minister's office are there to worry about the political challenges it may present (Shergold 2012a).

Weller is also aware of how much harder the mandarins' role has become as a result of the 'constant pressure to feed the demand of 24-hour news channels, [which] require instant responses' (Weller, Scott and Stevens 2011: 289). As processes of policy-making have become more frenetic and governing more complex, so the pressure on mandarins to provide instant advice has increased. I felt harried when I needed to respond immediately and continuously to the media as it brayed for the resignation of Governor-General Peter Hollingsworth; or to successive revelations of bribery by the Australian Wheat Board in Iraq; or to questions on whether the Australian government should have had forewarnings of the Bali bombings. These are the occasions when I felt most exposed as secretary of PM&C. Like any mandarin in similar circumstances, I was all too aware that I had limited information at a time when I was expected to provide answers.

As you would expect, Weller is well versed on the manner in which mandarins must exercise their power of advice on a daily basis—how often, and how vigorously, they must oppose or seek to modify the policy proposals of their ministers or continue to put forward initiatives that their ministers are reluctant to consider. Weller accepts, as do most mandarins, that at some point that represents 'the end of the day', ministers decide on policy and secretaries implement it. This practice does not represent the bended knee of political acquiescence—it is how Westminster democracy was intended to work. The question is for how long and with how much vigour do mandarins argue their case, and at what stage and with what grace do they accept defeat. There is no easy answer. As Weller, quoting an anonymous 1980 official, puts it epigrammatically: 'to object once is stupid, twice is desirable and three times is suicidal' (Tiernan and Weller 2010: 159).

The belief that mandarins are 'political' seems to be interpreted ever more widely. Consider the concept, derived by Weller from Professor Richard Mulgan, of 'managerial politicisation' (Mulgan: 1998a, 1998b). This relates to the proposition that mandarins may be selected, often replacing incumbents, not on the basis of their political partisanship but on their managerial capacity. Often they are chosen to symbolise a fresh start. What makes them 'political' are the circumstances of their appointment and the qualities on which they are selected. As Weller puts it bluntly, 'firing a secretary every now and again has a salutary effect' (Weller 2002: 62).

In 2002, I was called to the Prime Minister's Office, and asked by John Howard to take the role of his departmental secretary. He indicated that I had been chosen as the person best able to give administrative effect to the policies his government had been elected to implement. I willingly accepted the role, clear that I would actively seek to influence policy but, equally importantly, that I would do all I could to ensure that decisions, once made, were delivered on time, on budget and to the government's expectations. That ethos, indeed, underpinned my motivation in establishing a Cabinet Implementation Unit in PM&C. I was regarded as a 'can-do' secretary, and saw it as part of my role to explain policy decisions publicly (which could, of course, easily be perceived to be spruiking their virtue). In my attempt to drive a whole-of-government approach to delivery I was, as Howard recognised, 'a consummate public service networker' (Howard 2010: 239).[9]

The question is whether that means that, selected for conscientious display of these managerial qualities, I was 'politicised'. If my predecessor at PM&C had not retired, but had been removed or terminated in order to be replaced by me, would that have represented 'politicisation'? I am not persuaded. If senior executives are always selected on merit, on the basis of criteria such as strategic ability and conceptual capacity, why is it political if mandarins are chosen on a similar basis? I cannot conceive that it is political for a minister to indicate that they want a secretary with— for instance—strong subject knowledge, a record of implementation achievement, effective organisational leadership, an ability to operate under pressure and good people skills, even if it requires the replacement of a secretary not seen to possess such qualities. Choosing secretaries on the basis of managerial capability is not, in my judgement, political. Nor is the termination of their contract when a minister does not believe them able to demonstrate such qualities.

Implementing government policy

This consideration of preferring secretaries who can get things done provides a neat segue into the second role of the mandarin: that of implementer. A major responsibility of the mandarin, particularly outside the central agencies of government, is turning policy decisions—by either legislative or administrative means—into the programs and services that usually bring citizens into contact with public servants.

Implementation, of course, is largely a managerial matter. Weller notes that mandarins today are much more likely than in the past to be judged by their success in harnessing the capacity and building the capability of the agencies they lead. This is a role that most of them acknowledge. They were, after all, collectively responsible for advocating the reforms a generation ago that became known as 'new public management' (NPM). As Weller emphasises, to a significant extent managerial reform in Australia came from within. Indeed it was 'advocated with at times excessive zeal'. The paradox, he notes, is that a rigid bureaucracy was 'changed by those apparently socialised into its culture'. The mandarins, far from suffering institutional rigor mortis, were 'obviously open to new ideas' (Weller 1996: 1, 6).

Simplistically characterised by critics as applying principles of market competition to the more complex world of public administration, managerial reform in Australia has been seen most clearly in the attempt to price assets, to cost and allocate resources against outputs or outcomes and, on that basis, to measure and evaluate performance. The focus is on results rather than processes. Mandarins today must manage, not simply administer.

The good thing is that no longer can any secretary imagine that the role of management can be delegated to duller and less ambitious executives with less policy acumen. The bad thing is that the unthinking appropriation of private-sector language to ministers (a.k.a. clients or customers) and citizens (a.k.a. customers or consumers) has served to distort the conceptual distinctiveness of the public servants' role. The implicit contract between the state and the public, unlike in the corporate world, should be marked by a balance of rights and responsibilities, entitlements and obligations. The public's relationship with a department of health is quite different from its relationship with a department of David Jones. The modern mandarin needs to be a manager, but also a public administrator. The two roles are distinctive if complementary.

The now rather dated approach to public management evolved from the late 1980s. It emerged alongside the privatisation or corporatisation of public enterprise activities that had traditionally been regarded as the domain of government. Particularly at the state level, various forms of public–private partnership were actively pursued. The most far-reaching manifestation of this emerging 'commercial' ethos, however, was the benchmarking and outsourcing of government services through the contracting of agents. The scale of the change has been enormous. In the area of human services, much government delivery (valued at more than $26 billion a year in direct funding) is now undertaken by not-for-profit, community-based organisations (Productivity Commission 2010: 275).

I know, from my experience in establishing, overseeing and tendering out the Job Network in the mid-1990s, just how profoundly the new challenges of third-party delivery altered the role of a departmental secretary. For a time it dominated my life. Yet read Weller's *Australia's Mandarins* and you will not sense that significance. The book has only a small handful of relatively inconsequential references to outsourcing, contract management, corporatisation and privatisation. It is as if such issues remain peripheral to the life of a modern mandarin.

This is decidedly curious. Weller, after all, alone and in partnership with colleagues, was one of the first Australian academics to write about the emerging 'hollow crown'. The 'hollowing out of the state', he and Herman Bakvis suggested in 1997, had the potential to affect deeply the exercise of executive leadership in public administration. They note that as a consequence, 'the interests of bureaucracies have become more interwoven with client groups, reducing the capacity of the government at large to move forward and make decisions' (Weller and Bakvis 1997: 3). Weller, together with the distinguished mandarin Michael Keating, also wrote a perceptive account of the contracting out of government services in Australia (Keating and Weller 2001). They recognised that the outsourcing of service delivery would 'replace the hierarchical procedures of the traditional bureaucracy' (Weller 2001b: 199).

So why, I wonder, does Weller appear to ascribe to this profound change so little impact on mandarins? I have three working hypotheses. The first is that while much of his analysis focuses on the negative impact of the 'contract state' in undermining coherence among 'policy communities', he does not see that it affects leadership in any substantive way. The second is that he conceives the process of contracting as transactional rather than transformational. Perhaps he's talked to too many mandarins, who do not themselves yet sufficiently comprehend that the changing governance structures within which they operate are likely to become the precursors of disruptive innovation.

The third possibility is that Weller, perhaps unconsciously, distinguishes between the 'public sector manager' and the mandarin. Very early, Weller was perceptive in assessing the new world of public sector management—from the introduction of contracts, performance indicators and corporate plans to program budgeting, outcomes-based funding and 'customer service'. He anticipated the manner in which such concepts might undermine traditional bureaucracies and create looser, more open and less hierarchical structures (Wanna, O'Faircheallaigh and Weller, 1992: 3–9). Yet, when it comes to assessing the role of mandarins, Weller appears to regard such changes as of relatively little consequence. I think he is wrong. The days when a secretary or director-general could assign such matters to 'corporate services' are gone; in a world of public–private partnerships and outsourced service agreements, a mandarin has to be both a leader and a manager, an organiser as much as an adviser.

Facilitating

These ruminations lead me to consider the potential role of the mandarin as a facilitator. I sense that the days of 'new public management' are numbered. Evolution continues. Mandarins of the future will have the role of integrating the mandate of governments, building new forms of public value, and reasserting the significance of citizenship. Their responsibility will be to negotiate the complex interplay of a diverse range of state and non-state actors in setting policy, designing programs and delivering services. The emerging qualities that Weller attributes to the recent development of PM&C as a 'powerhouse'—coordinating, brokering, mediating, and acting as a catalyst—represent the leadership characteristics now required of a modern mandarin, who must seek cross-jurisdictional and cross-sectoral solutions to program design and delivery.

This is the most dangerous point of a personal essay, for I can no longer pretend to stand aside as an objective observer. I am, albeit in a small way, a player. Both through my writings and my actions, I have sought to promote new forms of partnership for the creation of public benefit (Shergold 2012b, 2013). I see the mandarin of the future standing at the central axis of 'network governance', commissioning innovative collaborations to deliver public goods. Mandarins, I hope, will become the lead facilitators. They will act as system stewards for democratic governance, forging partnerships and alliances with a range of public, private and community leaders.

Collegiality

Finally, and with these exciting possibilities at the forefront of my mind, let me turn to the issue of collegiality. *Australia's Mandarins*, quite explicitly, is intended to be a collective portrait. It is far more persuasive than Michael Pusey's more polemical account, *Economic Rationalism in Canberra*, written ten years earlier (Pusey 1991). Pusey's book, hailed (in *Arena*) as 'the most important intervention against the New Right carved out by an academic in recent years', was extolled (by *Australian Society*) as an approach that 'penetrates the club of free market bureaucrats to reveal the mind, manner and machination of Canberra's top men'.[10]

I enjoyed being interviewed by Pusey, but scarcely recognised the diversity of my senior colleagues in his portrayal of a homogeneous mandarin class that had imposed 'economic rationalism' on the will of the nation. I was also bemused by the politics of the polemic about the 'Canberra state apparatus': how could the leadership of the APS stand accused of exerting their sinister free-market orientation on their political masters while at the same time being attacked, elsewhere on the left of politics, as politicised and lacking influence? To Pusey, the 'top Canberra bureaucrats . . . are way to the right of centre'. They 'were the "switchmen" of history . . . When they change their minds the destiny of nations takes a different course' (Pusey 1991: 2, 5, 13). It was an exciting but unconvincing proposition.[11]

Of course, those who were ministers at the time did not feel that they had lost control to their mandarins. Graham Richardson, for example, denies he abrogated the responsibility of office; he fondly remembers writing 'rubbish' or 'nonsense' on the briefs provided to him by his bureaucrats. Since then, he believes, his successors have gone soft, and today 'far too many ministers always accept the advice their department serves up to them' (Richardson 2013). The story remains the same, only the names of the incumbents change.

Weller, in contrast to Pusey, understands that Canberra's mandarins do not share a common educational or social background. Silver-spoons are rare. They look and act like a meritocracy. Economically they may, in the broadest sense, share a belief in the benefits of competition, but much of their activity is focused—many business leaders would say far too vigorously—on market regulation. Socially, reflecting the generally high education level in Canberra, they tend to be liberal and tolerant.

It is nonsense to suggest that this rather vague world view takes the form of a Commonwealth Club cadre of mandarins who share a mission to foist a 'neo-liberal' agenda on Australia. To take just one important public policy issue on which I had a chance to play a significant role—whether and in what manner Australia should seek to limit greenhouse gas emissions—the distinctive perspectives of my secretarial colleagues (and our state counterparts) were well informed, wide-ranging and hotly contested. It would have been far easier, but much worse, if there had been a single pervasive viewpoint.

My own concerns are not about group-think among the mandarin elite, but whether they share a will to collaborate in the interest of better governance. On this score, there has been a concerted effort, both culturally and structurally, to work together as leaders of a 'joined-up' government. The value of a whole-of-government approach, which breaks down the barriers of bureaucratic demarcation, is today accepted by most secretaries. From my experience it is generally a custom honoured as much in the observance as in the rhetoric.

The importance of this change in behaviour should be highlighted. My former colleague, Roger Beale, remembered in his 2004 valedictory address just how intense and corrosive was the in-fighting he had witnessed between mandarins in the past: 'those great men of the post-war public service were also great haters and great players of time-wasting, self-indulgent bureaucratic games'. Beale left the service convinced that collegiality had become far more embedded in the behaviour of APS leadership: today's mandarins, he concluded, are 'much more inclined to take a whole-of-government view of issues rather than a narrowly departmental one' (Wanna, Vincent and Podger 2012: 2). Rick Smith, too, reflected at his retirement in 2006 that his most enjoyable times had been 'those occasions in which public servants from many agencies have come together to work as one team to deliver a clear result' (Wanna, Vincent and Podger 2012: 41). Weller, in some of his writings, reflects on the attempts by public administrators to ensure that the development and implementation of policy take place in a cohesive and integrated manner. He recognises the advantages. By contrast, I think he spends too little time assessing the inefficiencies that result from the continuing pervasiveness of vertical hierarchy. Mandarins, like any leaders, require followers if they are to succeed—and they need to listen to and learn from those who work for them. They need to harness the wisdom of the public service crowd.

I spoke to hundreds of forums, public and private, during my five years as 'national head' of the APS. I extolled the manifest virtues of joined-up government. I did so in order to make sense of the need for ongoing reform and, on a good day, to inspire all those who worked as public servants (no matter what their role) with the importance and integrity of the vocation they had chosen. However, with the wisdom of hindsight, I realise that I failed to advocate with sufficient force the way in which the design of programs could be significantly enhanced by harnessing the frontline knowledge of junior public servants and contracted community-based workers. There is a high level of creativity among the lower-level public servants. Unfortunately, their innovative impulse has to be directed to designing informal work-arounds to overcome the prescriptive process-driven guidelines that inhibit performance.

In short, mandarins today are generally more collegial with their fellows than in the past, but often they remain too removed from the experience and ideas of those at the bottom of the public service pyramid. I always enjoyed talking to the public servants who worked in regional offices and call centres. I learnt a lot from them. I tried to make sure that they were given the opportunity to participate in the meetings of national policy managers, interdepartmental committees or taskforces. It was not sufficient, and I wish that I could have harnessed their experience in a more systematic way.

CONCLUSION

There is a problem with contributing a chapter to a *festschrift*. How does one reach an epigrammatic conclusion without it sounding too much like a premature epitaph? The solution I have decided upon is to reverse the normal process and to let the person honoured enjoy the last word. The quote I have selected captures the essence of what I most admire about the manner in which Patrick Weller continues to approach the task of understanding Australia's mandarins. 'Finally, and as ever', he acknowledges, 'I want to thank all those public servants, past and present, who have spent time over the years talking about their roles and responsibilities. If there are insights of value . . . they are due to you, even if, of course, you may not recognise them' (Weller 2002: 104).

The sentiment is so warm and gracious that one almost doesn't feel the sting in the tail.

NOTES

1. The good news is that Sir William recovered from his nervous breakdown and, after recuperation in the Caribbean, returned to become Chairman of the Midland Bank and died as Baron Armstrong of Sanderstead.
2. I was interviewed for Weller's *Australia's Mandarins: The Frank and the Fearless?* (2001); *Cabinet Government in Australia, 1901–2006* (2007); and *From Postbox to Powerhouse* (2011).
3. Recent headlines on the transition to the Abbott government continue to characterise Australian public service leaders as mandarins: see, for example 'Abbott takes charge, axes mandarins', *The Australian*, 19 September 2013; 'When mandarins turn into lemons', *Daily Telegraph*, 20 September 2013; 'Mandarins to go', *Business Review Weekly*, 19 September 2013; 'Mandarins toppled in new order', *Brisbane Times*, 19 September 2013; and 'Top mandarins aren't forever', *The Australian*, 23 September 2013. It's even anticipated that Eric Beecher, publisher of *Crikey*, will in 2014 host a new website aimed at public servants called *The Mandarin* (*Australian Financial Review*, 23 September 2013, p. 45). My all-time favourite public service headline was when the 'femocrat' Helen L'Orange was appointed as head of the Office of the Status of Women in 1988: 'L'Orange amongst the Mandarins' was a tribute, if I remember correctly, to the wit of a *Canberra Times* sub-editor.
4. I am grateful to Glyn Davis for reminding me that Lord Astor was judged by the court not to have had sex with Ms Rice-Davies . . . which just goes to show that a memorable quote is always more powerful than the truth.
5. Weller has even explained the myth of Westminster with an allusion to the heroic charisma of John Wayne (Rhodes and Weller 2005: 11–12).
6. The oration title was turned into the article entitled, with equal extravagance, 'Lackies, Careerists, Political Stooges?' (Shergold 2004). The terms in the title were taken from Margo Kingston's entertaining rant, *Not Happy John!* which claimed: 'the public service is in ruins, reduced to mere caterers, lackies, careerists and political stooges' (Kingston 2004).
7. One of the most entertaining and perceptive insider books on public service leadership is Paul Hartigan's *The Public Service Unzipped: Memoirs of a mandarin*. It's a collection of cartoons. However, as Hartigan admits, 'I never got to be Secretary or Deputy Secretary and so I don't really know how they feel. Pretty good, I shouldn't wonder' (Hartigan 1995: 30).
8. The Hawke Review recommended that the exemptions for cabinet documents be widened to include policy 'considerations' and that there would be benefit in 'a comprehensive review of the FOI Act'.
9. The prime minister also generously described me as possessing 'a wonderfully creative policy mind'. On that score, I am less certain of his judgement.
10. The quotations are from Michael Pusey's website, <www.michaelpusey.com.au>, accessed 10 December 2013.
11. In the same year, Laura Tingle came to a similar conclusion, arguing: 'the government was being run effectively by the public service alone—that its political masters had

almost gone "out to lunch"' (Tingle 1992). Although Pusey's book appeared in 1991, he based his analysis on 240 90-minute interviews conducted with APS senior executives in 1985–86.

REFERENCES

ABC, 2008, 'Mandarin Shuns Millionaires' Professional Afterlife', *National Interest* transcript, 7 March

Bevir, M. & Rhodes, R.A.W., 2010, *The State as Cultural Practice*, New York, NY: Oxford University Press

Briggs, Lynelle, 2007, 'Public Service Secretaries and their Independence from Political Influence: The view of the public service commissioner', *Australian Journal of Public Administration*, vol. 66, no. 4, pp. 501–6

Button, James, 2012, *Speechless: A year in my father's business*, Melbourne: Melbourne University Press

Garett, John, 2013, 'Mandarins Who Live For Ever', *The Independent*, 15 June

Groves, Matthew & Lee, H.P., 2007, *Australian Administrative Law: Fundamentals, principles and doctrines*, Melbourne: Cambridge University Press

Grube, Dennis, 2011, 'What the Secretary Said Next: "Public rhetorical leadership" in the Australian public service', *Australian Journal of Public Administration*, vol. 70, no. 2, pp. 115–30

Hartigan, John, 1995, *The Public Service Unzipped*, Melbourne: The Text Publishing Company

Hawke, Allan, 2013, *Review of the Freedom of Information Act 1982 and Australian Information Commissioner Act 2010*, Canberra: Commonwealth of Australia

Hennessy, Peter, 1989, *Whitehall*, London: Secker and Warburg

Howard, John, 2010, *Lazarus Rising: A personal and political autobiography*, Sydney: Harper Collins

Keating, Michael & Weller, Patrick, 2001, 'Rethinking Government's Roles and Operations' in Glyn Davis & Patrick Weller (eds), *Are You Being Served? State, citizens and governance*, Sydney: Allen & Unwin

Kerr, Christian, 2006, 'Shuffling the Chairs of the Mandarin Emperors', *Crikey*, 15 August

Kingston, Margo, 2004, *Not Happy John! Defending our democracy*, Melbourne: Penguin

Leake, Christopher, 2008, 'Revealed: The day Britain's top civil servant rolled naked on the floor ranting about the end of the world', *The Daily Mail*, 20 September

Mulgan, Richard, 1998a, 'Politicisation of senior appointments in the Australian Public Service', *Australian Journal of Public Administration*, vol. 57, no. 3, pp. 3–14

—— 1998b, 'Politicising the Australian Public Service?', research paper, Commonwealth: Department of the Parliamentary Library, p. 3

Nethercote, John, 2012, 'Revisiting the History Wars', *Sydney Morning Herald*, 6 June

Podger, Andrew, 2007a, 'What Really Happens: Departmental secretary appointments, contracts and performance pay in the Australian public service', *Australian Journal of Public Administration*, vol. 66, no. 2, pp. 131–47

—— 2007b, 'Response to Peter Shergold', *Australian Journal of Public Administration*, vol. 66, no. 4, pp. 498–500

—— 2013, 'Mostly Welcome, but are the Politicians Fully Aware of What They Have Done? The Public Service Amendment Act 2013', *Australian Journal of Public Administration*, vol. 72, no. 2, pp. 77–81

Productivity Commission, 2010, *Contribution of the Not-for-Profit Sector*, research report, Canberra: Commonwealth of Australia, January

Pusey, Michael, 1991, *Economic Rationalism in Canberra: A nation-building state changes its mind*, Melbourne: Cambridge University Press

Rhodes, R.A.W. & Weller, Patrick (eds), 2001, *The Changing World of Top Officials: Mandarins or valets?*, Buckingham: Open University Press

Rhodes, R.A.W. & Weller, Patrick, 2005, 'Westminster Transplanted and Westminister Implanted: Exploring political change', in Haig Patapan, John Wanna & Patrick Weller (eds), *Westminster Legacies: Democracy and responsible government in Asia and the Pacific*, Sydney: UNSW Press

Rhodes, R.A.W., Wanna, John & Weller, Patrick, 2008, 'Reinventing Westminster: How public executives reframe their world', *Policy and Politics*, vol. 36, no. 4, pp. 461–79

Rhodes, R.A.W., Wanna, John & Weller, Patrick (eds), 2009, *Comparing Westminster*, Oxford: Oxford University Press

Richardson, Graham, 2013, 'Keep Political Power where the Buck Stops: With the elected minister', *The Australian*, 1 November

Shergold, Peter, 2004, 'Lackies, Careerists, Political Stooges? Personal reflections on the current state of public service leadership', *Australian Journal of Public Administration*, vol. 63, no. 4, pp. 3–13

—— 2007, 'What Really Happens in the Australian Public Service: An alternative view', *Australian Journal of Public Administration*, vol. 66, no. 4, pp. 367–70

—— 2008, 'Satisfactions of an Invisible Life', *Sydney Morning Herald*, 9 February

—— 2012a, 'Political Staffers Aren't Killing the Public Service', *The Conversation*, 26 October

—— 2012b, 'A Social Contract for Government', in *Government Designed for New Times*, New York: McKinsey & Co.

—— 2013, 'Reform of the Australian Public Service', in Don Markwell et al. (eds), *State of the Nation: Aspects of Australian public policy*, Ballan: Connor Court

Tiernan, Anne & Weller, Patrick, 2010, *Learning to be a Minister: Heroic expectations, practical realities*, Melbourne: Melbourne University Press

Tingle, Laura, 1992, 'Commonwealth Public Service: Looking severely sick', *Canberra Bulletin of Public Administration*, vol. 68, March

Wanna, John, Vincent, Sam & Podger, Andrew (eds), 2012, *With the Benefit of Hindsight: Valedictory reflections from department secretaries, 2004–11*, Canberra: ANU ePress

Wanna, John, O'Faircheallaigh, Ciaran & Weller, Patrick (eds), 1992, *Public Sector Management in Australia*, Melbourne: Macmillan

Weller, Patrick, 1996, 'The Universality of Public Sector Reform: Ideas, meanings, Strategies', in Glyn Davis & Patrick Weller (eds), *New Ideas, Better Government*, Sydney: Allen & Unwin

—— 2001a, *Australia's Mandarins: The frank and the fearless?*, Sydney: Allen & Unwin
—— 2001b, 'The Summit of their Discontents: Crisis or mere transition?' in Glyn Davis & Patrick Weller (eds), *Are You Being Served? States, citizens and governance*, Sydney: Allen & Unwin
—— 2002, *Don't Tell the Prime Minister*, Melbourne: Scribe Publications
—— 2007, *Cabinet Government in Australia, 1901–2006: Practice, principles, performance*, Sydney: UNSW Press
Weller, Patrick & Bakvis, Herman, 1997, 'The Hollow Crown: Coherence and capacity in central government', in Patrick Weller, Herman Bakvis & R.A.W. Rhodes (eds), *The Hollow Crown: Countervailing trends in core executives*, Houndmills, Basingstoke: Macmillan
Weller, Patrick, Scott, Joanne & Stevens, Bronwyn, 2011, *From Postbox to Powerhouse: A centenary history of the Department of the Prime Minister and Cabinet*, Sydney: Allen & Unwin
Wheen, Francis, 2010, *Strange Days Indeed: The golden age of paranoia*, London: Fourth Estate

6

PAT WELLER AND THE MACHINERY OF GOVERNMENT: THE EVOLUTION OF RESEARCH ON MINISTERIAL PORTFOLIOS[1]

Evert Lindquist

When one thinks of the research themes Pat Weller is best known for investigating, the topics of prime ministers, cabinet dynamics, cabinet offices, mandarins, and international organisations immediately come to mind—typically undertaken with a historical orientation and mix of archival and ethnographic research. Perhaps less of a headline theme, but an abiding one nonetheless, has been Pat's research and reflections on how prime ministers in Australia and across different jurisdictions have elaborated and consolidated the machinery of government. Interestingly, his scholarly career coincided with the growth of government and the modern welfare state in the developed world in the decades after World War II. With this as backdrop, it was only natural that one of Australia's few public administration specialists would explore the growth of government during the 1970s and beyond, not only with respect to the proliferation of departments and agencies, but also the efforts of successive prime ministers to govern and organise their cabinets and the machinery of government in order to move forward mandates and provide oversight of the increasingly vast array of public organisations. Pat often documented and analysed within a comparative frame, since the leaders of other jurisdictions in Canada, the UK, and New Zealand were grappling with similar challenges.

For many political and social scientists, the idea of monitoring and understanding the 'machinery of government' is like watching paint dry; for others, such as Pat Weller, machinery decisions are critical revelations of the aspirations and strategising of prime ministers with respect to maintaining the support of cabinet and caucus colleagues, the matching of technical capabilities with political realities, the beginning of another round of efforts of ministers to shape bureaucracy and guide public servants to achieve policy goals, and conversely to channel officials seeking to influence ministerial thinking and decision-making. For Pat, the challenge for prime ministers in balancing these considerations over the course of a mandate is like a high-wire act, with much at stake, and therefore deserving of close and recurring attention.

Writing on the machinery of government in Westminster systems presents an intriguing mix, ranging from historical accounts of the announcements of new cabinets and the names of the new set of departments, to empirical studies seeking to better understand cabinet-making by prime ministers, to studies seeking to gauge the evolving scale and reach of government over the decades. Many scholars have focused on the birth and proliferation of public organisations, while others have considered their termination or death. Some scholars have sought to inform how governments evaluate the need for, as well as design considerations for, significant machinery changes, while others have sought to gauge the effects of machinery changes on how departments and indeed entire public-service institutions perform, as part of larger reform efforts. The research questions, levels of analysis, and theoretical and empirical focus of the contributions to this literature vary enormously. Pat's work stands out because he is one of the few to view the machinery of government in a more holistic and integrated manner, striking an intriguing balance when drawing on practical and scholarly insights to contribute his own. Pat doesn't simply rely on the literature, colleagues and graduate students to assist with his research; he has regularly visited other countries to engage officials and scholars alike, in return providing a welcoming intellectual home to visit when they came to Queensland. He has sat at the nodes of several networks emerging from his various strands of research, which include scholars and practitioners. Pat has not hoarded his research data but has always been willing to openly discuss work-in-progress as well as completed research, and always takes an interest in the work of others and facilitating their lines of enquiry. His research has influenced highly regarded research in Canada in the machinery of government (Aucoin and Bakvis 1993) and is relevant to this day, as I find myself working with colleagues to publish a collection on the June 1993 restructuring of the Government of Canada, similar to the wholesale machinery changes announced in 1987 by the Commonwealth government.

The goal of this paper is to appraise Pat's contributions to understanding the machinery-of-government function in Westminster systems. The first part reviews Pat's key contributions to the literature and describes how he and his colleagues studied machinery changes. The second part considers how the distinct strands of research in the diverse literature on machinery changes have evolved from the 1960s to the present, allowing an assessment of what was distinctive and seminal about Pat's contributions. The third part identifies blind spots and opportunities for the next generation of researchers in this area, while the conclusion offers some final reflections.

WELLER'S CONTRIBUTIONS TO MACHINERY OF GOVERNMENT

Pat's earliest work on decision-making about the machinery of government emerged from research and reflections in the late 1970s, when many governments had been expanding rapidly since World War II with respect to the number of programs and the departments and agencies that delivered them, and there emerged greater interest in policy analysis and evaluation. One result was that prime ministers began to establish bigger and more complicated cabinet systems and central-agency apparatus, and the design challenges and solutions were appraised by scholars in every country. Pat's work examined the design challenge from two perspectives.

The first considered the movement by prime ministers away from traditional cabinet structures, which have 'inner' and 'outer' ministers, and introduced a great mix of substantive and executive committees to handle the increasing flow of business (Weller 1980b). This study compared recent practice in Australia and the UK, but was published in *Canadian Public Administration* and, as always, considered the challenge from the vantage point of the prime minister. For Pat, such designs, in addition to investigating representational imperatives for prime ministers, raised fundamental issues at the heart of prime ministerial versus collective responsibility for government, what ministers were actually minister for (department, issue, or nothing really at all) and had practical implications for the sharing of information among inner and outer members, junior and senior.

In the second paper, Weller considered the challenge for prime ministers less as one of cabinet-making and controlling a caucus, and more from the need of a government to control the rapidly growing and otherwise independent, non-partisan public service, which was unionised with many protections, and whose role was to 'assist government in the creation and implementation of programs' (Weller 1980a: 197). Here Pat was exploring how prime ministers were altering the broad departmental structures of the public service and specific functions relating to merit and staff, and their relationships with permanent heads from inside or outside the public service. (I am not exploring Pat's work on department secretaries and their relationships with ministers and the prime minister—see Chapter 5.)

The next round of contributions from Pat on machinery of government matters was stimulated by the massive reorganisation of the Commonwealth government structure by Prime Minister Hawke, which, along with introducing many 'managerialist' reforms, dramatically reduced the number of departments and established several mega-departments (from 27 to 16). Ministers and top officials were explicit about the policy and administrative goals they sought to achieve with the restructuring, so Pat and his colleagues secured funding for the Centre for Australian Public Sector Management to appraise the results. An early output from this research program was Pat's 1991 paper, 'Amalgamated Departments—Integrated or Confederal', which explored whether the new departments with broader scope would fully integrate the bigger baskets of programs or serve as holding companies for programs to function as they previously had. This was a precursor to the more substantial, collaborative project, culminating in the edited collection *Reforming the Public Service: Lessons from recent experience* (Weller et al. 1993), involving several scholars, graduate students, and high-ranking practitioners.[2]

The ambition of the project, which led to a fifteen-chapter volume, was to appraise—five years later—the extent to which the 1987 restructuring had achieved its stated multifaceted goals of facilitating policy coordination, broader perspectives on issues (what we now call horizontal management), a variety of policy and managerialist reforms, and operating efficiencies. Predictably, with so many stated goals, the many values and initiatives at play and the capacity of the group, the ability of the contributors to provide a definitive assessment was bound to disappoint. However, the collection produced a few general conclusions: there was more policy and administrative coordination; better balance with central agencies and support from officials; advantages of scale that provided more access to more operating resources and talent; significant transition costs for each department; less diverse advice and competition around the cabinet table; and less redundancy. More importantly, the restructuring marked a reversal of a sustained period of growth in size of government and proliferation of agencies. There is not the space to review all of the contributions and findings here, and other articles emerged from the project;[3] what follows will focus on Pat's final assessment.

In the final chapter, Weller (1993) focused on distilling what was achieved by the 1987 restructuring and whether one could systematically evaluate the outcomes. Pat outlined the main challenges in appraising the success and effects of the reforms: what was really trying to be accomplished; ascertaining the winners and losers in terms of key roles and responsibilities of key individuals (ministers, department secretaries, etc.) and institutions (central agencies, departments); how making this assessment would boil down to values that were considered most important in the eyes of beholders either involved in or observing the drama; and whether anyone, despite the strong interest in measuring outcomes, could satisfactorily identify robust and sufficiently nuanced measures. At the broadest level, Pat concluded that there was general approval of the worth of the restructuring and accompanying reforms—that the restructuring had led to more coordination and coherence in advice from ministers and top officials—and the proof was in the pudding: the machinery had remained intact over five years; a smaller group of ministers could allocate budgets across programs and exercise control which, in turn allowed central agencies to deal with aggregates and monitor a reduced number of departments; secretaries could manage departments on a rolling three-year basis; and program managers were freer to focus on service delivery in larger departments but likely had less influence on policy in departments.[4]

There were lessons to be had about launching such reforms, such as fidelity to Westminster governance principles, and sensitivity to the strategic political context of the prime minister and his government, and involving senior officials in the design, and ongoing assessment of programs and efficiencies during implementation. But rather than be categorical, Pat identified and queried critical trade-offs informed by the different values and vantage points: whether the restructuring really served the prime ministers and ministers (political logic) or senior and middle managers in departments (administrative logic); whether accountability was increased or diminished depending on administrative scale (programs or departments); whether coordination had increased for providing advice to ministers or improving service delivery for citizens, which might involve action across larger departments; and whether the 1987 restructuring was de facto politicisation of the Australian public service because it institutionalised, at a higher level, the policy and program reforms associated with economic rationalist and managerial values.

The next round of machinery-of-government research flowed naturally from this earlier collaborative work. Similar large-scale restructurings had occurred in the UK (in 1960s and 1980s), Australia (in 1987) and Canada (in 1993). Since Pat had undertaken comparative research for the Canadian Centre for Management Development for a project on Canada's June 1993 restructuring (Weller 1995), it was natural to attempt a more systematic comparison of these experiences. The outcome was yet another significant collaborative effort, seeking to chronicle and explain machinery change across three countries from 1950 to 1997 at the level of creating ministerial portfolios and departments (Davis et al. 1999). This research is remarkable for several reasons. First, the contributors undertook an extensive review of diverse literature pertaining to machinery changes, identifying streams of relevant work: government and commission reports; studies of organisational change in departments and agencies; evaluations of wholesale government restructurings of specific governments; diverse theoretical and comparative perspectives; longitudinal studies of machinery change; and studies of machinery-of-government per se which, however, tended to focus on cabinet-making.

Second, taking cues from Osbaldeston (1992), they converted data assembled from previous studies and cabinet offices into visual charts to display each government's ministry changes and patterns over time, and at points in time, something not typically found in scholarly journals.[5]

Third, they created an important taxonomy for classifying the scale of reorganisation based on the number of implicated departments (simple: 1–5; low: 6–10; medium: 11–15; high complexity: 16 or more). This categorisation not only enabled them to identify patterns, such as periods of stability and great change over time, but also to conduct finer-grained comparison across countries (i.e., Australia had more significant reorganisations, but Canada had many more simple ones). They concluded that departments may come and go, but many functions simply get moved around while certain core departments are long-standing, and governments provide weak explanations of machinery changes.

Fourth, they returned to the literature to provide explanations of patterns (Aucoin 1986; Bakvis 1988; March and Olsen 1989b; Peters 1988; Pollitt 1984; Hogwood 1992; Osbaldeston 1992), arriving at a relatively simple heuristic developed by Davis (1995), which usefully captured the often competing political, policy and administrative logics at play, with the prime minister balancing these considerations whenever establishing cabinets or considering machinery-of-government changes.

This stream of work from Pat Weller and his colleagues constitutes a significant contribution in its own right, but it is only one element of his corpus. Like his other work, it has a historical, comparative, and analytic character, always tapping relevant literature even from different analytic and methodological approaches, and always revealing a detailed understanding of roles, responsibilities, and precedents. His research has involved collaborations with Australian scholars and practitioners, as well as colleagues in other countries. Pat has an abiding empirical focus on Australian machinery-of-government changes, but his assessments have been always informed by frameworks and comparison with other jurisdictions, leading to clarity about the distinctiveness of the evolving Australian model. The particular nature of his contribution will become clearer as we consider, in the next section, how the machinery-of-government literature has evolved over the years.

WELLER'S PERSPECTIVE: THE LITERATURE ON GOVERNMENT MACHINERY

The work of Pat Weller and his colleagues has always been well informed by the literature, but where does Pat's work on the machinery of government fit into the literature? What follows considers a very diverse stream of studies—historical accounts, Australian sub-national comparative studies, accounts of births and deaths of public organisations, theoretical and empirical studies of machinery and cabinet-making, and practical guides—which allows consideration of what makes Pat's work distinctive. Until the 1980s, the writing on government machinery was similar to literature on budgeting before Wildavsky (1964) published *The Politics of the Budgetary Process*: historical and dry. In Canada, for example, des Roches (1962) documented machinery change for the government of Canada since 1867, essentially chronicling the priorities of early governments when key central and oversight agencies were established, and the effects of wars and economic upheavals, identifying periods of great change and of relative calm, and surges of new kinds of economic activity or social aspirations that required responses from new ministers and departments. This work also considered why new non-departmental forms of public entities were established.

To the extent that efforts were made to interpret change, des Roches relied on Gulick (1937) to categorise the focus of the changes—function, clientele, process, internal administration, and area—but the complexity of considerations going into machinery design meant such categorisations were too simplistic. He also considered the government's efforts to classify these organisations in statutes and with royal commissions. Similar examples of this approach can be found in Australia (e.g. Hughes 1984; Nethercote 2000) and the UK (Chester and Willson 1968), but subsequent theoretically inclined scholars have found such work very useful. Pat and his colleagues joined a larger wave of interest from UK scholars in machinery-of-government questions, no doubt driven by the extensive reforms introduced by Prime Minister Thatcher during the 1980s. For example, Pitt and Smith (1981) surveyed how government was organised, and while not providing an account of machinery decisions, they did apply contemporary organisation theory to probe how departments were structured and worked, and why managerialist perspectives on departments and agencies might not capture or point to all that was important to understand in the public sector.

Two seminal studies (Hood and Dunsire 1981; Pollitt 1984), one from York University's Machinery of Government Project and a dissertation, were initiated in the late 1970s, and sought to move from historical, descriptive accounts of machinery decisions and shed light on what had been a closed, concentrated decision-making process using theory and quantitative and qualitative data.[6] Both surveyed a great deal of literature and informed Pat's work on the machinery of government. Hood, Dunsire and Thompson's (1982) *Bureaumetrics* sought to measure how machinery changes had impacted on different types of agencies, the allocation of portfolios, the appropriate size of departments, and the alignment of task structures with task environments for performance. Rather than explain machinery-of-government change at the macro level, the authors identified variables from organisation theory and explored how departments were affected by measuring and comparing overall budget and broad allocations, total staff and field staff, occupational groups and grading, administration, grants, etc.[7]

Pollitt's (1984) *Manipulating the Machine*, which focused on departments and agencies, and included interviews with decision-makers and advisers involved in machinery decisions (prime minister, head of civil services, and the prime minister's principal private secretary) and the machinery-of-government unit. It also included case studies of decisions made by prime ministers from 1960 to 1983. Pollitt details the multiple considerations that inform decision-making; intriguingly, he sought to articulate what amounted to shared and competing 'practitioner theories' underpinning decisions and advice, as well as their interpretations of such changes, while paying equal attention to the 'social science theories' from history, political science, and organisation theory. As a result, he shares the metaphors of births, deaths, marriages, amputations to describe the effects of machinery decisions on departments and agencies, notes that the British experience, despite the coming and going of prime ministers, could be described as having periods of calm, with sequential change in selected portfolios, and more episodic change.

Presaging the important work of March and Olsen (1987a), Pollitt pointed to the symbolic and political dimensions of machinery change, which often trumped the policy or administrative rationale for increasing effectiveness, which Hood, Dunsire and Thompson (1981) sought to measure. Nevertheless, he flagged the cost of machinery decisions and need for policy signalling. An interesting strand of work emerged, contemporaneous to the 1987 Commonwealth restructuring, but focused on machinery changes in Australia's states. Moon (1987) briefly examined some of the challenges of machinery-of-government activity in order to consider the evolving scope of government and whether there was convergence or divergence across state jurisdictions. He reviewed the benefits of different streams of data—legal designation of ministerial portfolios versus expenditures versus employment levels versus laws versus organisations—for measuring scope, but surprisingly concluded that relying on changes in ministerial portfolios would be best (Moon 1987). Later, Moon and Sayer compared the growth in number of portfolios at the state and Commonwealth levels from 1890 to 1997 (Moon and Sayers 1999). They also reviewed state government responsibilities and explored partisanship as an explanatory variable of evolving scope, with the broad categories of defining, physical resource mobilisation, and social (Sayers and Moon 2002). They discovered that the scope of states does expand over the decades, with the 'defining' portfolios initially created, followed by physical resource, and later the social portfolios. However, they could not identify patterns of convergence across states, and did not find that 'partisanship of government' explained these patterns. Since what Sayer and Moon measured was the name of portfolios, they could not consider their reach, size or influence.

Another research question posed by scholars looking over similarly long time periods was: what kinds of departments and agencies were created or eliminated? Much of this literature focuses on the births of new departments and agencies, essentially revealing the evolution and growing reach of government (see Moon 1987; Osbaldeston 1992; Moon and Sayers 1999; Sayers and Moon 2002), but other studies were stimulated by the provocative work of Kaufman (1976), *Are Organizations Immortal?*, and are more focused on whether departments and agencies die. A more interesting question is, when departments and agencies are eliminated as part of a machinery change, do all the organisations and their parts disappear, or do some of the policies, programs and functions get transferred to another organisation? Many writers who explore this question appeal to policy-termination literature (Bardach 1976; DeLeon 1978; Daniels 1997), and like Weller (1991), there is some acknowledgement that many restructurings are not 'eliminations' and may result in mergers or marriages (Peters and Hogwood 1988). There is a general dismay and wonderment about the long lives of many public organisations, leading authors to identify factors such as intellectual and political resistance, permanence and resilience and resistance of policies and programs, transaction and start-up costs, as well as strategies for effecting policy, program and organisational terminations (Zhang 2009; Adam et al. 2007).

Adam et al. (2007) provide a nice survey of the various variables used by researchers as well as their empirical strategies, along with efforts to better classify kinds of organisations and transformations (Roness 2007; Rolland and Roness 2010) and country case studies (e.g. MacCarthaigh 2010; Kuipers and Boin 2005). Antecedents to this interest in the longevity of public organisations can be found in the organisation theory literature in Stinchcombe (1965) and population and organisational ecology models (e.g. Hannan and Freeman 1977, 1989) which led to efforts in the 1980s and 1990s to measure the rise and fall of populations of organisations. Glor (2011) recently surveyed the international literature and compares the survival and mortality rates of Canadian public organisations to mortality rates of private sector and non-profit sector counterparts, as well as the track record of births and terminations under different prime ministers (inter alia, Carpenter and Lewis 2004; Park 2013). Recent work is getting more precise with respect to data and definitions (e.g. foundings, terminations, secession, splitting, absorption, merger, complex reorganisation) in order to get more comparable cross-country comparisons (e.g. MacCarthaigh 2010; MacCarthaigh and Roness 2012; Lewis 2002). Interestingly, though, none of these authors evince much interest in how these decisions are made and by whom, nor the underpinning logics. Other research pertaining to machinery-of-government decisions has emerged from political scientists relying heavily on principal–agent and game theory models to logically deduce how prime ministers make decisions about the structure and membership of cabinets and ministerial portfolios (e.g. Laver and Shepsle 1996). Dewan and Hortala-Vallve (2011), for example, adapt these models to the Westminster government context and explore different facets of how prime ministers might go about forming a government and appointing ministers, as well as what portfolios and specific responsibilities in those departments to allocate to ministers. Kam and Indridason (2005) explore what might influence the timing of cabinet reshuffles, and involves some high-level empirical work, largely looking at political as opposed to other drivers of machinery decisions. Their focus is not the composition of portfolios per se, but rather, on the ministers and their interest in retaining power, the timing of decisions with respect to the electoral cycle, party rules for appointing and removing leaders, and if re-assignments of ministers are viewed as promotions, demotions or neutral in nature. Indridason and Kam (2008) focus on the 'agency loss' of prime ministers and how cabinet shuffles and machinery decisions can be used to reduce 'ministerial drift' or the moral hazard of or delegating responsibility to ministers. Such writing is essentially a logical-deductive approach in contrast to the historical inductive approach of Weller and many other colleagues with a focus on capturing political dynamics (prime ministerial popularity, coalition dynamics, party leadership selection rules, etc.) and almost totally ignoring policy or administrative considerations.

A final strand in the literature is comprised of more practically oriented research, drawing on the public administration literature, interviews, and comparative experience to inform those advising or making machinery-of-government decisions. For example, the OECD considered machinery decisions with respect to spinning off core functions of government into arm's-length agencies and potentially commercialisation or privatisation, which fits into a long line of alternative service delivery thinking over the last decade and more (see also Nuffield College 1999). More interesting is White and Dunleavy's (2010) *Making and Breaking Whitehall Departments: A guide to machinery of government changes* for the Institute for Government, intended to inform a newly arriving Prime Minister Cameron, who would soon have to make numerous machinery changes.

Like Pollitt (1984), White and Dunleavy (2010) interviewed machinery officials and undertook case studies of machinery changes in the UK, but they also interviewed officials responsible for machinery change in Australia and Canada. After considering the drivers for machinery change (external change, administrative challenges, political and cabinet-making), they also delineated how changes announced by prime ministers can affect departments—mergers, de-mergers, start-ups, major acquisitions or transfers of functions, termination—and the case studies explore examples of each scenario. A critical finding is that while cabinet-making and shuffles are relatively inexpensive, departmental-level changes are very costly—largely because of diverse IT and HR compensation systems, and rough re-apportioning of budget and staff due to time pressures—and often followed by productivity dips. Accordingly, White and Dunleavy explored more agile and supported ways to plan, approve, implement, and monitor such changes. They suggested that ministerial changes could be de-coupled from administrative restructuring. I am confident that, given Tiernan and Weller's book and primer on *Learning to Be a Minister*, Pat would find the White and Dunleavy work compelling. A more detailed survey and citation tracking would show that Pat's single-authored and collaborative work on the machinery of government has been regularly cited by scholars in Australia, Canada, and the UK, and not simply on the topics he focused on. I find the most interesting contributions to this literature are Pollitt (1984), Weller, Forster and Davis (1993), Davis et al. (1999), and White and Dunleavy (2010), because all of them depict machinery-of-government decisions as complex, often over-determined, difficult decisions for prime ministers to make, which occur at the intersection of political, policy, and administrative logics, requiring the navigation and balancing at different levels of analysis: government-wide and cabinet considerations (macro); impacts on departments and agencies (meso); and program or service consequences (micro). When Pat's work is compared to contemporary and more recent contributions to this literature, one can see that although his research is theoretically informed, his work has fallen squarely into the historical, descriptive tradition, relying heavily on documents as well as interviews and exchanges with senior officials. On the other hand, many of the logical-deductive, empirical, and explanatory work by others in the literature desperately need the historical context that Pat so naturally gravitates to as his point of departure.

Pat has sought to illuminate how machinery decisions are made and identify patterns, but unlike other contributors to the literature, he has not striven to develop an analytic and theoretical framework arising from his empirical forays. Part of this reluctance, I am sure, is that Pat believes there are so many factors at play—personalities, historical peculiarities as well as the different factors noted above—that to distil a theory of judgements made at points in time would be to miss what was interesting. Research that parses out only one set of influences, or focuses only on one level of analysis, or simply tests theory for its own sake, essentially removes what is really interesting and often beguiling about the machinery-of-government challenge and function, and what makes it difficult to theorise and comprehend with simple empirical methods. Pat, building on his early work (Weller 1980a, 1980b, 1991) and his other work on prime ministers, cabinets and departmental secretaries, never seems to have lost this bigger picture and it is reflected in the regard for his work.

MISSED OPPORTUNITIES AND NEW DIRECTIONS

Having reviewed the contributions of Pat Weller and his colleagues on the machinery of government, and having reviewed the broader literature, it is possible to identify several gaps in research. In what follows, five topics are identified that could usefully be taken up. Many build on the trails that Pat and his colleagues have already blazed.

What about the rest of typical ministerial portfolios?
A surprising oversight of the literature emerges from its focus on the appointment of ministers and the departments they are assigned, but little attention has been given to the composition of full ministerial

portfolios, that embrace the core department and its programs as well as the agencies, boards, commissions and Crown corporations that are also part of the ambit of the minister's accountabilities. Building on Pat's distinction between integrated and confederated programs inside departments, a similar set of questions could be asked of the entities comprising the larger ministerial portfolio: how connected are they? What sort of ministerial direction, control, and accountability is exercised? Is there a more general strategic direction for the portfolio as a whole or is it simply a holding company for relatively independent entities? How affected are non-core entities by machinery-of-government changes made for other purposes?

Do ministry boundaries matter for horizontal governance?

Weller, Forster and Davis (1993) pointed out that one of the primary reasons for the 1987 restructuring of the Commonwealth government was to facilitate what we would now call 'horizontal coordination' by building bigger departments of related activities, which would facilitate better alignment and coordination, and by limiting the number of ministers in cabinet, which presumably would also facilitate more coordination across portfolios. Similar rationale was given for the June 1993 restructuring in Canada (Aucoin and Bakvis 1993), but we also know that if prime ministers declare an issue to be a top priority, ministers and secretaries or deputy ministers will quickly align. We also know that in Australia and Canada, governments have come to the conclusion that there is insufficient horizontal coordination, despite these significant machinery changes. This raises the important question of whether leadership, culture, fiat, or structure facilitate the right amount of cross-boundary policy advising and service delivery, and when, depending on the gap or initiative requiring cross-boundary work, a restructuring at the micro, meso or macro level is useful.

What are the evolving contours and character of government?

Many readers might argue that far too much ink has been spilled on discussing the impact of the New Public Management and hollowed-out government. However, the gap that I see is similar to some concerns raised by Hood, Dunsire and Thompson (1981). Exploring machinery-of-government changes does not get one too far in understanding how the work, means and reach of government is evolving through the programs it delivers. There has been no shortage of interesting work exploring the expanding range of policy instruments, but far less effort has been devoted to considering what work governments—either through core departments or agencies—are really doing, which has profound consequences for how one evaluates higher-level machinery changes. We need more research on, as well as means for describing, what government has become: government could be considerably smaller in the size of many programs and sectors in terms of budget and staff complement, and yet be more influential given how it controls resources and shapes discourse; or prime ministers could appoint more ministers and increase the number of departments and portfolios, yet function in a 'smaller' way. Although 'bureaumetrics' and similar studies (Hood, Dunsire and Thompson 1982; Light 1995), as well as a small literature on organisational systematics (Kaufman and Seidman 1970; McKelvey 1975, 1982), have tried to encourage more research, we do not have good ways of collecting data and depicting these important dimensions of portfolios and the programs they contain—here I am thinking what lies underneath the high-level diagrams found in Osbaldeston (1992) and Davis et al. (1999), which is where public administration research needs to start investing in data analytics and different visualisation techniques (Lindquist 2011).

Can we better model how prime ministers navigate and balance different logics?

A simple but compelling diagram capturing the dynamic, pressure-cooker environment of prime ministers comes from Davis (1995) and Davis et al. (1999). Figure 1 below captures how prime ministers sit at the juncture of overlapping political, policy and administrative logics. This broad perspective is critical to understanding how machinery-of-government decisions are really made, and yet much of the modern literature does not show this broader, dynamic, always-evolving circumstance, which would allow for a broader range of explanations of machinery decisions. Moreover, even though Davis (1995) initially used this framework to capture competing and clashing routines and considerations, the framework could be modified to capture dynamics and flows over time, showing how prime ministers surf and balance considerations over the course of government mandates, emphasising that machinery-of-government decisions are always a temporary balancing of competing priorities, and providing a foundation for more systematic theorising. Different analytic frameworks could be adapted to capture these considerations, such as Kingdon's (1984) adaptation of garbage-can decision-making formulations to policy-agenda setting and decision-making—a streams and policy window approach might better convey the already sophisticated analysis found in Weller, Forster and Davis (1993), Davis et al. (1999) and Pollitt (1984). There would be potential for distilling Wellerian insight in a more logical-deductive manner.

Figure 1: Prime ministers balance three streams of pressures

Adapted from Davis (1995: 28); Davis et al. (1999: 39).

Are restructuring, reform and change in government the same?

Of course not! Pat and his colleagues have always recognised that restructuring the machinery of government was not necessarily the same thing as deep reform, although the 1987 Australian restructuring had the ambition of changing how government worked with respect to improving policy coordination, introducing managerialism, and reducing the size of government as part of sweeping reforms to the state. But many other restructurings are merely reshuffling the chairs on the deck or bureau-shuffling, often for symbolic or political reasons Hood, Huby and Dunsire (1985). So, at a broad level, they are not about reform at all, but rather, legitimate internal and external political considerations. This also raises the question of whether, with or without structural change or announced reforms, government and its programs might be changing in any event. Change is always happening inside organisations (Benson 1977; see Nethercote 2000, p.106), which is not always induced by machinery, reform or policy decisions—new staff, new technology, and new sensibilities from outside government can steadily influence what happens within. Indeed, sometimes reforms and restructuring are simply catching up with what organisations and services have already become. It raises the possibility that departments and portfolios across jurisdictions could be similarly named, but work very differently in terms of policies, programs, reach, and accountability.

Though a scholar with interests that have long since gravitated to other topics beyond the machinery of government, I think Pat would be receptive to a younger scholar approaching him with one of these research topics. He always delights in younger scholars getting involved in new research: he would work with the younger colleague to find a pragmatic way to take up the topic, he would not hesitate to lend his name in support of grant proposals, he would throw his shoulder behind a team if that is what the research called for, and he would share the credit and further careers with the results.

MACHINERY AND BEYOND: FINAL REFLECTIONS ON PAT WELLER'S CONTRIBUTIONS

Pat has approached the machinery of government from many angles, often mobilising teams and drawing on his many other lines of research to do so. Pat's work has been acknowledged widely in the literature, even by scholars asking different questions and relying on different empirical approaches.

This acknowledgement is partly due to the quality of his work, but also because he makes it interesting and authentic, connecting his analysis to the real decisions of prime ministers; they have to balance various considerations in a multi-level context, sometimes reactively and other times proactively, often leading to incremental and sometimes episodic changes. He has rightly depicted machinery decisions as one of many tools available to prime ministers for governing, and certainly a critical fulcrum for moving or containing the system, with the often brutal political pressures always at play.

In his effort to fathom machinery of government decisions, Pollitt (1984) made an important analytic distinction and supplied language that allows us to capture an essential feature of Pat's research and writing style: it has always reflected a dialectic between *practitioner logic*, which he has always taken seriously and always tried to ascertain and convey to others; and *academic logic*, which sought to chronicle, measure, and explain decisions at varying levels of analysis. Pat's work throughout his career has sought to bridge these logics, showing that many considerations are always at play. I have argued that, on the one hand, several strands of the literature could be better situated within the broader perspective that Pat has always brought to analysing machinery of government issues; and, on the other hand, the entire literature on machinery of government is ripe for being taken further with a combination of more theory-driven and finer-grained empirical approaches.

Pat has done more than join up practitioner and academic logics when exploring machinery of government developments: he has also provided a personal bridge among individuals who work in these different worlds. In reflecting on public administration scholarship in Canada, Kernaghan (2009) notes the critical role of a few current and former public servants who function as 'pracademics', linchpins for moving information and insight across often deep practitioner and scholarly divides, and encouraging scholars, young and old, to take up important topics. However, it also takes alter-egos on the scholarly side to take the hand extended by pracademics—whether top officials or politicians—and to reach back across the divide, or from time to time extend their own hand. Pat's many encounters with the Codds, Keatings, Frasers, and Rudds—and the list could easily be extended—and his encouragement of others to do the same, have immeasurably improved the quality of public administration research in Australia.

NOTES

1. I would like to acknowledge the impressive research assistance of Irene Huse, a doctoral candidate with the school of Public Administration at the University of Victoria.
2. This work-in-progress had an important influence on Canadian research (Aucoin and Bakvis 1993) on a similar restructuring of its own cabinet and the machinery of government announced on 23 June 1993.
3. For example, Craswell and Davis (1994) was published as a tighter version of Chapter 13.
4. This was a central concern of the Moran Review launched by the Rudd government in 2010 (Lindquist 2010).

5   See Lindquist (2010) on different traditions in the use of visual displays to convey complexity and large amounts of data.
6   Other seminal work was Dunleavy's (1989a, 1989b) 'The Architecture of the British State' in *Public Administration*, but this was less on the machinery-of-government function, and more an effort to introduce and evaluate 'bureau-shaping' models. This work shared an aspiration, though, with Hood, Dunsire and Thompson (1981) and Hood et al. (1985) of getting facts into the debate about the nature of different functions of government. It is also important work for one of the themes taken up below.
7   They used glyphs (in this case, faces) to summarise the diverse streams of data associated with each department or agency. Follow-up research was reported in Hood, Huby and Dunsire (1985), which focused on what they called 'bureau-shuffling' and tested three hypotheses: changes in scale create more or less administrative economies, reorganisation leads to cost increases, and reorganisation has little effect on bureaucratic structure and work.

REFERENCES

Adam, C. et al., 2007, 'The Termination of Public Organizations: Theoretical perspectives to revitalize a promising research area', *Public Organization Review*, vol. 7, pp. 221–36

Aucoin, P., 1986, 'Organizational Change in the Canadian Machinery of Government: From rational management to brokerage politics', *Canadian Journal of Political Science*, vol. 19, no. 1, pp. 3–27

—— 1996, 'Introduction: An overview of the restructuring', and 'Conclusion: Learning points in managing change', manuscript for the Canadian Center for Management Development

Aucoin, P. & Bakvis, H., 1993, 'Consolidating Cabinet Portfolios: Australian lessons for Canada', *Canadian Public Administration*, vol. 36, no. 3, pp. 392–420

Bakvis, H., 1988, 'Regional Ministers, National Policies and the Administrative State in Canada', The regional dimension in cabinet decision-making 1980–1984', *Canadian Journal of Political Science*, vol. 21, no. 3, pp. 539–67

Bardach, E., 1976, 'Policy Termination as a Political Process', *Policy Sciences*, vol. 7, no. 2, pp. 123–31

Benson, J.K., 1977, 'Organizations: A dialectical view', *Administrative Science Quarterly*, vol. 22, no. 1, pp. 1–21

Boston, J., 1991, 'Reorganizing the machinery of government: Objectives and outcomes', in J. Boston, J. Martin, J. Pallot & P. Walsh (eds), *Reshaping the State*, Auckland: Oxford University Press

Carpenter, Daniel P. & Lewis, David E., 2004, 'Political learning from rare events: Poisson inference, fiscal constraints, and the lifetime of bureaus', *Political Analysis*, vol. 12, no. 3, pp. 201–32

Castleman, B.D., 1993, 'Changes in the Australian Commonwealth departmental machinery of government 1928–82', *Australian Journal of Public Administration*, vol. 52, no. 4, pp. 442–55

Chester, D.N. & Willson, F.M.G. (eds), 1968, *The Organization of British Central Government 1914–1964*, London: Allen & Unwin

Craswell, E. & Davis, G., 1994, 'The Search for Policy Coordination: Ministerial and bureaucratic amalgamation in a federal parliamentary system', *Policy Studies Journal*, vol. 22, no. 1, pp. 59–73

Daniels, M.R., 1997, *Terminating Public Programs: An American political paradox*, New York, ME Sharpe

Davis, G., 1995, *A Government of Routines: Executive coordination in an Australian state*, Melbourne: Macmillan

Davis, G. et al., 1999, 'What Drives Machinery of Government Change? Australia, Canada and the United Kingdom, 1950–1997', *Public Administration*, vol. 77, no. 1, pp. 7–50

DeLeon, P., 1978, 'Public Policy Termination: An end and a beginning', *Policy Analysis*, vol. 4, no. 3

Des Roches, J.M., 1962, 'The Evolution of the Organization of Federal Government in Canada', *Canadian Public Administration*, vol. 5, no. 4, pp. 408–27

—— 1965, 'The Creation of New Administrative Structures: The Federal Department of Industry', *Canadian Public Administration*, vol. 8, no. 3, pp. 285–91

Dewan, T. & Hortala-Vallve, R., 2011, 'The Three As of Government Formation', *American Journal of Political Science*, vol. 55, no. 3, pp. 610–27

Doern, G.B., 1987, 'The political administration of government reorganization: The merger of DREE and ITC', *Canadian Public Administration*, vol. 30, no. 1

Doerr, A.D., 1981, *The Machinery of Government in Canada*, Toronto: Methuen

Dunleavy, P., 1989a, 'The Architecture of the British Central State, Part I: Framework for Analysis', *Public Administration*, vol. 67, no. 3, Autumn, pp. 249–75

—— 1989b, 'The Architecture of the British Central State, Part II: Empirical Findings', *Public Administration*, vol. 67, no. 4, December, pp. 391–417

Gill, D., 2006, 'By Accident or by Design—Changes in the Structure of the State in New Zealand', *Policy Quarterly*, vol. 2, no. 4, pp. 27–32

Glor, E.D., 2011, 'Patterns of Canadian Departmental Survival', *Canadian Public Administration*, vol. 54, no. 4, pp. 551–66

Greenwood, R. & Miller, D., 2010, 'Tackling Design Anew: Getting back to the heart of organizational theory', *Academy of Management Perspectives*, November, pp. 78–88

Gulick, L., 1937, 'Notes on the Theory of Organization', in L. Gulick & L. Urwick (eds), *Papers on the Science of Administration*, New York: Institute of Public Administration, Columbia University

Hamilton, S., 1990, 'The restructuring of the Federal Public Service,' in A. Kouzmin & N. Scott (eds), *Dynamics in Australian Public Sector Management*, Melbourne: Macmillan

Hannan, M.T. & Freeman, J., 1977, 'The Population Ecology of Organizations', *American Journal of Sociology*, vol. 82, no. 5, pp. 929–64

—— 1989, *Organizational Ecology*, Cambridge, MA: Harvard University Press

Hodgetts, J.E., 1973, *The Canadian Public Service: A physiology of government 1867–1970*, Toronto: University of Toronto Press

Hogwood, B.W., 1992, *Trends in British Public Policy: Do governments make any difference?*, Buckingham: Open University Press

Hood, C., Dunsire, A. & Thompson, K.S., 1981, *Bureaumetrics: The quantitative comparison of British central government agencies*, Farnborough: Gower

Hood, C., Huby, M. and Dunsire, A., 1985, 'Scale Economics and Iron Laws: Mergers and demergers in Whitehall 1971–1984', *Public Administration*, vol. 63, no. 1, pp. 61–8

Hughes, C.A., 1984, 'The Proliferation of Portfolios', *Australian Journal of Public Administration*, vol. 43, no. 3, pp. 257–74

Hughes, C. & Graham, B., 1968, and supplements, *A Handbook of Australian Government and Politics*, Canberra: ANU Press

Indridason, I. & Kam, C., 2008, 'Cabinet Reshuffles and Ministerial Drift', *British Journal of Political Science*, vol. 38, no. 4, pp. 621–56

Kam, C. & Indridason, I., 2005, 'The Timing of Cabinet Reshuffles in Five Westminster Parliamentary Systems', *Legislative Studies Quarterly*, vol. 30, pp. 327–63

Kaufman, H., 1976, *Are Government Organisations Immortal?*, Washington DC: Brookings

Kaufman, H. & Seidman, D., 1970, 'The Morphology of Organizations', *Administrative Science Quarterly*, vol. 15, December, pp. 439–52

Keating, M., 1993, 'Mega-Departments: The Theory, Objectives and Outcomes of the 1987 Reforms', in P. Weller, J. Forster & G. Davis (eds), *Reforming the Public Service: Lessons from recent experience*, Brisbane: Centre for Australian Public Management, Griffith University, pp. 1–15

Kernaghan, K., 2009, 'Speaking Truth to Academics: The wisdom of the practitioners', *Canadian Public Administration*, vol. 52, no. 4, pp. 503–24

Kingdon, J.W., 1984, *Agendas, Alternatives, and Public Policies*, Boston: Little, Brown

Kuipers, S. & Boin, A., 2005, 'The life and death of public organizations: Revisiting the New Deal agencies', Paper presented at the 21st EGOS colloquium, Berlin: 30 June – 2 July

Laver, M. & Shepsle, K.A., 1996, *Making and Breaking Governments: Cabinets and legislatures in parliamentary democracies*, New York: Cambridge University Press

Lewis, D.E., 2002, 'The Politics of Agency Termination: Confronting the myth of agency immortality', *Journal of Politics*, vol. 64, pp. 89–107

Light, P.C., 1995, *Thickening Government: Federal hierarchy and the diffusion of accountability*, Washington, DC: The Brookings Institution

Lindquist, E., 2010, 'From Rhetoric to Blueprint: The Moran Review as a concerted, comprehensive and emergent strategy for public service reform', *Australian Journal of Public Administration*, vol. 69, no. 2, pp. 115–51

—— 2011, 'Surveying the World(s) of Visualization', paper prepared for the Australian National University's HC Coombs Policy Forum Roundtables on Policy Visualization, <https://crawford.anu.edu.au/public_policy_community/content/doc/Visualisation_roundtable_2_Background_Paper.pdf>

—— 2014, 'The responsiveness solution: Embedding horizontal governance in Canada', Chapter 12, in J. O'Flynn, D. Blackman & J. Halligan (eds), *Crossing Boundaries in Public Management and Policy: The international experience*, London: Routledge

MacCarthaigh, M., 2010, 'Where Do Agencies Go When They Die? A longitudinal analysis of agency termination', Institute of Public Administration & Geary Institute, UCD

MacCarthaigh, M. & Roness, P.G., 2012, 'Analyzing Longitudinal Continuity and Change in Public Sector Organizations', *International Journal of Public Administration*, vol. 35, no. 12, pp. 773–82

MacCarthaigh, M., Roness, P.G. & Sarapuu, K., 2012, 'Mapping Public Sector Organizations: An agenda for future research', *International Journal of Public Administration*, vol. 35, no. 12, pp. 844–51

McKelvey, B., 1975, 'Guidelines for the Empirical Classification of Organizations', *Administrative Science Quarterly*, vol. 20, December, pp. 509–25

—— 1982, *Organizational Systematics: Taxonomy, evolution, classification*, Berkeley: University of California Press

McKelvey, B. & Aldrich, H., 1983, 'Populations, Natural Selection, and Applied Organizational Science', *Administrative Science Quarterly*, vol. 28, March, pp. 101–28

March, J.G. & Olsen, J., 1989a, 'Organizing Political Life: What administrative reorganization tells us about government', *American Political Science Review*, vol. 77, pp. 281–96

—— 1989b, *Rediscovering Institutions: The organizational basis of politics*, New York: Free Press/Macmillan

Moon, J., 1987, 'Convergence/Divergence Hypotheses of Governments' Activities: Some methodological considerations', *Politics*, vol. 22, no. 2, pp. 36–45

Moon, J. & Sayers, A., 1999, 'The Dynamics of Governmental Activity: A long run analysis of the changing scope and profile of Australian ministerial portfolios', *Australian Journal of Political Science*, vol. 34, no. 2, pp. 149–67

Nethercote, J., 2000, 'Departmental Machinery of Goverment Since 1987', *Australian Journal of Public Administration*, vol. 59, no. 3, pp. 94–110

Nuffield College, 1999, *Machinery of Government Reform: Principles and practice*. Available at <www.nuffield.ox.ac.uk/Politics/Whitehall/Machinery.html>, accessed November 2013

Osbaldeston, G., 1992, *Organizing to Govern*, London: University of Western Ontario

Park, S., 2013, 'What Causes the Death of Public Sector Organizations? Understanding structural changes and continuities in Korean Quangos', *International Public Management Journal*, vol. 16, no. 3, pp. 413–37

Peters, B.G., 1988, 'Introduction', in C. Campbell & B.G. Peters (eds), *Organizing Governance: Governing Organizations*, Pittsburgh: University of Pittsburgh Press

—— 1992, 'Government Reorganization: A theoretical analysis', *International Political Science Review*, vol. 13, no. 2, pp. 199–217

Peters, G.B. & Hogwood, B.W., 1988, 'Births, Deaths and Marriages: Organizational change in the U.S. federal bureaucracy', *American Review of Public Administration*, vol. 18, pp. 119–33

Pitt, D.C. & Smith, B.C., 1981, *Government Departments: An organizational perspective*, London: Routledge Direct Editions

Pollitt, C., 1984, *Manipulating the Machine: Changing the pattern of ministerial departments 1960–83*, London: Allen & Unwin

Rolland, V. & Roness, P., 2010, 'Mapping Organizational Change in the State: Challenges and classifications', *International Journal of Public Administration*, vol. 33, no. 10, pp. 463–73

Roness, P.G., 2007, 'Types of State Organizations: Arguments, doctrines and changes beyond new public management', in T. Christensen & P. Lægreid (eds), *Transcending New Public Management: The transformation of public sector reforms*, Aldershot: Ashgate, pp. 65–88

Savoie, D.J., 1995, 'Restructuring the government of Canada: Leading from the centre', manuscript for the Canadian Center for Management Development

Sayers, A. & Moon, J., 2002, 'State Government Convergence and Partisanship: A long-run analysis of Australian ministerial portfolios', *Canadian Journal of Political Science*, vol. 35, no. 3, pp. 589–612

Singh, J.V., 2006, 'Ecology, Strategy and Organizational Change', in J.A.C. Baum, S.D. Dobrev & A. Van Witteloostuijn (eds), *Ecology and Strategy (Advances in Strategic Management, Volume 23)*, Emerald Group Publishing, pp. 177–214

Stinchcombe, A., 1965, 'Social Structure and Organizations', in J.G. March (ed.), *Handbook of Organizations*, Chicago: Rand McNally, pp. 142–93

Tiernan, A. & Weller, P., 2010, *Learning to be a Minister: Heroic expectations, practical realities*, Melbourne: Melbourne University Press

Warriner, C.K., Hall, R.H. & McKelvey, B., 1981, 'The Comparative Description of Organizations: A research note and invitation', *Organization Studies*, vol. 2, no. 2, pp. 173–80

Weller, P., 1980a, 'Controlling the Structure of the Public Service', *Politics*, vol. 15, no. 2, pp. 197–203

—— 1980b, 'Inner cabinets and outer ministers: Some lessons from Australia and Britain', *Canadian Public Administration*, vol. 23, no. 4, pp. 598–615

—— 1991, 'Amalgamated Departments—Integrated or Confederal', *Canberra Bulletin of Public Administration*, vol. 65, July, pp. 41–7

—— 1993, 'Reforming the Public Service: What has been achieved and how can it be evaluated?', in P. Weller, J. Forster & G. Davis (eds), *Reforming the Public Service: Lessons from recent experience*, Brisbane: Centre for Australian Public Management, Griffith University, pp. 222–36

—— 1995, *Machinery of Government in Canada 1993: A comparative perspective*, Ottawa: Canadian Centre for Management Development

—— 2001, *Australia's Mandarins: The frank and the fearless?*, Sydney: Allen & Unwin

Weller, P., Forster, J. & Davis, G. (eds), 1993, *Reforming the Public Service: Lessons from recent experience*, Brisbane: Centre for Australian Public Management, Griffith University

Weller, P. & Wood, T., 1999, 'The department secretaries: A profile of a changing profession', *Australian Journal of Public Administration*, vol. 58, no. 2, pp. 21–32

White, A. & Dunleavy, P., 2010, *Making and Breaking Whitehall Departments: A guide to machinery of government changes*, London: Institute for Government

Wildavsky, A., 1964, *The Politics of the Budgetary Process*, New York: Little, Brown

Zhang, L., 2009, 'Study on Obstacles to Policy Termination', *Journal of Politics and Law*, vol. 2, no. 4, pp. 99–102

PART 4

HISTORY AND BIOGRAPHY

7

'IT IS NOT A BIOGRAPHY...', IT IS EXECUTIVE PRACTICE

James Walter

Patrick Weller is acknowledged as an expert on executive practice, bureaucracy and political institutions in Westminster systems, especially in Australia. He is less commonly thought of as a biographer. Indeed, with the exception of one book, he might himself cavil at being so identified. Yet the recurrent resort to life history is integral to his method of analysing executive politics. My purpose here is to highlight this element of his work, asking how it illuminates his broader enterprise, and what it contributes to biography not as a humanistic pursuit, but as a social science.

Attention to the actors in core leadership positions has become increasingly salient. Many scholars accept that the recent augmentation of executive resources, the media attention to leaders as party narratives and ideological differentiation decline, and the acceleration of decision-making with globalisation have shifted the political balance in favour of the 'big beasts' in executive positions. Some argue that modern polities are moving towards 'leader democracy' (Pakulski and Körösényi 2012). Weller would not agree. At least, he would first insist that we overlook the media-soaked dazzle of executive politics (Helms 2012; Boumans et al. 2013) to see how individuals work within institutions, before arguing over whether anything has changed. Thus, for example, he once commissioned me to contribute a chapter on prime ministers and their influence on evolving staff structures to one of his books (Walter 1992), but later he took mischievous delight in challenging my exposition of the increasing licence granted to contemporary prime ministers by describing the ways in which the early-twentieth-century prime minister Billy Hughes' imperiousness, authoritarianism and eccentricity outstripped any of the more extreme recent incumbents. This was not a challenge to the potential for leaders to exercise agency, simply to the argument that a trend had been identified. Power and influence, he would say, waxes and wanes: 'twas ever thus.

Well, there can be vigorous dispute about the dimensions and effects of contemporary trends, but there is little doubt that there has been a renaissance of the debate over the structure versus agency question, which has dogged the social sciences ever since the Carlylean proposition that history is made by 'great men' was quite properly dispensed with. Weller, I will argue, contributes to this debate in innovative ways. But first, consider the context.

LIFE HISTORY AND HISTORICAL INSTITUTIONALISM: CREATING AN INTERSECTION?

As the social sciences developed in the twentieth century, emphasising broad, law-like generalisations, there was increasing scepticism about the fundamental indeterminacy of biography, diverting attention to approaches—such as broad statistical studies and institutional elucidation—that gave limited credence to individual influence in politics and society. Political scientists have been especially cautious about embarking on individual case studies. Yet biography continued to flourish, as public demand for the 'lives' of influential figures scarcely waned, and in the academy there were serious attempts to promote rigorous practice (Davies 1972; Edinger 1964; Pimlott 1994), driven not by the romance of individual 'journeys', but by questions integral to politics. The point made by these authors was that political biography should be driven not (or not purely) by an interest in a life 'on its own terms'. Rather, social scientists should turn to individual cases that could address larger questions—reaching plausible generalisations—about processes such as leadership, decision-making, the acquisition and exercise of power, the dynamics of policy-making, and the constraints and opportunities generated by institutions. Even so, the most respectable of academic practitioners, such as the distinguished biographer of Keynes, Robert Skidelsky, acknowledged that political biography was regarded as a not quite respectable subsidiary (Skidelsky 1988), and it was recurrently dismissed as inappropriate to the disciplines of either politics or history (e.g. O'Brien 1998).

In the late twentieth century, this long-standing scepticism was given fresh impetus with the rise of 'new institutionalism', whose advocates opted strongly for the determining impact of structure over agency, arguing that social science should try 'to avoid unfeasible assumptions that require too much of political actors ... The rules, routines, norms, and identities of an "institution", rather than micro rational individuals or macro social forces, are the basic units of analysis' (March and Olsen 2005: 20). And yet, as institutional approaches, too, proved incapable of resolving the indeterminacy of disciplines that dealt with the vagaries of individual and group action—relationship-based behaviour—fresh demonstrations arose advocating the necessity for both structure and agency through behavioural case-study research (e.g. Flyvbjerg 2006), and for an 'interpretive' approach, including biography (Rhodes 2012).

In Australia, these debates were particularly intense. There was no lack of biography (for instance, only one Australian prime minister—Billy McMahon, the 'also ran' in this as in other forms of evaluation—lacks a biography). And there were certainly examples of inventive and theoretically informed biography—indeed, Rhodes (2012: 166) suggests that, in some respects, innovative Australian biographers overcame the caution that hobbled their British counterparts. But there was no local equivalent to, say, the late Ben Pimlott as an emblematic, respected British practitioner, and the stridency of biographical critique ensured that the field remained marginal, despite able defenders of the genre (e.g. Brett 1997). Much of what was produced came from insiders, acolytes and journalists.

Patrick Weller, however, was an exception. He demonstrated the importance of understanding agency in executive roles, but largely flew under the radar of those engaged in biographical advocacy and their critics. How he did it can tell us much about the potential for research on individuals in studies of the executive, and how to overcome the structure/agency conundrum by close attention to individual practices *and* to institutional context. But, as noted earlier, Weller himself would likely acknowledge only one of his books as biography—the 'Labor life' of John Button (Weller 1999). Indeed, he explicitly disavows biography in his study of Malcolm Fraser as a prime minister: 'It is not a biography, but a study in the exercise of power and influence . . .' (Weller 1989: 13). Yet his work, while concentrating largely on political institutions—the public service (especially Prime Minister & Cabinet), cabinet government, ministerial office, the role of prime ministers—is replete with experiential narratives drawn from actors within those institutions, and intends to demonstrate how power is exercised within and constrained by those institutions. For my purposes, then, he satisfies the key criterion of those who argued for a more rigorous form of political biography by demanding that it be driven by questions about politics; Weller pursues questions about power, influence and their limits by drawing on the working lives of political actors. Dispensing with a limiting definition of biography (including Weller's own) allows us to explore the full range of Weller's use of life studies in politics.

Weller was trained as a historian, and while he has much to say about contemporary politics, he remains wedded to a historian's data, to documents and interviews rather than statistics, relying on close observation and inductive interpretation rather than theory. He is best described as a practitioner of historical institutionalism, giving primary attention to how institutions are 'understood as sets of regularized practices with rule-like qualities, structure action and outcomes' (Schmidt 2010: 10). Yet in drawing on illustrative material concerning the way individuals work within institutional bounds, he escapes the path dependency often assumed by historical institutionalism; the observational method allows him to show the potential for individual agency. Certainly institutions 'can shape and constrain political strategies in important ways, but they are themselves also the outcome (conscious or unintended) of deliberate political strategies, of conflict and of choice' (Thelen and Steinmo 1992: 10). This is best illustrated in Weller's books dealing primarily with a single actor—his studies of Fraser (1989), of Button (1999) and, we might guess, of Kevin Rudd (forthcoming). Appreciating Weller's full range, however, entails also looking at his resort to experiential narrative as it crops up in those works dealing primarily with institutions (e.g. Weller 1985, 2007; Tiernan and Weller 2010; Weller, Scott and Stevens 2011), and also his exercises in collective biography (e.g. Weller 2001; Rhodes and Weller 2001).

SINGLE ACTOR STUDIES

Pat Weller's account of purpose and method in the prologue to *Malcolm Fraser PM* (Weller 1989: xi–xvii) is a useful primer on the concerns informing all of his research on the core executive: he is concerned with power, how it is attained, how it is exercised, how closely it approximates the expectations (and myths) of the political culture, how it is expressed (and managed) through a working life, and what its limits are. Fraser, he suggests, was seen by both supporters and critics as a dominant figure, a perception at odds with Australia's political design: 'a parliamentary system, for the Australian system of responsible government is collective in its rhetoric, its form and its presentation . . . meant to be based on cabinet and parliament, not presidential or prime ministerial in its style' (Weller 1989: xii–xiii). But how powerful was Fraser, and how real was the institution of cabinet when he presided? This generates more fundamental questions: 'How do prime ministers have an impact on the procedures and policies of government—what can they do and what can't they do? . . . what does an appreciation of the working styles of, and limitations on, prime ministers tell us more generally about the difficulties of governing Australia?' (Weller 1989: xiii). Weller takes a cumulative approach to addressing these questions, dealing first with Fraser's management of the machinery of government (parliament, advisers, ministers, cabinet), then with presentation (relations with the public), and then with illustrative examples of policy-making (budgets, federal–state relations, foreign policy) to arrive at a representation of decision processes themselves: a picture of 'a prime minister in action'.

Along the way, Weller offers an illuminating aside on biographical models he admires: Fred Greenstein's revisionist account of Dwight Eisenhower (Greenstein 1982) and the first volume of Robert Caro's monumental (and still incomplete) biography of Lyndon Johnson (Caro 1982). These are valued because both authors 'explain the methods that their subjects adopted to achieve their ends. They place them in the confines of an institution and ask how they took their opportunities and to what degree their actions were shaped by institutional demands' (Weller 1989: 8). One might perhaps add that Caro's voluminous detail vindicates Weller's choice of induction based on close observation. For Caro's multiple volumes on Johnson, written over many years, challenge Lytton Strachey's insistence that the complete life can never be told.

Caro's implication is that if you watch someone long and closely enough all will be revealed.

Not surprisingly, then, Weller's forensic examination of Fraser's working life concentrates on his methods, and the extent to which he was able to capitalise on institutional levers, or was constrained by what he saw as institutional imperatives. The concluding chapters, on decision processes and on Fraser as prime minister, effectively draw the threads together to show how Fraser managed the tensions between what he had to do, and what he wanted to do. What he wanted was an Australia in which people had relative freedom of choice (so the state was appropriately constrained), but prosperity and security were assured (so the state was still capable of intervention when needed): 'To argue that governments were too large and intrusive was not to assert that they had no proper and necessary role' (Weller 1989: 403). This was a problematic position for Fraser to take when some in his party were prepared to abandon this Deakinite tradition in favour of neo-liberalism; it would be a persistent problem for him, and would influence negative assessments of his achievement thereafter. Yet what Fraser felt he had to do was to restore due process after the chaos of the Whitlam years, which meant a commitment to cabinet and avoidance of the perceptions of conflict: 'Being elected under a cloud meant that there was a constant search for legitimacy, a desire to govern without taking decisions that were divisive' (Weller 1989: 403).

While Fraser appeared tough and dominating, no prime minister can be all powerful; Fraser was both more cautious and more consultative than he appeared at the time. While he was by far the most influential policy player in his government, and used his knowledge and formidable personality to drive decisions, he did not make them alone, nor did he act unilaterally—he consulted exhaustively. Though constantly involved in the daily running of policies, cabinet was central to his mode of governing: 'He argued aggressively, interrogated ministers, pushed hard for preferred policies; yet he did not dictate nor often demand' (Weller 1989: 398). Yet ministers felt pushed to perform, and some felt his persistent attention signalled a lack of trust. Fraser's reputation for ruthlessness and indifference to others had its source in shyness: he was task-oriented, but uncomfortable dealing with individuals and their problems—compassion was instead expressed through large-scale measures (resettlement of Vietnamese boat people; a concern for human rights; and liberal, third-world oriented foreign policies).

Weller carefully marshals the evidence that Fraser's performance is to be understood as dependent not only on personal style, but also on the imperatives of party management and, especially, of cabinet government, which 'still means collective decision-making because of the need to maintain support, because the authority and administrative capacity still lie with the departments, and because only cabinet government allows the variety of views to be expressed and tested' (Weller 1989: 408). Finally, Weller not only addresses the question of how particular methods can be deployed within a particular institutional environment (and this remains one of the best studies we have of 'a prime minister in action'), but also uses the Fraser instance to confirm the position he outlines in his opening pages: that debates about 'prime ministerial' versus 'cabinet government' depend on a mistaken dichotomy:

> prime ministerial and cabinet government are presented as alternative models of behaviour. Analysts have not defined when the one shifts to the other: when is cabinet government no longer 'real' or how often must a prime minister lose before the government is no longer prime ministerial? Nor could they. The problem is that one model posits individual decision making and the other collective action. The distinctions in reality are never so clear-cut. It may, for instance, be possible for every decision to be taken by cabinet and yet for the prime minister still to dominate. The two models are points on a spectrum defining the exercise of power, not distinct alternatives.
>
> The power of prime ministers can only be properly understood if the two perspectives are combined, to understand prime ministers in their environment. How influential they are will depend on personal, institutional and intellectual factors. For particular leaders the question is how they use the potential of their office. (Weller 1989: 2–3)

Weller's second major study of a political actor was his biography of John Button, *Dodging Raindrops* (1999). With a focus on the 'life', the book is more conventionally biographical, with an orthodox depiction of origins and formative influences (especially the childhood experience of the expressed idealism and harsh discipline exercised by his father), and a temporally organised account of Button's career trajectory. The professed purpose this time was to draw on Button's experience 'to provide some light on the way that the Labor Party Button joined in 1953 became the party he left in office in 1993' (Weller 1999: xi). Ultimately, however, the book deals more satisfactorily with Weller's long-standing concerns: how people learn to become ministers and what it takes to succeed. This is not to say that the book avoids the subject of party change—there is detailed discussion of the Victorian 'participants' whose agitation led to intervention in Victoria, of party conferences, caucus operation and the like—but curiously Button almost drops from view in much of this discussion. Weller concentrates instead on the settings in which Button's ambition could play out: historical institutionalism comes to the fore and our protagonist seems at most a subsidiary actor. Where the book comes to life is in demonstrating Button's skills as 'a strategist, realist and tough operator' (Weller 1999: 240): the means by which he gained power and influence to become a central figure in the parliamentary executive and an effective minister.

Especially impressive is Weller's persuasive teasing out of the way Button understood the institutions in which he must perform (the 'weather' common to all), but played his own game ('dodging the raindrops'). He was a loner who could nonetheless master the delicate factional negotiations needed to reinforce his own insecure position; a man who could charm and amuse but maintained a distance; a shrewd (and outspoken) analyst of the propensities and potential of others, but whose public servants and staff often remained unsure of what he wanted; a pivotal player in cabinet (and in successive leadership transitions), yet always regarded as in the team but not of the team; a well-informed idealist, alert to ideas, but essentially a realist suspicious of 'vision'; a minister capable of left-field innovation, but largely given to pragmatic solutions; a man committed for a lengthy period to one portfolio, but often inattentive to his department's wishes and unwilling to defend it. Weller is captivated (as is the reader) by Button's unusual capacity to realise his ambitions as a tough strategic operator while playing against the expectations of collectives—the party, his department and even his executive colleagues.

Writing at a time when there was much debate about whether the ALP had been 'hi-jacked' by neo-liberals, Weller sets out to show that this is a 'perverse' debate, looking backwards for continuity when outcomes are a matter of hard work, contingency and chance; and of what a government can do, and what it can't. As in the Fraser book, he lays down his cards at the outset:

> Policy choices are the consequences of consultation, pressures of time and an agonising appreciation that there are always losers . . . Political battles depend on fortuitous numbers. Few ministers, if they are being entirely honest, will end up where they anticipated when a policy is developed. The Hawke ministers may have had a broad ambition to open up Australia and slow its economic decline, but the details were developed as they went along. Governments just do not have enough power to operate otherwise . . . What in retrospect may seem to be a staged and logical process of reform could at the time have been a number of small steps, followed by an analysis of where the game was. (Weller 1999: x)

The Button depicted by Weller, making it up as he went along (and tempering ideals) according to his assessment of what would work rather than conforming to expectations, seems ideally suited to this project. Button later wrote one of the most trenchant critiques of the ALP, pleading that imagination must not be 'constrained by illusory ambitions and an innate fear of rocking the boat', but insisting that it 'has to be sure what it stands for . . . guided by the idea of a social democratic Australia' (Button 2002: ix–x), suggesting, however, that Weller's own pragmatic incrementalism may be begging the question of what drives party reform, and occluding the nature of the change his book professes to illuminate. His 'life' of Button is, on the other hand, a consummate demonstration of the capacity of an individual to exercise agency within the institutions of party, parliament and government.

INSTITUTIONAL VIGNETTES

Turning from individual cases to explicitly institutional studies, Weller's operating assumptions are clarified: he is intent on showing that the exercise of power is often misunderstood or over-rated because we are 'dazzled' by the media, institutional machinery is 'taken for granted', and powerful political actors 'are often more limited than they appear' (Weller 1985: 210–11). His commitment is to elucidate institutional machinery in order to challenge such misconceptions. But he maintains an eye for idiosyncrasy and personal style so long as these are seen to operate within institutional bounds. Eschewing theory, especially psychological theory, he nonetheless has a historian's eye for the comment or anecdote that reveals character. The remark of an acquaintance, for instance, is used to capture much that theoretical analysis might arrive at more tortuously: of Billy Hughes, for instance, Weller notes an early party colleague's telling summary: 'want of tact; brilliant no doubt, but ballast none' (Weller 1975: 30). This is a tactic that draws on the observational common sense thought to be the strength of conventional biography. It is recurrent in Weller's work, where prime ministers, cabinet members and bureaucrats alike are effectively encapsulated by such means.

Once the institutional machinery with its possibilities and constraints is mapped, Weller can (as in his individual actor studies) explore the possibilities of agency. His study of cabinet government (Weller 2007), for instance, provides a linear history of the evolution of cabinet in Australia, followed by an elaboration of systematic processes, showing how these ultimately give a range of powers to the prime minister. It provides a comparison for other Westminster systems. Having established limits, cleared away media 'dazzle', and challenged widespread misconceptions, Weller shows the means by which prime ministers can exercise power: through patronage, control of resources, veto ability, monopoly of advice, capitalisation of media attention, definition of the agenda through public commitments, management of cabinet as a source of support, containment of factions by integrating their leaders in cabinet, and use of cabinet to legitimise decisions made elsewhere. If such measures are deployed skilfully, establishment of authority 'gives prime ministers an ability to operate individually that is effectively untrammelled. Consequently, it is easy to point to occasions where prime ministers have set the tone and direction of government and/or policy' (Weller 2007: 257). He peppers the discussion with vignettes that illuminate the ways each prime minister has exercised such powers differently, not only in (sometimes) acting unilaterally, but also in maintaining unity and support in cabinet. He also alerts us to those occasions when a prime minister gets bogged down by losing the balance between administrative and political imperatives (for instance, Fraser, in Weller 2007: 267), or, more consequentially, when prime ministerial authority fails (for instance, Scullin in 1930 and Hawke in 1991, see Weller 2007: 255–6 and 252).

Interestingly, while Weller's periodisation of cabinet evolution is not overtly tied to particular prime ministers, his contribution to the history of the Department of Prime Minister and Cabinet (Weller, Scott and Stevens 2011)[1] is more clearly biographically inflected. The chapters in part one (again a linear history, this time of departmental evolution) are subtitled with reference to the succession of departmental secretaries. And in this case, the illustrations of key players at work serve not only to reveal the possibilities for agency within the institutional carapace, but also to signify the importance of departmental secretaries as the driving intelligence behind the changes that took place. They, too, had to be understood in an institutional context and never worked alone—they were responsive to prime ministers and their staff, to other departmental actors, to the contingent challenges of their times. Indeed, reference to their personal stories reveals the limits within which each had to work. But we are left in little doubt that key players were never merely subject to the institutional script with which they were presented: they set the 'tone and direction' of the department.

Moments of transition make this especially clear. John Bunting (secretary in 1959–68 and 1971–75), for instance, developed a close relationship with Robert Menzies, and was always prepared to offer a personal view: he ran a department where policy influence was quietly garnered but was not to be overt; propriety dominated. Weller relies on the views of a colleague (and successor) to capture Bunting's strengths:

> He was a fantastic listener. He would draw out other people's views. He'd never rush to make a judgement himself. He might have a very strong view . . . of where it ought to end up, but he'd always draw everybody else out first. He'd only come to an expressed view about what should happen at the end of that kind of process. He just exuded wisdom and calmness. (Weller, Scott and Stevens 2011: 78)

Bunting's successor, Lenox Hewitt (1968–71) brought in by John Gorton, however, was very different: aggressive, intimidating, controlling and far more willing 'to openly contribute his policy views' (Weller, Scott and Stevens 2011: 68). He recruited 'sharp and aggressive policy specialists' (Weller, Scott and Stevens 2011: 69) and so the departmental culture changed. It was not only a matter of personal style, however, since Hewitt provided what

> Gorton needed and could not immediately get . . . He guided him, supported him and helped him cut through time-honoured practices. But for Gorton to be more successful he had to have the full co-operation of the public service and Hewitt had made things

difficult for him by alienating too many senior public servants. (Ian Hancock, Gorton's biographer, cited in Weller, Scott and Stevens 2011: 69)

Bunting would be returned for a period after Gorton's fall, but Hewitt was a portent of the significant policy role that was to come, establishing 'a more assertive place for PMD in policy generation and advice that came to be accepted over the following decade' (Weller, Scott and Stevens 2011: 69).

Thus, by the late twentieth century, departmental secretaries fulfilled not only a service role, they were 'policy driving'. Their gifts and proclivities therefore cannot be ignored in this institutional history, and we are given a strong sense of how the interaction of their preferences and governmental demands shaped the character of the department as it developed the capacity to lead. Mike Codd (under Bob Hawke) was interested in improving the machinery, and finding better systems for running policy; Mike Keating (under Paul Keating) focused on policy content, designing solutions to the immediate problems confronting government; Max Moore-Wilton (under John Howard), the prime minister's man in the bureaucracy, was intent on ensuring that Howard's wishes were carried into the APS and put into effect; Peter Shergold (also under Howard) was forensic and disciplined, an enthusiast for the big picture, but concerned that policy advising was informed by evidence and the political climate; Terry Moran (under Kevin Rudd) wanted 'a department that can find new ways of collaborating across the public service . . . a department that could give a reliable read to the prime minister on paper coming into the cabinet process . . . a department that could itself lead or cooperate in major strategic projects, using new and better approaches to public policies' (Weller, Scott and Stevens 2011: 146), and when he found it wanting, he set out to re-shape and revitalise it. In each case, Weller, Scott and Stevens introduce the lead player with a synopsis of his background; in each case there is an assessment of how his intentions and activities transformed the institution: this is biography with purpose.

COLLECTIVE BIOGRAPHY

Political scientists have sometimes adopted the collective study of elites as a means of overcoming the supposedly individualist (and ungeneralisable) bias of biography. Now known as prosopography, 'the investigation of the *common background characteristics of a group of actors* ... by means of a collective study of their lives' (Stone 1971: 46, emphasis added), social scientific collective biography was pioneered by Lewis Namier as a blend of statistics and social history (see Namier 1957). In the Australian context, Ian McAllister has been a notable practitioner (McAllister 1992), but Weller too has made notable contributions. His studies of the roles of ministers, first with Michelle Grattan (Weller and Grattan 1981) and again, 30 years later, with Anne Tiernan (Tiernan and Weller 2010) contain both demographic and statistical overviews of the sort pioneered by Namier (see, for instance, Tiernan and Weller 2010: chapter 2), and a considerable reliance upon experiential narrative, in order to capture the nature of the people drawn to, and the expectations attached to, the ministerial job. In these books, the purpose is not to develop vignettes about key players, but instead to draw on narratives of experience to advance our understanding of the working lives of ministers. While individuals are not identified, the results can be read not only as a depiction of demand and response within the ministerial institution but also as a form of collective biography, as patterns of shared background and common experience are elaborated. In the process, we gain a social history of political elites from decades apart, allowing for a comparison that highlights how much has changed: the professionalisation and 'younging' of politics (cf. Weller and Fraser 1987); the heightened expectations of and demands on ministers; the institutional evolution of cabinet, parliament and bureaucracy; the increasing size of ministerial offices and—with this—the potential for forms of 'court politics' (cf. Rhodes 2013) simply unimaginable 30 years ago.

Ministers, of course, are only one element of the political elite—'the public servants provide the sinews and muscle that make the body politic work' (Weller 2001: 3). True to his broader interest, Weller has also applied the tools of prosopography to the bureaucracy, both in Australia (Weller 2001) and beyond (Rhodes and Weller 2001). For purposes of this discussion I refer only to the first. In this instance, as in his study of the ministers, Weller also introduces a demographic- and statistics-based collective portrait (Weller 2001: chapter 3). This usefully identifies changing characteristics at different periods (such as age and levels of education/qualification at entry) and career patterns (such as mobility; length of service before Senior Executive Service appointment; years between SES appointment and assumption of departmental head; central agency experience). This, in turn, shows that silos have been reduced, there is more lateral movement—careers are now within the APS rather than in an individual department—but promotion to secretary is still largely from within the APS. Again, that is followed by the thematic mining of experiential narrative to elucidate the key elements of, and the changes over time in, the roles of 'the mandarins', with particular attention to the efforts of ministers to exert more control and to the attempts of the APS itself to ensure more responsiveness. The distinction in this case is that respondents are named and quotations attributed.

While there is not the recurrent resort to the sort of vignettes that established departmental secretaries as driving figures in his later book on the evolution of Prime Minister & Cabinet (see above), it is possible to piece together coherent impressions of key figures. And in one chapter (Weller 2001: chapter 8), Weller concedes that 'collective portraits can only take us so far', and allows some key individuals 'to speak for themselves' (Weller 2001: 181). Here we are given concise biographies of, and consolidated views from, representative 'mandarins' active in different periods: Sir Roland Wilson (1940s and 1950s), Tony Ayers (1970s and 1980s), Mike Codd (1980s) and Mike Keating (1980s and 1990s). It is an effective way of bringing focus to the preceding mosaic of voices speaking to particular themes. And it acknowledges a degree of agency: 'particular choices and decisions that had an impact on the world of the departmental secretaries were not inevitable. They were made because of the intersection of people and ideas at a given time' (Weller 2001: 227). But in this instance it is less about agency than about outlining 'changes in the social conditions and expectations [that] provide the background and conditions within which the role of the departmental secretary must be understood', and by 'identify[ing] and explain[ing] these changes . . . to determine what implications they have for the governance of Australia' (Weller 2001: 3).

This was, Weller asserted, an exercise in collective memory—hence the importance of testimony from successive cohorts of departmental secretaries—as well as an assessment of the current state of play. On that subject, he concludes:

> there has been no long period of stability. There is no given target for reform, no agreement on what is an ideal situation . . . Rather there is constant evaluation of how the APS might be organised and where the departmental secretaries should stand in that new

world ... Competition for the ear of the minster can be fierce, solutions are uncertain, the battle for good ideas continuous and the traditional grounds for dispute constantly shifting ... [D]epartmental secretaries have to fight for attention. They have to make their case and deliver programs in a way that satisfies government. (Weller 2001: 228)

While the old system of appointing secretaries for life, who long survived their ministers, was problematic, the new world of flexibility and heightened accountability has made the relationship with the minister paramount, but also introduced the potential for capriciousness (Weller uses the sacking of Paul Barratt to underscore this point). 'That can only breed insecurity. And insecurity is not good for the quality of advice' (Weller 2001: 235). Weller's answer, then, to the question implied by his subtitle—'the frank and the fearless?'—is that the conditions revealed by his respondents may militate against the quality of advice. 'There is therefore a particular requirement that the career service be maintained and nurtured' (Weller 2001: 237). It is a lesson well supported by the experiential narrative on which the book relies.

A CRITICAL APPRAISAL

It has been rightly observed that Patrick Weller 'has produced the only substantial and sustained body of work on the Australian core executive', that he is its 'narrator in chief' (Rhodes and Wanna 2009: 121). This paper argues that, though resistant to being identified as a biographer through his uses of political 'lives' and experiential narrative to address fundamental questions about how the executive works, Weller has made a significant contribution to political biography—which should always be driven by such questions rather than by the romance of individual 'journeys' (Walter 2014). His range—covering individual cases, illustrative vignettes within institutional histories, and collective biography/prosopography—has been unusual and innovative. His attention is always directed to the nature of political work (questions of private life are rarely broached), and always within specific institutional contexts: the machinery of state is never to be taken for granted. We are left in no doubt that institutions themselves are the source of opportunities and constraints—that should be our main objective if we are to appreciate how the executive functions and evolves—but individual agency makes a crucial difference. This is a salutary lesson both to political biographers (many of whom remain implicitly wedded to the 'great man' theory of history), and to those 'new institutionalists' who assert that we should avoid 'unfeasible assumptions that require too much of political actors'.

Weller relies almost wholly on qualitative data (documentary records and interviews): this reliance is very much in the vein of what some regard as the 'commonsensical, humane and empirical' bent of good biography (Homberger and Charmley 1988: ix–xv). He is perceptive, measured, not prey to ideological leanings, usually non-judgemental (though he will quote both positive and critical peer assessments to capture character) and rarely polemical (his account of 'children overboard'—Weller 2002—is the exception). These are well-chosen tactics: caution and even-handedness have allowed him to prosper for a lengthy period in this field, and without this exhaustive engagement such a substantial contribution could not have been achieved. Politicians and the policy community continue to respond willingly to his questions because of his reputation as a safe pair of hands. He is wary of theory, certainly of that deployed by 'psychobiographers', but even—when it comes to prosopography—of the 'interpretive' turn to ethnomethodology urged by his long-time associate and occasional co-author Rod Rhodes. He is usually sceptical about normative claims, suggesting that in their pursuit of what 'ought' to be, their exponents lose sight of what executives actually and, sometimes, must do (see Tiernan and Weller 2010: 11). But at times—as in his advocacy for the 'mandarins' (Weller 2001: conclusion)—his own work assumes a normative dimension.

Cautious empiricism has allowed Weller to remain onside with his subjects, perhaps even to fly under the radar of critics who have taken issue with more experimental or theoretically contentious methods. But what are the limits to such an approach? What are the questions it fails to address? I suggest four areas for consideration.

First, it is curious that, while in most respects a practitioner of historical institutionalism, Weller pays relatively little attention to the 'exogenous shocks'—war, economic collapse, national crisis—that are said by its advocates to drive change. This leads to a very linear version of history: change is incremental and the policy cycles stimulated and destroyed by such shocks remain in the background (and the theorists of 'political time' who attend to such cycles—e.g. Skowronek 1997—are ignored). Is he *too* focused on internal institutional dynamics and key players within the elite?

Second, Weller's pursuit of biography without theory is very successful in showing how an individual can 'work the machine' in a particular context, at a particular moment, but it begs the question of whether the strengths and weaknesses that Fraser, for instance, exhibited might illuminate the potentials and limitations of other such individuals in disparate institutions at different times. (Hence, there is no dialogue with, say, Graham Little's interpretation of Fraser as a 'strong leader' or engagement with a broader debate, see Little 1988: 178–255.) Weller, in dispensing with theory in favor of description, is also better on the 'what' and 'how' questions of action rather than the 'why'. (Again one turns to Little, in relation to Fraser, for reflection on why he acted as he did.)

Third, Weller poses limiting questions about just when the transition from cabinet government to 'prime ministerial' government might be identified, and suggests that, based on the evidence he will admit, it is essentially unanswerable. Thus, he explicitly positions himself alongside the continuity theorists, such as George Jones (Blick and Jones 2010), and against the 'institutional stretch' thesis adopted by, say, Peter Hennessy (2001) or Michael Foley (2001)—or in Australia, James Walter and Paul Strangio (Walter and Strangio 2007). That thesis contends that, with resource intensification enhancing their power, and party decline pushing them to the fore as the object of political identification and differentiation, leaders have become ever more central to the way politics is understood. Consequently, they have been given more licence to 'stretch' the office by exceeding the conventions and expectations that once applied to the leader's role. Weller's engagement in this debate is long-standing and vigorous, and a salutary caution against its normative theorists (e.g. Walter and Strangio) and some of its more polemical manifestations (e.g. Oborne 2007). But it is a position that relies on limited evidence—cases of excessive leadership behaviour and autonomous decision-making (Billy Hughes is his standout example) that long predate the supposed trend,[2] and the internal behaviours of the groups to which he has had access. At the same time, it ignores countervailing evidence of international patterns (e.g. Pakulski and Körösényi 2012: chapter 3) and of the linkage between reduced liberal democratic restraints on leaders due to institutional change, and mass political psychology (e.g. Blondel and Thiebault 2009). His is a form of rational actor thesis that does not engage with such debates and the bigger questions they suggest (e.g. Gill 2012).

Fourth, positioning himself with the 'continuity' theorists precludes Weller from engaging with contemporary debates about the interpretation of executive behaviour in terms of court politics (see Rhodes, this volume: chapter 2). While there are differences in that interpretation (cf. Rhodes, above; Rhodes 2013; Walter 2010), the essential point is that court politics attempts to map the relational interdependencies between core executive positions without resort either to misleading metaphors of 'presidentialisation' on the one hand, or reversion to institutional rationality on the other. While Weller has skilfully shifted the 'either/or' focus of contention about structure versus agency to 'both/and', his preoccupation with limiting questions about 'prime ministerial' government causes him (perhaps unwittingly) to revert to traditional concerns with actors identified in particular positions. The field has moved on. We need neither succumb to the 'leader democracy' thesis, nor accede to functional analysis of discrete institutional roles. The operations of core executives can be understood as variants of 'the court': the interplay of loyalties, beliefs, institutional traditions and practices within elite networks. Those networks are constituted by relational interdependency, mutability of power relations and Realpolitik.

CONCLUSION

The sheer range of Patrick Weller's engagement with life history—biography, institutional vignettes, role studies and prosopography—is a corrective to political scientists' reluctance to dwell on 'the individual'. He invites us to look at the political process through a variety of different windows—from the situations of prime ministers, ministers, policy activists, mandarins, staffers, collectives—allowing every angle to enhance our perspective. By always linking his enterprise to questions of engagement, action, the acquisition and exercise of power, and the way actors can 'work' the matrix of institutional conventions, he transcends these individual cases to produce plausible generalisations about politics at large. We thus see the potential of life history as a tool for social science rather than (or as well as) a humanistic endeavour. His achievement of a fruitful intersection between biography and historical institutionalism demolishes arid speculation about the provenance of structure versus agency.

There are limits to Weller's research: an inherent scepticism about most theory, a conservative bent towards continuities that screens out qualitative change, some reluctance to acknowledge when the field has moved on, and hence a failure to engage with some of the bigger questions that theory, complex change and disciplinary/practitioner disputation have generated. But without his comprehensive empirical groundwork, his exemplary attention to what political actors actually do, and his ability to work the middle ground between pure institutionalism and biographical individualism, we in Australia would not even have arrived at the starting point for such discussions.

NOTES

1   In a jointly authored publication such as this, it must be acknowledged that individual contributions are difficult to identify, but when Weller is cited as senior author, it will be assumed that he is at least the organising intelligence behind the work.
2   One colleague, challenged in this manner by Weller, remarked: 'It's a bit like a climate change denialist asserting, "But we've always had storms!"'

REFERENCES

Blick, A. & Jones, G.W., 2010, *Premiership: The development, nature and power of the office of the British Prime Minister*, Exeter: Imprint

Blondel, J. & Thiebault, J.-L., 2009, *Political Leadership, Parties and Citizens: The personalisation of leadership*, Hoboken: Taylor & Francis

Boumans, J., Boomgarden, H. & Vliegenthart, R., 2013, 'Media Personalisation in Context: A cross-national comparison between the UK and the Netherlands, 1992–2007', *Political Studies*, vol. 6, no. 1, pp. 198–216

Brett, J., 1997, 'The Tasks of Biography', in J. Brett (ed.), *Political Lives*, Sydney: Allen & Unwin, pp. 1–15

Button, J., 2002, 'Beyond Belief: What Future for Labor?', *Quarterly Essay*, no. 6, Melbourne: Black Inc.

Caro, R., 1982, *The Years of Lyndon Johnson, Volume 1, Means of Ascent*, New York: Knopf

Davies, A.F., 1972, 'The Tasks of Biography', in A.F. Davies, *Essays in Political Sociology*, Melbourne: Cheshire, pp. 109–72

Edinger, L., 1964, 'Political Science and Political Biography', *The Journal of Politics*, vol. XXVI, pp. 423–39, 648–76

Flyvbjerg, B., 2006, 'Five Misunderstandings about Case-Study Research', *Qualitative Inquiry*, vol. 12, no. 2, pp. 219–45

Foley, M., 2001, *The British Presidency*, Manchester: Manchester University Press

Gill, S., 2012, *Global Crises and the Crisis of Global Leadership*, Cambridge: Cambridge University Press

Greenstein, F.I., 1982, *The Hidden Hand Presidency: Eisenhower as leader*, New York: Basic Books

Helms, L., 2012, 'Democratic Political Leadership in the New Media Age: A farewell to excellence?', *The British Journal of Politics and International Relations*, vol. 14, pp. 651–70

Hennessy, P., 2001, *The Prime Minister: The office and its holders since 1945*, New York: Palgrave

Homberger, E. & Charmley, J. (eds), 1988, *The Troubled Face of Biography*, Houndmills, Basingstoke: Macmillan

Little, G., 1988, *Strong Leaders: Thatcher, Reagan and an eminent person*, Melbourne: Oxford University Press

McAllister, I., 1992, *Political Behaviour: Citizens, parties and elites in Australia*, Melbourne: Longman Cheshire

March, J.G. & Olsen, J.P., 2005, *Elaborating the 'New Institutionalism'*, Oslo: Centre for European Studies, Working Paper No. 11, at <www.arena.uio.no>, accessed 5 December 2009

Namier, L., 1957 [first published 1929], *The Structure of Politics at the Accession of George III*, London: Macmillan

Oborne, P., 2007, *The Triumph of the British Political Class*, London: Simon & Schuster

O'Brien, P., 1998, 'A Polemical Review of Political Biography', *Biography: An Interdisciplinary Quarterly*, vol. 21, no. 1, pp. 50–7

Pakulski, J. & Körösényi, A., 2012, *Toward Leader Democracy*, London: Anthem Press

Pimlott, B., 1994, 'The Future of Political Biography', in B. Pimlott, *Frustrate their Knavish Tricks: Writings on biography, history and politics*, London: Harper Collins, pp. 149–61

Rhodes, R.A.W., 2012, 'Theory, Method and British Political "Life History"', *Political Studies Review*, vol. 10, no. 2, pp. 161–76

—— 2013, 'From Prime-Ministerial Leadership to Court Politics', in P. Strangio, P. 't Hart & J. Walter (eds), *Understanding Prime-Ministerial Performance: Comparative perspectives*, Oxford: Oxford University Press, pp. 318–33

Rhodes, R.A.W. & Wanna, J., 2009, 'The Executives', in R.A.W. Rhodes (ed.), *The Australian Study of Politics*, Houndmills, Basingstoke: Palgrave Macmillan, pp. 119–30

Rhodes, R.A.W. & Weller, P. (eds), 2001, *The Changing World of Top Officials: Mandarins or valets?*, Buckingham: Open University Press

Schmidt, V.A., 2010, 'Taking ideas and discourse seriously: Explaining change through discursive institutionalism as the fourth "new institutionalism"', *European Political Science Review*, vol. 2, no. 1, pp. 1–25

Skidelsky, R., 1988, 'Only Connect: Biography and truth', in E. Homberger & J. Charmley (eds), *The Troubled Face of Biography*, Houndmills, Basingstoke: Macmillan, pp. 1–16

Skowronek, S., 1997, *The Politics Presidents Make: Leadership from John Adams to Bill Clinton*, Harvard: Harvard University Press

Stone, L., 1971, 'Prosopography', *Daedalus*, Winter, pp. 46–79

Thelen, K. & Steinmo, S., 1992, 'Historical Institutionalism in Comparative Perspective', in S. Steinmo, K. Thelen & F. Longstreth (eds), *Structuring Politics: Historical institutionalism in comparative perspective*, Cambridge: Cambridge University Press

Tiernan, A. & Weller, P., 2010, *Learning to be a Minister: Heroic expectations, practical realities*, Melbourne: Melbourne University Press

Walter, J., 1992, 'Prime Ministers and their Staff', in P. Weller (ed.), *Menzies to Keating: The development of the Australian prime ministership*, Melbourne: Melbourne University Press, pp. 28–63

—— 2010, 'Elite Decision Processes: The "Court Politics" Debate', paper to the Australian Political Studies Association Annual Conference, University of Melbourne, 27–29 September
—— 2014, 'Biographical Analysis', in R.A.W. Rhodes & P. 't Hart (eds), *The Oxford Handbook of Political Leadership*, Oxford: Oxford University Press
Walter, J. & Strangio, P., 2007, *No, Prime Minister: Reclaiming politics from leaders*, Sydney: UNSW Press
Weller, P., 1975, *Caucus Minutes, 1901–1949: Minutes of the meetings of the federal parliamentary Labor Party*, vol. 1, Melbourne: Melbourne University Press
—— 1985, *First Among Equals: Prime ministers in Westminster systems*, Sydney: Allen & Unwin
—— 1989, *Malcolm Fraser PM: A study in prime ministerial power in Australia*, Melbourne: Penguin
—— 1999, *Dodging Raindrops: John Button—A Labor life*, Sydney: Allen & Unwin
—— 2001, *Australia's Mandarins: The frank and the fearless?*, Sydney: Allen & Unwin
—— 2002, *Don't Tell the Prime Minister*, Melbourne: Scribe Books
—— 2007, *Cabinet Government in Australia, 1901–2006*, Sydney: UNSW Press
Weller, P. & Fraser, S., 1987, 'The Younging of Australian Politics or Politics as a First Career', *Politics*, vol. 22, no. 2, pp. 76–83
Weller, P. & Grattan, M., 1981, *Can Ministers Cope? Australian federal ministers at work*, Melbourne: Hutchinson
Weller, P., Scott, J. & Stevens, B., 2011, *From Postbox to Powerhouse: A centenary history of the Department of Prime Minister and Cabinet*, Sydney: Allen & Unwin

8

ADMINISTRATIVE HISTORY AS BIOGRAPHY
John Wanna

Threescore and ten I can remember well,
Within the volume of which time I have seen
Hours dreadful and things strange, but this sore night
Hath trifled former knowings.

—William Shakespeare, *Macbeth*, Act 2, scene 4

For forms of government let fools contest:
whate'er is best administered is best.

—Alexander Pope, *An Essay on Man*, Epistle 3

In the introduction to this *festschrift*, Rod Rhodes recounts how he had met Pat Weller only a couple of 'fleeting times' before he invited him to attend the ESRC workshop held at the University of York in April 1992; from which point they began a collaborative working relationship that was to last well over two decades. At that time, Pat was already a scholar of executive politics with an international reputation, but it was a pivotal moment for Rhodes as he began to move into executive studies. I had gone to York University in early 1992 to take part of a sabbatical and finish off some writing, at that stage never having done any serious research on the political executive. I had first met Pat a decade earlier in Christchurch, New Zealand, where I was a contractual lecturer and he had come to visit Professor Keith Jackson as part of the fieldwork research for his comparative book on prime ministers in Westminster systems (*First Among Equals*), and also to get in a bit of skiing on the ski fields of the South Island. Pat had then appointed me in 1985, along with Glyn Davis, as his two inaugural appointments at the about-to-be-named School of Politics and Public Policy at Griffith University.

Although the York workshop became a pivotal moment for Rhodes in terms of subsequent collaborations, it was what Pat Weller said at the workshop that was the most telling and illuminative. His interjections at the workshop neatly encapsulate his approach to qualitative research in the discipline and, more generally, his contribution to scholarship in political science and public policy.

Rhodes had called the workshop as part of the preparation process for the so-called 'Whitehall Project'—a concerted program of research into modern government in the UK. The most eminent British political scientists had been invited to attend, and they soon began to lament that British scholars had not been able or prepared to produce decent studies on many of the core institutions of British government (or in some cases had not produced *any* studies at all). The list of omissions included: national parliament, the core executive, key central agencies, line departments, political parties, prime ministers and senior ministers, advisers, senior mandarins, etc. But selecting exactly *what* research projects to frame and commission proved somewhat difficult. At one stage, Rhodes could be seen rolling his eyes in exasperation after one senior Don suggested in all sincerity that one of the most pressing issues the British academy could contemplate was a study of how many questions in parliament the prime minister or government of the day actually answered!

After hearing these laments, an unabashed Pat Weller was able to tick off an entire list of similar studies that had *already* been done in Australia. Many of these studies he had contributed himself, or had participated in, or had built on, and his list was extensive. Australian academics, he argued, had shown initiative, taken up the challenges, and generally found that the sometimes ticklish matter of 'access' had not been a problem—senior officials were cooperative with research endeavours and willing, indeed happy, to talk. Hugh Heclo and Aaron Wildavsky had found the same in Whitehall with their 1974 study of the private government of public money, as had Peter Hennessy (1989) in his compendia of executive politics and administration in Whitehall. While some workshop attendees might have regarded Weller as a jumped-up 'colonial' (which he wasn't), his main point was well made: Australian political scientists had charted the territory of core executive administration and institutional governance at the centre long before many of their British counterparts had thought of attempting the task or dared to approach those in power. And these corresponding comparative observations were made not by a native Australian boasting of his parochial ostentatiousness, but by an English-born scholar who had crafted his career in Australia and saw an opportunity for cutting down the tall poppy that was British academia.

• • •

This chapter seeks to locate the works of Patrick Weller in the conspectus of the field of Australian administrative history. The argument pursued in this chapter is that throughout his career Weller has maintained an abiding interest in historical analysis and uses history as a backdrop to his scholarship in political science. He was originally trained as a historian and still approaches the study of politics through the lens of historical empiricism (see an earlier essay on the 'narrator in chief' in Rhodes and Wanna 2009: 119–30). He has occasionally produced works of administrative history, such as commissioned agency studies (institutional history) and sporadic case studies of administrative practice (case histories), and some of his major opuses could later be 'read' by scholars as fine examples of contemporary administrative studies (for instance, his acclaimed study of *Malcolm Fraser PM* which explores the interface between politics and administration in great detail); but he is no conventional administrative historian and has maintained only intermittent involvement in the field. Hence, as a political scientist his influence in the field of administrative history is more nuanced than seminal. However, and in contrast to many of his contemporaries, he approaches administrative history through the eyes of the inquisitive biographer—the narrative historian interested in charting how key personalities exercise power. So, perhaps unexpectedly, as a social scientist his notable influence may be in bringing an appreciation of history to bear on political science. Throughout his career he has championed the significance of 'good' history to 'good' political analysis, while reserving a particular disdain for shallow ahistorical espousals. In short, he has long advocated the importance of the value of historical grounding, and knowledge of administrative history, to inform the study of political institutions, political actors and the practices of modern government.

ADMINISTRATIVE HISTORY CONSTITUTES A SUB-SET WITHIN THE GENRE OF ADMINISTRATIVE STUDIES

Administrative history is a small sub-set of the genre of public administration and administrative studies. Together they have a long pedigree dating back to the nineteenth century with classic writers (in rough chronological order) such as William Wentworth, James Macarthur, Henry Melville, J.D. Lang, John West, Henry Parkes, William Lane, William P. Reeves, Robert Garran, John Quick, Catherine Spence and even Anthony Trollope and slightly later Gordon Childe. There were occasional flurries of interest in administrative topics in Australia, especially in the years after Federation and in the 1920–30s, 1950–60s and post-1980s (see Parker 1993). Yet, throughout the twentieth century these fields have not always gained the recognition and prominence they might deserve, nor the enthusiasm to remain vibrant areas of scholarship. Some writers have even complained that administrative history is a 'relatively neglected field' where interest blows hot and cold (Wettenhall 1975: 216 [1968]). Gerald Caiden also bemoaned the lack of interest in the serious study of administrative history, arguing that 'contemporary administrative problems are more interesting, more challenging and more compelling of attention' (Caiden 1963: 1). By implication, administrative history co-existed as a marginal or subsidiary interest of public administration (for instance, many studies of domestic administration merely charted current developments and were far more likely to discuss future directions than past trajectories). It is worth noting that in the Institute of Public Administration's journal begun in 1937—the *Australian Journal of Public Administration* (AJPA—see www://onlinelibrary.wiley.com)—there were virtually no articles on administrative history contained in the journal of record for the first three to four decades of its existence, although it did carry a regular 'administrative chronicle' covering most jurisdictions over many decades until the late 1990s—see Curnow 1984; Curnow 1989 (and the rest of the special issue of *AJPA*); Wettenhall 1997; and Althaus 1997, who lists under 6 per cent of articles dealing with administrative history over a 25-year period).

Defining the sub-field of administrative history is perhaps inevitably problematic. Its content matter is not the sole prerogative of any one discipline, but rather it is a multi-disciplinary endeavour and a 'catch-all' repository of various ad hoc contributions from authors of different backgrounds and with different motivations—much of which is contained in diverse academic journals, the main ones being: the *AJPA*, the *Australian Journal of Politics and History*, *Labour History*, the *Australian Journal of Historical Studies/Australian Historical Studies*, and the *Australian Journal of Economic History*. There is little developmental progression or theoretical development evident in the administrative history literature; every purveyor apparently begins from scratch and eschews any theoretical disposition bar realist empiricism. Research design and project structuring are important but not the finer epistemological issues or debate over rival theoretical approaches to the transmission of knowledge. The more significant intellectual contributions to administrative history (see below), now constitute a small but important and informative field of Australian scholarship (see Wanna 2003; Scott and Wanna 2005). Traditionally, the format is almost always exclusively 'modernist empiricist' in approach, chronological in structure, narrative and descriptive, with a bias towards realist preoccupations (see Wettenhall 1975). Most are locked in the confines of traditional 'old' institutionalism, although some important accounts have introduced 'new' institutionalist thinking or adopted a political economy approach (see the NSW parliamentary and executive studies to mark the sesquicentenary of responsible government—*The Administration of NSW*, Volumes 1 and 2, 2005–6; and Tsokhas 1990). Almost all these studies are written from the authorial perspective of an external observer providing 'objectified' commentary and assessments of institutions, people, activities and events. Many are underappreciated at the time they are written by fellow scholars and administrative practitioners but prove to be invaluable to later researchers and historians as they grapple to piece together the contours of previous times, periods and subjects.

Although administrative history could conceivably include a potentially wide range of subject matter and domains of interest (public and private spheres, non-government organisations, community and voluntary bodies) it has tended to focus on three topics: administrative institutional histories of public bodies; past events often captured by administrative cases; and administrative biographies of significant historical figures (two earlier surveys of the field include: Wanna 2003 and Ahamed and Davis 2009).

Institutional histories typically record the particular history of enduring organisations or agencies, such as departments of state, statutory authorities, corporations, defence bodies, special offices of state such as the Auditor-General's Office, regulatory boards. As a field of scholarship, administrative history has charted organisations and bureaucracies across a number of public spheres: political, legal, economic and regulatory institutions, and documented a range of prominent social and environmental bodies, voluntary and charitable associations, pressure groups and industrial associations, even sporting and community clubs, and the occasional private firm such as General Motors Holden (Davey 1961). Many of these studies are top-down rather than bottom-up and offer descriptive chronologies based on historical archives and records of institutional achievement (reflecting persistence and perseverance in the main). Many are worthy, but even their most ardent enthusiasts will often admit they may not be the most riveting examples of the social sciences. As a former professor of government at the University of Sydney, R.N. 'Dick' Spann, once said: although the empirical study of administrative practices was one of the 'most important things in the world' the topic often has 'little sex-appeal' (Spann 1955).

Administrative cases of past events tended to focus on pivotal moments or real-world dilemmas reported by researchers as providing some illumination to the politics of the day. They are written as case studies applied to areas of administration or contained events; they are snapshots rather than longitudinal histories. Many are intended as 'windows' into a previous world, trying to capture the particular incidents, decision-making processes and proximate actors, and usually to draw lessons—perhaps for subsequent administrators or for teaching purposes. Scandals, failures or natural disasters often provide a subtext for these studies. Many prominent administrative researchers have produced historical administrative cases, including R.S. Parker (1993: chapters 7 and 8 on both the Bazeley and Creighton cases), Schaffer and Corbett 1965; Wettenhall 1975; Smith and Weller 1976; Scott and Wettenhall 1981). The Spann series on public administration beginning in 1965 and running to 1981 contained many administrative cases, as did other specific teaching texts (Forward 1974; Byrt and Bowden 1989; Peachment and Williamson 1993). The Hawker, Smith and Weller (1979) policy compendium contained five insightful historical administrative cases written to illustrate the interplay of politics, policy and administrative systems; or in their words to 'link the general with the specific' (1979: 26).

The ANU's public policy program issued a regular series of 'policy cases' and administrative cases as discussion papers from the mid-1980s to early 2000s, as did other universities eventually (e.g. Melbourne, Griffith, Canberra, Curtin). The School of Administrative Studies at the University of Canberra produced administrative studies of every Commonwealth government from the first Hawke government of 1983—concluding to date with the first Rudd government (Aulich and Evans 2010).

There is also a smaller but growing interest in administrative biographies of significant historical figures (see Nethercote 2006). While Weller and his colleagues were able to state that 'few public servants have written in an illuminating way about their roles' (Hawker et al. 1979: 25), an increasing number of prominent administrators (and an occasional minister) have penned personal reflections of their careers in government, including providing primary administrative historical accounts. More interestingly, some influential administrators have now become the subjects of detailed scholarly biographies—tracing political and administrative contours through their life and careers. Nethercote provides an idiosyncratic listing of these studies, and comments on their contributions.

So, who writes administrative history? There is a small group of scholars who explicitly define themselves as 'administrative historians' and who have dedicated their career to the sub-field. They are relatively few not least because there is little demand for their skills in tertiary institutions (few courses, no teaching departments, no research centres) and limited interest or sponsorship from governments or organs of public service. Their interest is largely a personal proclivity and their commitment a life-long dedication to the craft. The stalwarts of this tiny self-identified field would include F.A. Bland, Gerald Caiden, Selwyn Cornish, Ross Curnow, John Nethercote, Martin Painter, R.S. Parker, Roger Scott, Dick Spann and Roger Wettenhall. Other scholars from different disciplines occasionally enter the fray charting administrative legacies although they are not primarily administrative historians—we might regard these writers as 'the intermittents'. They research and write these studies to fill gaps in the field, fulfilling a special interest or to accept a particular challenge (and some to fulfil a consultancy). Intermittent authors who have all written some administrative histories include: Geoffrey Bolton, Troy Bramston, Deborah Brennan, Claire Burton, Peter Carroll, Ralph Chapman, Stephen Duckett, Sol Encel, Fin Crisp, Paul Finn, John Halligan, Geoff Hawker, Chis Hood, Carol Johnston, Paul Kelly, Marilyn

Lake, Scott Prasser, Tim Rowse, Marian Sawer, Marian Simms, Gwyn Singleton, Jenny Stewart, Doug Tucker, John Warhurst, Pat Weller, Greg Whitwell, Peter Wilenski, Ken Wiltshire, and perhaps I would include myself. Administrative history in Australia is a world inhabited mostly by two groups that are simultaneously both its purveyors and its critical audience; they consist of knowledgeable practitioners with immense insider information, and practically minded scholars anxious to research the 'real world'. The extant literature is produced almost exclusively from these two sources, with practitioners describing what they were doing or what was going on within government and outside scholars negotiating special access to governmental institutions or actors with the intention of reporting on and analysing their dynamics. Many of these researchers and writers produced their contributions while at the top of their respective professions. Such prominent practitioners included: Jack Bunting, Clair Burton, Jack Crawford, H.C. 'Nugget' Coombs, Meredith Edwards, Allan Fels, Robert Garran, Paul Hasluck, Robert Hyslop, Mike Keating, John Nethercote, John Paterson, Fred Wheeler and Peter Wilenski. A small but dedicated group of public administration scholars who have largely remained in the academy (besides those already mentioned above) include: Mark Considine, Hugh Emy, Jean Holmes, Owen Hughes, Ainsley Kellow, Peter Loveday, John Power, Joanne Scott, Amanda Sinclair and Anna Yeatman. There have also been occasional professional hybrids who have managed to maintain a successful career in both camps—such as: Francis Bland, Neal Blewett, David Corbett, Glyn Davis, Tom Kewley, Russell Mathews, John McMillan, Geoff Sawer and Spencer Zifcak.

Although space does not permit a complete listing, there are some key scholars and works that must be noted from this field. Robert Parker's monumental contribution dates from the early 1940s and runs to the 1990s and although he mostly wrote journal articles and book chapters, his main works were finally brought together by Uhr (Parker 1993; see also Uhr's 2007 assessment). Although his work is usually very detailed, Parker's discussion of public administrative practices and cases is used to raise important questions of political science (accountability, ethics, and ministerial responsibility); his work taken as a whole is probably the stand-out compilation of scholarship in this field. Roger Wettenhall's life opus documenting institutional structures/organisational changes to government, including statutory authorities (QUANGOs), is a notable contribution. Gerald Caiden's studies of the Commonwealth public service are rich sources of information at a time when Weberianism had finally triumphed in the federal bureaucracy. Three of the best historical administrative cases are Parker's dissection of the Creighton case in Queensland, Viviani and Wilenski's post-mortem/eulogy to the Australian Development Assistance Agency (1978), and Weller's devastating critique of Treasury's role in destabilising the framing of the 1974 budget (see Hawker et al. 1979). Among the best administrative biographies are Peter Edwards' study of the autocratic Arthur Tange (2006), Tim Rowse's Nugget Coombs (2002), and Jack Bunting's autobiographical reflections of the Menzies regime (1988).

WELLER'S INTEREST IN ADMINISTRATIVE HISTORY AS BIOGRAPHY AND PERSONALISED ACCOUNTS OF POWER

Patrick Weller began writing on government and administration in the late 1970s. So, we might reasonably ask: how has the sub-field of administrative history in Australia developed since Weller began making his contributions and accepted the challenge to chart the core institutions of government? The first point to reiterate, from the anecdote at the forefront of this chapter, is that many of the core national Australian political and administrative institutions (and their core functions) have been studied and have attracted detailed analysis. There are now well over 50 very thorough institutional accounts of Australia's central agencies, cabinet and the executive, and many of the operational departments (PM&C, Defence, Treasury, Finance, Foreign Affairs) and specialist agencies (the High Court, the Auditor-General's office, Centrelink, Aboriginal Affairs, the Industry Assistance Commission, and some of the postwar reconstruction agencies). Some administrative histories describe major policy innovations (e.g. Medicare, tertiary education and HECS, and arts policy), while others compare state-level institutions and the occasional study of local government administration.

Second, the older traditional institutionalism that focused on the formal structures, legal authorities and detailed internal processes of public organisations (which could risk producing dry, dull studies of administrative architecture that were 'worthy' rather than 'compelling'), gradually gave way to a more 'issues-based public policy' drawing on themes that would later be termed 'new institutionalism'. This latter approach was influenced by the sceptical Berkeley school of public policy, centred on Aaron Wildavsky, that focused on policy outcomes and portrayed public institutions as living and breathing entities, getting inside and up-close, exposing their external and internal politics, their foibles and shortcomings—in essence combining the participant observations of an anthropologist or ethnographer with those of an astute political historian. A good example is Geoff Hawker's *Who's Master, Who's Servant?* (1981), a much-underappreciated analysis.

Third, some of the more talented political scientists who were Weller's contemporaries, including David Corbett, Sol Encel, Brian Galligan, Geoff Hawker, Peter Loveday, Marian Sawer, Bob Smith, John Warhurst, and later Mark Considine, Ainsley Kellow and Stephen Bell, shifted the analysis of institutions towards the interplay between their internal actors or influential processes and the political context within which they were operating. Though not self-identifying administrative historians their work contributed to the field. As 'public policy' researchers interested in Realpolitik interpretations they chose to ask: who were the key decision-makers, how did they shape decisions and wield power, how did they come to make decisions, what internal capacities did they exhibit, and how did they actually execute their responsibilities? Their self-consciously political accounts formed an implicit critique of the 'old institutionalists' who while dominating administrative studies had nonetheless shied away from overt political comment.

Fourth, the emergent area of 'public policy' prospered through the development of cases studies grounded in administrative history; and Weller and his colleagues stimulated the production of illustrative policy studies from the 1970s onwards. They highlighted pivotal events or aberrant incidents, occasional crises, key turning points, celebrated stoushes, the creation or demise of agencies, and the fall of outgoing governments and the arrival of new ones in transitional mode—because these showed the system at its most vulnerable and also how it conducted politics in the raw. One of Weller's first major publications (Hawker, Smith and Weller 1979) was a university textbook largely containing public policy case studies, some of which are fascinating diagnostic studies of actors, institutions and processes in dynamic context, and an outstanding example of extraordinary scholarship.

Weller's prime focus (and arguably his main legacy) has been to lay bare the internal politics associated with governmental decision-making processes at the very centre of government. His abiding interest was always in the question of *who exercises power* and *how do they exercise it* in the complicated institutional structures found at the heart of government. Yet, Weller almost invariably adopts a personalised narrative account, almost biographical in construction, with power and events interpreted through the eyes of the main protagonists. His portraits of Malcolm Fraser in power as the frustrated political conductor at the head of a resolute government, or John Button as a mercurial Labor fighter on the outer, leave the reader with the impression they are shadowing the main characters, watching their movements and hearing their rationalisations. He was less interested in questions of *why* power was being exercised and to *what effect*—those questions are for others to explore. Accordingly, he acknowledges the formal positions of power actors possess, but is especially interested in the informal ways power is negotiated. When exploring power he adopts a 'weak structuralist' position that comes down to the personal adage: 'where you stand depends on where you sit' (meaning a person's position on an issue is usually dependent upon where that person sits in the constellation of politics).

So, Weller is no straightforward administrative historian (a label that would better apply to scholars already mentioned such as Dick Spann, Roger Wettenhall or Gerald Caiden). He tends to enter the fray episodically when the subject matter really interests him sufficiently. Weller's research and writings touch on many aspects of administrative history in the Australian context and in selected Westminster systems. He was originally trained as a historian and still approaches politics through the lens of historical empiricism (see our earlier essay on the 'narrator in chief' in Rhodes and Wanna 2009: 119–30). On some occasions he has tackled administrative history directly (as with historical studies of agencies and institutions), at other times his work on contemporary politics can constitute administrative history for later audiences (for instance, his book *Malcolm Fraser PM* is a rich source of administrative history of this government).

Not surprisingly, therefore, Weller's influence is pervasive in some aspects of administrative history (such as, the administration of central government, the ministerial-administrative interface), but in others it is more tangential (such as with parliament, political parties, interest groups in policy-making, administrative federalism).[1] In some areas Weller is *the* pivotal figure, in others he plays a bit-role, offering the occasional contribution. Although he later produced some seminal studies, his early *curriculum vitae* reads like he was a bowerbird picking this and that issue because it interested him, because fortuitously he had good access to evidence, or it provided a prism through which to view political behaviour. Some of Weller's passing interests in administrative history developed from his original work as an academic consultant to the Coombs Commission.[2] But Weller's interest and output in these areas does not indicate a sustained contribution—he was keen to move on, not descend into ever shrinking circles.

There are some important gems in his publication profile that Weller investigated but to which he never really returned. His work on the Treasury as a powerful adviser to government, using the Heclo and Wildavsky ethnographic approach, included an analytical exposé of Treasury undermining the Whitlam government's 1974 budget(s). It remains a masterful diagnosis of budget-making in central government, interweaving the political, personal, partisan, and venal bureaucratic politics into a powerful story of intrigue and catastrophe (see Hawker et al. 1979). Weller had earlier mentioned conflicts between Treasury and the Labor government in his 1976 *Treasury Control in Australia* book (one of his best institutional accounts and study of core administrative functions), but he did not at the time have access to a rich record of the decision-making process in 1974. Once available from a confidential source, he skilfully teased out the evidence into a compelling read (corroborating his account with some of the leading officials of the day). His particular interest at the time was in analysing Treasury as a powerful beast in the political jungle of Canberra—assertive, jealous of its turf, monopolistic and monological in its advice, and seeking to dictate to governments, but with a core set of key expertise. This ended with Weller speculating on Treasury's future as a monolithic entity arguing against any separation of the department—only to experience the misfortune of the book being launched on the very day that Malcolm Fraser split Treasury into two departments. He advocated what I have called elsewhere a 'bob-each-way' proposal for retaining a single department with two senior ministers rather than a complete separation (Wanna et al. 2000). Weller went on to write about potential advantages of a separate budgetary department (that would become the Department of Finance) before arguing in 1977 that the new structure would not defeat the old habits and the old department may have to come together again for coordination purposes (or some other administrative cultures would have to be devised). The once unified Treasury has remained split for almost 38 years now.

Two of Weller's principal administrative histories are of core political institutions—produced to mark a centenary anniversary or (an almost) sesquicentenary—on the Department of Prime Minister and Cabinet

(*From Postbox to Powerhouse*, Weller et al. 2011) and the Queensland Premier's Department (*The Engine Room of Government*, Scott et al. 2001). With both books, Weller worked as part of a team, so his individual contribution is somewhat refracted although his framing influence and biographical orientation is still apparent. He chose to work through a team to combine skills, divide the research endeavour and spread the workload—his fellow collaborators were administrative historians Joanne Scott and the late Ross Laurie, and his wife Bronwyn Stevens. Weller worked closely with Peter Hamburger and co-wrote other departmental studies with him. These histories of two very different central agencies are broadly chronological, documenting how the organisation came about, its initial intentions, formative developments, key actors and the influence of context on its emerging cultures and behaviours. However, both also adopt an explicit thematic structure, focusing on how significant actors in each agency dealt with the issues of the day, fulfilled their functions, reconciled their powers, assisted in coordinating across government to provide some greater coherence.

Both histories are told through the interplay of personalities, who was appointed and promoted and who was deposed, how they dealt with the events that occurred and the happenstance of history, how blind luck and fate intervened, the quirky moments and the inexplicable. The biographical approach certainly makes the books interesting, lively and a racy read. For instance, *The Engine Room of Government* has chapters which begin 'Everyone's Problems are on Your Desk', and working in a 'Jumble Store of Administrative Oddments'. He begins the book by describing the Colonial Secretary (Premier Robert Herbert) and his departmental head Under Colonial Secretary Abram Moriarty surveying the condition of the new capital Brisbane; they were both well-connected and well under 30 years of age when appointed. On Herbert, he writes:

> Herbert was an old Etonian and an Oxford graduate; a former fellow of All Souls, he was urbane in a manner representative of his class, born to rule and to condescend. So was his constant companion, John Bramston, another Oxonian and All Souls fellow ... Both had acted as secretaries to Governor Bowen before entering parliament for a few years. Gentlemen they remained, more comfortable with the routine of civil service life than the rough and tumble of colonial politics. Indeed, in 1871 Herbert became Permanent Under Secretary of the Colonial Office in

London and held the post for twenty years. He was a civil servant of influence and distinction. (2001: 2–3)

The first six chapters of *From Postbox to Powerhouse* classify the departmental culture and evolving orientations according to the influential heads of the Prime Minister's department as it gradually increased in standing and influence, commencing as a minor administrative unit to becoming a significant policy outfit driving prime ministerial agendas. We have the era of the 'Three Clerks' perennially dealing with correspondence in the early years, then the 'Cerebral' leaders who gradually built coordination capacities in the postwar years. A group of 'Second Opinion' repositories of wisdom was followed by the 'Policy Drivers' who thought *they* were the government of the day, before finally there arrived the 'Can-do' secretaries who were more interested in 'making it happen'. Prime Minister and Cabinet as an institution is written up as if it were an extension of the secretary's style and the preferences of the prime minister of the day. The research technique employed to capture these stories involved the extensive use of interviews with former and serving leaders and agency heads, insights and often lengthy quotes were then used to build the narrative. Weller had earlier used this particular technique in his study of *Australia's Mandarins*, 2001: Chapter 8).

Weller has spent his academic career talking to people in power, probing perceptions, gaining impressions, layering observations, and gradually building a picture of how power operated in a given context. One of the immediate advantages in adopting this administrative history as biography approach is that it gives intimacy and freshness as it records personal achievements. The downside is that it can descend into faux soap-opera and dwell on the foibles of the passing parade of characters (the explanation of the transition from John Bunting to Lenox Hewitt in the PM's department may be an instance of this). When adopting such a personalised biographical approach it is not always easy to remain impartial and dispassionate about the protagonists as they go about shaping history.

WELLER'S LEGACY AND THE FUTURE OF ADMINISTRATIVE HISTORY

After four decades as one of Australia's most prolific political science scholars, Weller has out-produced most of his own generation of peers (by a long measure) and arguably produced in his professional career about as much as all the preceding generations of political scientists writing about Australia stretching back to the nineteenth century. He has deservedly earned a reputation as the definitive scholar on prime ministers and executive government. This is a truly outstanding achievement. But it is all the more remarkable because he has also researched and published across a wide range of political/government/public administration sub-fields in the style of a true polymath.

Weller has long puzzled the main historiographic problematic underlying administrative history: *who* and *what* makes history. For Weller *people* make history in a given context. It is a gladiatorial struggle played out with sometimes malleable rules of engagement. Above all, politics cannot be removed from the interplay of people, institutions and events. Weller customarily places enormous importance on history, accumulating facts and providing a detailed knowledge of events. He rejoices in the richness of politics and its many delectable components (some intentional and planned, some surprising and unintentional). Politics was predominantly ad hoc with no immutable 'iron laws'; he would agree with the late Fred Daly that in politics you are a rooster one day and a feather duster the next. History rolls on, combining renewed opportunities with a lurking fatalism and perhaps even a Faustian compact.

Yet the subject matter of *administrative* history is organisational structures and institutional resources, in which people operate. Exploring these bodies and practices through the key individuals that run them is one way to study, but not the only one. Structural accounts and organisational theory can de-emphasise the importance of individuals, focusing instead on enduring patterns and predictable behaviours. Comparative research is likely to point to 'soft structures' as being more determining of administrative dynamics, especially where policy transfer and learning are factors. Constructivist accounts are likely to probe the various interpretations, meanings and understandings that actors profess—whether through traditions and beliefs or through other hermeneutic approaches. Alternatively, those interested in extensive data-sets and longitudinal evidence will be less moved by individualised narrative accounts of particular cases, and more interested in statistically significant correlations. However, scholars such as Weller have remained highly critical of these partial mathematical 'models' that used available statistical data to tally abstracted instances often to produce naïve observations or spurious correlations.

There are other aspects of administrative history that have been less well explored to date; particularly neglected themes and topics. There is still much scope in using administrative history to explore wider concerns of political science, such as accountability and responsibility, ethics and integrity, the legitimacy of government, the representativeness of government and its agencies, executive capacities, the comparative performance of public provision and the hybridisation of delivery modes, the effective implementation of desired policies, and the engagement of citizens in decision-making.

Other topics which had not yet attracted attention can be framed, such as the changing nature and dynamics of government organisations, the nature of bureaucratic cultures and 'groupthink', hybrid organisations engaged in policy-work, diversity in administrative organisations and careers, the changing significance of gender in public employment, trust and new forms of accountabilities, and the impact of citizen engagement strategies. These themes and topics, and perhaps others, will lend themselves more to mixed-research methods and approaches and will be more open to the range of approaches mentioned above. It will largely be left to the next generations of scholars who succeed Weller to begin to address seriously these concerns.

NOTES

1   For instance, it was not until I began researching whether the House of Representatives should establish its own estimates committee system (to match the scrutiny of the Senate at estimates hearings) that I realised the only other article I could find on the topic was by Weller in the 1970s, although there was also a parliamentary paper produced in 1979 and some much earlier discussion by Bland when he convinced Menzies to re-establish the public accounts committee in the 1950s.
2   Royal Commission on Australian Government Administration (1974–76) and the later work that subsequently appeared from those research commissions.

REFERENCES

The Administration of NSW, 2005–6, *Volumes 1 and 2, Patronage and Public Works* (H. Golder) and *Humble and Obedient Servants* (P. Tyler), Sydney: UNSW Press

Ahamed, S. & Davis, G., 2009, 'Public Policy and Administration', in R.A.W. Rhodes (ed.), *The Australian Study of Politics*, London: Palgrave Macmillan

Althaus, C., 1997, 'What Do We Talk About? Publications in AJPA, 1970–95', *Australian Journal of Public Administration*, vol. 56, no. 1, March

Aulich, C. & Evans, M., 2010, *The Rudd Government*, Canberra: ANU E-press
Bunting, J., 1988, *R.G. Menzies: A portrait*, Sydney: Allen & Unwin
Byrt, W. & Bowden, P., 1989, *Australian Public Management: Principles and case studies*, Melbourne: Macmillan
Caiden, G., 1963, 'The Study of Australian Administrative History', Department of Political Science, RSSS, ANU
—— 1967, *The Commonwealth Bureaucracy*, Melbourne: Melbourne University Press
Curnow, R., 1984, 'Journals of Public Administration', *Australian Journal of Public Administration*, vol. 48, no. 4, December
—— 1989, 'Fifty Years of AJPA: Still muddling not yet through', *Australian Journal of Public Administration*, vol. 48, no. 4, December
Davey, F., 1961, 'General Motors in Australia', GMH Ltd., Adelaide (unpublished manuscript)
Edwards, P., 2006, *Arthur Tange: The last of the mandarins*, Sydney: Allen & Unwin
Forward, R., 1974, *Public Policy in Australia*, Sydney: Cheshire
Hawker, G., 1981, *Who's Master, Who's Servant?*, Sydney: George Allen & Unwin
Hawker, G., Smith, R.F.I. & Weller, P., 1979, *Politics and Policy in Australia*, St Lucia, Queensland: University of Queensland Press
Heclo, H. & Wildavsky, A., 1974, *The Private Government of Public Money*, Berkeley and Los Angeles: University of California Press
Hennessy, P., 1989, *Whitehall*, London: Secker & Warburg
Nethercote, J., 2006, 'Anonymous in Life, Anonymous in Death: Memoirs and biographies of administrators', in T. Arklay et al. (eds), *Australian Political Lives*, Canberra: ANU E-Press
Parker, R.S., 1993, *The Administrative Vocation*, Brisbane: RIPA
Peachment, A. & Williamson, J., 1993, *Case Studies in Public Policy*, Public Sector Research Unit, Perth: Curtin University
Rhodes, R.A.W. & Wanna, J., 2009, 'The Executives', in R.A.W. Rhodes (ed.), *The Australian Study of Politics*, London: Palgrave Macmillan
Rhodes, R.A.W. & Weller, P. (eds), 2001, *The Changing World of Top Officials: Mandarins or valets?*, Buckingham: Open University Press
Rowse, T., 2002, *Nugget Coombs: A reforming life*, Melbourne: Cambridge University Press
Schaffer, B. & Corbett, D., 1965, *Decisions: Case studies in Australian administration*, Melbourne: Cheshire
Scott, J., Laurie, R., Stevens, B. & Weller, P., 2001, *The Engine Room of Government*, St Lucia, Queensland: University of Queensland Press
Scott, J. & Wanna, J., 2005, 'Trajectories of Public Administration and Administrative History in Australia: Rectifying a "curious blight"', *Australian Journal of Public Administration*, vol. 64, no. 1, March, pp. 11–24
Scott, R. & Wettenhall, R., 1981, 'Public Administration as a Teaching and Research Field', in R. Curnow & R. Wettenhall (eds), *Understanding Public Administration*, Sydney: George Allen & Unwin
Smith, R.F.I. & Weller, P., 1976, *Public Servants, Interest Groups and Policy-making*, Department of Political Science, ANU, Occasional Paper, no. 12

Spann, R.N., 1955, 'Public Administration and the University', *Public Administration*, vol. 40, no. 1

Tsokhas, K., 1990, *Markets, Money and Empire*, Melbourne: Melbourne University Press

Uhr, J., 2007, 'Parker, Robert', in B. Galligan & W. Roberts (eds), *The Oxford Companion to Australian Politics*, Melbourne: Oxford University Press

Viviani, N. & Wilenski, P., 1978, *The Australian Development Assistance Agency*, Brisbane: RIPA

Wanna, J., 2003, 'Public Policy and Public Administration', in I. McAllister, S. Dowrick & R. Hassan (eds), *The Cambridge Handbook of Social Sciences in Australia*, Melbourne: Cambridge University Press

Wanna, J., Kelly, J. & Forster, J., 2000, *Managing Public Expenditure in Australia*, Sydney: Allen & Unwin

Weller, P., 1976, *Treasury Control in Australia: A study in bureaucratic politics*, Sydney: Ian Novak

—— 1989, *Malcolm Fraser PM: A study in prime ministerial power*, Melbourne: Penguin

—— 1999, *Dodging Raindrops: John Button—A Labor life*, Sydney: Allen & Unwin

—— 2001, *Australia's Mandarins: The frank or the fearless?*, Sydney: Allen & Unwin

—— 2002, *Don't Tell the Prime Minister*, Melbourne: Scribe

—— 2006, *Cabinet Government in Australia 1901–2006*, Sydney: UNSW Press

Weller, P. & Grattan, M., 1981, *Can Ministers Cope?*, Melbourne: Hutchinson

Weller, P. & Tiernan, A., 2010, *Learning to be a Minister: Heroic expectations, practical realities*, Melbourne: Melbourne University Press

Weller, P., Scott, J. & Stevens, B., 2011, *From Postbox to Powerhouse*, Sydney: Allen & Unwin

Wettenhall, R., 1975, 'History and Public Administration', in R.N. Spann & R. Curnow (eds), *Public Policy and Public Administration*, Sydney: Wiley

—— 1997, 'Reflections on AJPA and Other Public Administration Journals', in *Australian Journal of Public Administration*, vol. 56, no. 1, March

PART 5

INTERNATIONAL ORGANISATIONS

9

AGENTS OF INFLUENCE: WELLER AND XU ON INTERNATIONAL ORGANISATIONS FROM A PUBLIC POLICY PERSPECTIVE

J.C. Sharman

Renowned for his study of Australian politics, public policy, and the comparative politics of Westminster democracies, Pat Weller has increasingly turned his attention to the study of international organisations in the last ten years. This chapter reviews his published work on the World Trade Organization (WTO), the World Bank and other similar international institutions, all co-authored with Xu Yi-chong. Weller and Xu have pioneered the application of insights from public policy to international organisations, traditionally the bailiwick of international-relations scholars. In doing so they have fostered a process of cross-fertilisation and exchange between these two sub-fields. The sections below first put Weller and Xu's contribution in context by looking at the international relations literature that informs their starting point, then considering their particular approach and the main findings of their research on international organisations (IOs). The conclusion speculates on the rise of a prospective school or sub-field of 'international public policy' or 'global public policy', as the attention of public-policy scholars is drawn 'up' from the domestic setting to the institutions and processes of global governance. Perhaps the most valuable contribution of Weller and Xu's scholarship on IOs thus far is to demonstrate the potential of this new trend, and to seek to bring this perspective into dialogue with international relations.

A POINT OF DEPARTURE: INTERNATIONAL ORGANISATIONS IN INTERNATIONAL RELATIONS SCHOLARSHIP

For decades after 1945, the study of international organisations was something of a niche interest, or even a dead-end. There was a prevailing mood of scepticism about the ability of international bodies and treaties to restrain states' supposedly primal drive to maximise power above all else, an attitude that reflected experience of the failure of the League of Nations in the 1930s, and the paralysis of the United Nations during the Cold War thanks to superpower rivalry. While there was some tradition of legal and descriptive analysis of international organisations, as well as a modest body of analysis of roll-call votes in the UN General Assembly, these bodies were mainly seen as talk shops, with the 'real' politics happening elsewhere. One leading international relations scholar rhetorically asked why anyone would study the puppets, i.e. international organisations, when they could be studying the puppeteers, i.e. states. The work that international organisations did outside of the security realm, exactly the sort at the centre of Weller and Xu's studies, was too often seen as exemplifying distinctly unglamorous 'low politics', as opposed to the 'high politics' of war and peace. Though there were important and often quite brilliant individual exceptions, with scholars including Inis Claude, Ernst Haas, and Robert Cox and Harold Jacobson researching in this area, until the 1980s those studying international organisations in international relations were a very select group. The end of the Cold War, the stop-start progress of European integration, and the general growth in the prominence and number of international organisations transformed this situation and stimulated a massive expansion of scholarly interest in this area.

Two strands of scholarship in particular are important in providing foils and points of departure for Weller and Xu's work on international organisations. The first draws heavily on microeconomics, applying a rational choice framework to explain the relationship between states and the international organisations they form. The second draws loosely on Weber's writings on bureaucracy and rational-legal authority, as well as more general theory from the humanities and sociology that has come to be termed 'constructivist'.

The influence of economics on US political science is not news to any corner of the discipline, but international relations was (rather typically) a late adopter. Many of the areas of interest to Weller and Xu, such as free trade, guarding intellectual property, fighting pandemics, lender of last resort facilities and so on, came to be seen as examples of potential or actual market failure or collective action problems. International-relations scholars drew upon the writings of economists such as George Akerloff, Mancur Olson and Charles Kindleberger in both framing their understanding of such problems, and in considering solutions. The goals of non-security international organisations came to be seen as public goods, and the major obstacle to providing these goods was held to be states' tendency to free-ride, failing to bear their share of the costs involved. The potential solution was argued to be mechanisms that monitor and exclude free-riding states from the benefits of future cooperation, thus overcoming the short-term incentive to free-ride by consuming but not contributing to public goods (Axelrod 1984; Keohane 1984; Oye 1986). International organisations could play just this role, whether it was the General Agreement on Tariffs and Trade or the World Intellectual Property Organization. In this rendering, though international organisations were definitely the instruments of states, they nevertheless played a vitally important role in fostering and maintaining cooperation that individual states could not manage in isolation.

A further development of this rational-choice-inspired scholarship granted an important measure of autonomy to international organisations, based on the principal–agent framework first developed to explain the relationship between shareholders and company managers. Of course, principal–agent work based on the key concepts of goal diversity and information asymmetry is well known to scholars of public policy for modelling the relationship between voters and elected politicians, or even more so between elected politicians and bureaucrats. In the international relations version, states are the principals that create and fund international organisations, while the IOs themselves are the agents who enjoy de facto autonomy, thanks to their superior detailed knowledge of the task at hand and their own efforts to complete it (Nielson and Tierney 2003; Hawkins et al. 2006). IOs are vested with some significant political autonomy in pursuing their own goals, rather than being just unthinking tools of states. As detailed below, this picture is much closer to Weller and Xu's version of IOs as genuine political entities worth studying in their own right, and not mere talk shops, or arenas for negotiation, or instruments of states. The cover of one of the major volumes of this principal–agent work references the metaphor noted earlier by having a stylised puppet cutting the strings held by the puppeteer. A particular focus of those working from a principal–agent perspective is the special challenges faced by a collective principal, i.e. rather than just one minister running a department, a group of perhaps dozens of states hold their ostensible servants accountable.

The second, 'constructivist' perspective takes more inspiration from sociology than economics, and in particular the works of Max Weber. Constructivism in international relations holds that ideas, shared beliefs and culture are all important in shaping international politics, which is said to be more than just a Darwinian struggle for power and riches. These scholars share a common starting point with the principal–agent perspective, and Weller and Xu's work also, in that they view IOs as political actors in their own right that may or may not stay true to their founders' desires. This strand of work is associated above all with Michael Barnett and Martha Finnemore. They maintain that international organisations gain autonomy through embodying rational-legal authority, and through their ostensibly apolitical control over technical information. These organisations exert influence in the way that they classify and categorise the world, organise knowledge, and spread norms and models. They suffer pathologies of goal displacement, and of being bound to a bureaucratic culture that shapes perception and action. In this portrayal, IOs are thus explicitly theorised as bureaucracies first and foremost, and therefore of the same ilk as the domestic bureaucracies that are a central focus of those studying public policy. Barnett and Finnemore note: 'Scholarship on organizations generally (not just IOs) has made it abundantly clear that organizations routinely behave in ways unanticipated by their creators and not formally sanctioned by their members' (Barnett and Finnemore 2004: 2). To the extent that IOs are organisations like 'normal' bureaucracies, this suggests that international-relations scholars have a great deal to learn from their colleagues in public policy, and it provides a point of entry for the public policy analysis of these bodies.

There are some important similarities between Barnett and Finnemore on the one hand, and Weller and Xu on the other, in terms of how they study international organisations. Both duos are interested in the internal workings of IOs. Both adopt a qualitative approach based on interviews and fieldwork. Indeed, in Barnett and Finnemore's case they each spent a year working *in situ*, Barnett in the United States mission to the United Nations Security Council, by fluke ending up as the Africa 'expert' at the time of the Rwanda genocide, while Finnemore worked for a year in the World Bank. Yet there are also important differences between the two teams, explored below.

BEYOND INTERNATIONAL RELATIONS SCHOLARSHIP IN STUDYING THE WORLD TRADE ORGANIZATION

International-relations scholars are often preoccupied with various internecine battles between different research 'paradigms', and particular pieces of research may reflect the perceived need to attack or defend a position in this over-arching struggle, beyond the immediate explanatory goal. Thus scholars studying IOs through the lens of the principal–agent model are implicitly or explicitly arguing that the political world can be best understood through the tools of microeconomics. Conversely, constructivists define themselves in opposition to this 'rationalist' position. Sometimes the actual international organisations get lost as a result. Weller and Xu are never distracted from the topic in the same way. Although international-relations scholars have moved some way from the assumption of states as unitary actors (a position that would be risible in any other sub-discipline of political science) and international organisations as mere venues or puppets, there is still relatively little effort to disaggregate. Each IO is assumed to have either a transitive preference schedule (singular), usually focused on maximising turf, or a unified culture (again, singular), instantiated in organisational discourse and practices. In this way, the claims about looking inside IOs seem somewhat hollow, or at least incomplete. Here Weller and Xu's work marks a sharp break, in that they delve much further into the internal workings and politics of the WTO, the World Bank, and other IOs in their more recent comparative work. But specifically how do Weller and Xu link with and advance the international relations literature on IOs?

According to Weller at least, the origins of the collaborative research program began with a discussion about the role of international civil servants, the supposedly apolitical and powerless functionaries of international organisations. When Xu explained that the conventional wisdom styled these individuals as completely irrelevant to the study and functioning of IOs, Weller pointed out the improbability of this line from a public policy perspective (Xu and Weller 2004: vi). Even as early as the turn of the twentieth century, theorists such as Robert Michels and Max Weber had persuasively argued that those presented as apolitical and powerless officials were often anything but, and that rule by such bureaucratic officials in fact constituted perhaps the defining modern mode of authority and governance. Decades of subsequent public-policy scholarship have only deepened this conclusion, with civil servants wielding huge influence behind the scenes, thanks to their expertise, institutional memory, agenda-setting powers, and control of the flow of information, among other levers of power. Given this consensus position, how could international civil servants be the exception to the rule? Weller and Xu decided to go looking, in particular by shifting the level of analysis to people, rather than reified collective actors (in some cases to the level of individual biographies, as with Chrik Poortman of the World Bank and Transparency International, discussed later). They first turned their attention to the WTO, precisely because this body was meant to be the epitome of a member (i.e. state)-driven organisation where the secretariat exercised no independent influence of any note or interest: 'to be, but not to be seen', in the phrase of one international civil servant interviewee that became the title of an associated article in *Public Administration* (Xu and Weller 2008). In testing Weller's supposition about the previously neglected importance of officials in IOs, the WTO thus constituted a least-likely case, and as such a tough test of the contrary thesis.

Weller and Xu begin by bringing out the common-sense but nevertheless generally overlooked point that bureaucrats in the WTO share the same prerogatives that make bureaucrats important in any other similar organisation: 'their power of routine, power to sift, power to initiate, power to shape the direction of debate' (Xu and Weller 2008: 37). As a general rule, this influence may be wielded in a manner that protects and enhances the ability of the IO to supply the global public goods it was created to provide and guard against states' efforts to subordinate the organisation for their own selfish, narrow ends. In the case of the WTO this might apply to bolstering the free-trade regime against the short-term temptations of protectionism, which is sought to favour politically influential domestic constituencies according to the demands of pork-barrel politics. Or these civil servants' influence might be employed in a much more self-seeking manner, furthering personal career prospects and subverting mechanisms of accountability, even at the cost of imperilling the chances of achieving the mandated goals. In either case, the degree of (potential) influence exercised by international bureaucrats is said to depend above all on two factors: first, the formal institutional mandate and structure of the IO, and second, informal points of opportunity, including such matters as expertise and legitimacy.

Just as states can be unitary or federal, with many veto points or few, IOs can be more or less centralised in their formal institutional structure. The case of the WTO is especially illuminating given its change of personality from the postwar General Agreement on Tariffs and Trade (GATT) to the much more formal and binding WTO. To what extent was the transformation in formal institutional structure affected, directed or frustrated by informal practices? Even when concentrating on one case, Weller and Xu have tended to adopt a comparative approach, not just in breaking down the barrier between 'international' and 'domestic' politics, but also in comparing different IOs to capture variation and contrasts in the nature and content of their founding documents and governing rules.

Turning to the informal levers of influence, one of the most important is collecting and disseminating information. At first this observation may seem like a simple restatement of the principal–agent model's focus on information asymmetry between states and IOs. But for Weller and Xu this is less bureaucratic subterfuge and more prudent management of otherwise overwhelming information flows. They make the interesting observation that the more security-oriented organisations, which depend on staff temporarily seconded from member governments, are less likely to possess the independence that comes with the long tenure and separate career ladder that characterise most of the non-security organisations.

Individual leadership is also said to be important. While the heads of IOs cannot oppose a relatively united and determined coalition of member governments, more often than not governments are divided or not particularly engaged when it comes to the routine business of IOs, leaving room for leaders to steer. Even in politically fraught and contentious negotiations, directors can play an important role in crafting compromises, with the classic example coming from trade negotiations within the GATT. At critical points in the Uruguay Round, the secretariat and especially the Director-General Arthur Dunkel played a vital role in moving negotiations forward. Thus in 1991, Dunkel set a deadline for states to resolve their outstanding differences on the text of the final agreement, after which time he himself would choose from the disputed options on offer. Although the so-called Dunkel Draft was the subject of much horse-trading after the deadline, this did force the pace of negotiations well beyond what state representatives had thought was possible, and 90 per cent of his text was eventually included in the final agreement (Xu and Weller 2004: 116–17).

A NEW PERSPECTIVE ON THE WORLD BANK

How many of Weller and Xu's conclusions about the power of international civil servants within IOs carry over from the WTO to the World Bank, their second major case study in their IO research? In setting the stage, Weller and Xu observe how both bodies have attracted excoriating criticism for supposedly representing the vanguard of a particularly vicious brand of neo-liberalism (Xu and Weller 2009a; Weller and Xu 2010). Once again, the theoretical poles of the spectrum are defined as the rationalist principal–agent view, and Barnett and Finnemore's focus on bureaucratic culture. In terms of the formal institutional axis discussed earlier, the differences between the two bodies are stark. In particular, the Bank has a genuinely global footprint, not just in its remit, but also in the physical distribution of its staff. The WTO secretariat, in contrast, is concentrated in Geneva. This geographical diversity of the Bank coincides with a decentralised structure in the secretariat, with powerful country directors exercising a very great degree of independence in relation to far-away Washington DC. Weller and Xu's fieldwork itinerary matched this diversity as they travelled to Bangladesh, China, Nepal, India and Indonesia as well as Washington. Even at the centre, the Bank has a particular 'matrix' structure, a hybrid of organisation by sector and geographical region, rather than any sort of unified hierarchy. Though the 'trade and' agenda (trade and the environment, trade and intellectual property rights, etc.) greatly broadened the WTO's field of responsibilities compared with its predecessor, the GATT, it still has nothing like the breadth of the Bank. Finally, the Bank is simply a much larger organisation than the WTO, with a secretariat of 10,000, the most of any IO, compared to approximately 500 for the WTO, although even this total is significantly larger than the staff of the pre-1995 GATT.

To some extent, these formal institutional differences translate directly into cultural differences, especially with regards to the independence of the Bank's country directors. But in other important aspects, the parallels were just as notable. At the most basic level, the staff of both institutions are highly educated professionals who put a strong premium on their autonomous ability to 'puzzle' (in the sense of Heclo and Wildavsky's 1974 work), as well as their serving power (i.e. state members). The staff share similar specialised, technocratic expertise and reasonably long tenure in their organisations (Xu and Weller 2009a: 2–3), rather than being on short-term secondments from member governments. As with any comparable bureaucratic organisation, domestic or international, patterns of delegating responsibility and filtering, screening and aggregating information empower bureaucrats, sometimes individually, but most certainly in institutional terms. Unlike domestic government agencies, however, both international organisations are afforded the autonomy provided by having collective principals, as member states exhibit a range of preferences that flow through into latent or actual conflicts, and a corresponding degree of room to manoeuvre among IO staff. Although there were no direct equivalents to the GATT/WTO trade rounds with their final agreements, Bank staff are faced with the opportunity, and often the necessity, of mediating between different governments to craft mutually acceptable solutions.

With the significant exception of their de-centralised fieldwork away from the organisational headquarters, Weller and Xu's strategy for coming to grips with the workings of the Bank is similar to that employed in their research on the WTO. In particular, they make highly effective use of interviews, showing an incredible talent for opening doors to the top level of the Bank, and encouraging their interlocutors to share the sensitive everyday practices and politics of the Bank, conceived of as a globe-spanning network of affiliated units. Indeed, throughout their extensive collaborative studies of IOs, these two scholars have achieved a quantity and quality of interview evidence that would be the envy of most others. In part, this reflects a suspicion of deductive certainties and over-arching paradigms in favour of a strongly inductive research strategy that seeks to build up conclusions from the evidence, rather than fill in micro-foundations of initial defining assumptions. The international relations axiom, that states and international organisations can be meaningfully described as if they are unitary actors, receives particularly short shrift. More positively, the authors describe their approach as 'impressionistic, anecdotal, iterative', anchored in the idea that 'The only way to discover the perspective of staff or the influence of routine is to ask them' (Xu and Weller 2009a: 15, 17).

Despite the authors' scepticism towards abstract debates about epistemology and ways of knowing, the focus on interviews shares some strong similarities with Rod Rhodes' championing of interpretivism in his public-policy scholarship (Weller and Rhodes are long-time collaborators, and have published many works together). In brief, Rhodes studies (among others) the staff of British ministers by employing the insights and techniques that anthropologist Clifford Geertz used in entering into the cultural world of Moroccan sheep-thieves and Balinese puppeteers. Despite the vast gap that separates the exotic subjects of the anthropologist from the quotidian world of departmental committees and memos, Rhodes argues that the central goal of the researcher in each instance is fundamentally the same: to understand what actors think they are doing through their actions and words. Though Xu and Weller lack the programmatic fervour of Rhodes when it comes to intepretivism, and they generally eschew the use of this term, the parallels are nevertheless striking in their attention to the telling detail, and in their curiosity as to how IO officials understand and reflect upon their actions (Xu and Weller 2009a: 15). What sort of insights do we get as a result of this fine-grained attention to organisational dynamics and actors' self-understandings?

First, there is a strong refutation of the more alarmist and critical work portraying the Bank as a monolithic juggernaut serving the interests of transnational capitalism, or the US government. According to Weller and Xu, the Bank may be many things, but it is certainly not amenable to caricature as any kind of unified instrument serving a single will. Furthermore, and perhaps as a result of the wealth of interview material, the successes of the Bank, qualified and reversible as they may be, come to the fore. Weller and Xu note the obvious selection bias by which the Bank's failures (which they do not deny) are highlighted by NGOs and international critics, while the more modest but still significant successes tend to pass unnoticed. These may range from rebuilding the historic bridge in Mostar destroyed by shelling during the break-up of Yugoslavia, to improving access to justice for Jakarta's poor, or helping to manage traffic flows in Chongqing.

Less flattering for the Bank, the debacle of Paul Wolfowitz's brief tenure and removal as president becomes much more understandable with Weller and Xu's detailed narrative of everyday politics in the Bank. For example, Wolfowitz's decision to remove and publicly snub Chrik Poortman, vice president of the Middle East and North African section and one of the institution's most respected leaders, was a spectacular 'own goal' in terms of the president's own informal standing among his subordinates (Xu and Weller 2009b). They responded to this and other missteps by progressively withdrawing support in a manner that ultimately brought down Wolfowitz. But it is perhaps at one level down, that of the country directors, that Weller and Xu paint their most vivid portraits in their study of these 'agents of influence' (Weller and Xu 2010).

The 40-odd country directors represent the Bank in especially important borrower countries, but they also serve the function of representing these countries to the Bank's management in Washington. One interviewee described this dual role as: 'During the day, I lobby my country on behalf of the Bank. At night, I lobby the Bank on behalf of my country' (Weller and Xu 2010: 217). This captures the idea that directors are situated within a cascading chain of principal–agent relationships, especially considering that each country office might itself have a staff of up to 100 officials. By 2001 these country offices decided 80 per cent of the loan portfolio (Weller and Xu 2010: 219). While successive reforms in 1987 and 1997 delegated sweeping powers to these representatives in the field, the public and scholarly picture of the Bank remains myopically and (Weller and Xu argue) erroneously fixed on its president and Washington DC. Devoting attention to country directors captures critical variation in Bank policy across the world, and also reflects that, for most national governments, the country director is the World Bank. In the day-to-day relations at the country level, the local cultural context matters a great deal. National governments may be happy to be compared with perceived role model countries, but not to others who are seen as laggards. Some governments welcome the Bank as a valuable source of assistance in achieving their goals, others are suspicious, defensive or even resentful. For smaller and more aid-dependent nations, country directors may be important actors on the domestic political scene, while in larger states their contacts are largely confined to mid-level technocrats. Depending on their personal standing, they may be the informal leader of the whole donor sector within a particular country.

For Weller and Xu the Bank is irreducibly plural, and as such is highly resistant to simple depictions. Thus while they draw on aspects of principal–agent work and constructivist international-relations scholarship, Weller and Xu cannot contain themselves to operate within the strictures of any one framework. In choosing to take a bottom-up approach that focuses on the day-to-day workings of the Bank in the field, rather than the rarefied commanding heights of the board of directors in Washington DC, they present a richly detailed complement to what has become something of a cottage industry of research on the World Bank.

After the WTO and the Bank, what next for Weller and Xu in the study of international organisations? As noted previously, however much they have immersed themselves in particular case studies, Weller and Xu's approach has remained firmly comparative, not only in their ambitions to generalise across different organisations, but even more so in their healthy disrespect for artificial divides between the study of domestic and international institutions. Their current work stays true to these principles. The central aim is to explain the actions and decisions of IOs, or more particularly how various actors within IOs form their preferences, the effect of the formal institutional set-up and logic, the culture and history, and the internal process of contestation over ideas. The answers are sought in the interaction between three sets of key players: country representatives on the managing board or council, IO leaders, and the secretariat. Cases are drawn from their earlier work on the WTO and the World Bank, but also from the International Monetary Fund, the World Intellectual Property Organization, the Food and Agriculture Organization and World Health Organization. Weller and Xu's talent for securing funding is certainly equal to the scope of their ambition in pursuing the extensive fieldwork necessary to understand the inner workings of each institution (these two have an outstanding record of success in applying for highly competitive Australian Research Council grants). Yet at this point it is appropriate to pull back from the details of particular studies and put Weller and Xu's work in the broader scholarly context with reference to the potential of an emerging 'international public policy' or 'global public policy'.

CONCLUSIONS AND FUTURE DIRECTIONS: TOWARDS AN INTERNATIONAL PUBLIC POLICY?

In many ways, Weller and Xu's new comparative project together with their previous work on IOs is leading something of a growing scholarly move towards 'international public policy' as a potential new sub-field or hybrid of international relations and public policy. In terms of practice, more and more rules affecting domestic outcomes are made by bodies with ambitions to govern the globe in some specific area (Avant, Finnemore and Sell 2010). The study of public policy is thus being drawn 'up' to the traditional sphere of international relations. In terms of scholarship, this chapter has earlier remarked on how international-relations scholars increasingly study international organisations as 'normal' (i.e. domestic) bureaucracies, often drawing on frameworks such as the principal–agent model that have long been familiar to those studying policy-making in a wide range of areas. Thus, public-policy scholars bring to the study of international organisations an intellectual toolbox honed in the study of domestic agencies and processes.

An example of this trend might be the creation of the journal *Global Policy*, which defines its role as research on 'globally relevant risks and collective action problems; policy challenges that have global impact; and competing and converging discourses about global risks and policy responses', and including 'case studies of policy with clear lessons for other countries and regions; how policy responses, politics and institutions interrelate at the global level; and the conceptual, theoretical and methodological innovations needed to explain and develop policy in these areas' (Global Policy). This editorial statement might function as something of a manifesto for the new proto-field. Such a generalist journal is complemented by a plethora of more specialised outlets that are international (e.g. *Global Health Governance*), not in the sense that they compare policy practice in one specific area across different countries, but rather they focus on policy above the level of individual states, as well as policy-making in international organisations. These journals are often interdisciplinary, and at least aspire to bring academics and practitioners into more regular conversation. As a result, their articles tend to be somewhat less preoccupied with the theoretical concerns that may animate or even define particular disciplinary or sub-disciplinary communities.

In the context of this possible future international public policy, Weller and Xu's work stands out as a powerful and intriguing statement of what this new current of work might have to offer. Aside from the substantive concern with global policy and international institutions, the concern with the concrete details of policy-making, the close contact with practitioners, the willingness to cross disciplinary boundaries and the relative lack of theory are all of a piece.

To the extent that Weller and Xu do employ theory, a recurring conceptual motif present in their work is the importance of institutionalist scholarship, and especially the writings of James March and Johan Olsen and Douglass North. This theoretical work is significant more broadly in marking a potential bridge between international relations and public policy. March and Olsen are those rarest of scholars who have had a substantial impact on international relations from, if not quite a public-policy background, then one that is very close to it (organisational studies), as evidenced especially be their landmark contribution to the flagship journal *International Organization* (March and Olsen 1998). As pioneers of the 'garbage can' model of organisational decision-making, these two share Weller and Xu's reservations about the abstracted elegance of rational-choice models of how organisations work. Though less thorough in his rejection of rationalist work, North is keen to emphasise the importance of history, historical legacies and path dependency (key concerns for Weller), as well as the cultural aspects of institutional and human behaviour more generally (North 1990). To the extent that Weller and Xu (and other international public policy scholars) were looking to make a more explicit theoretical contribution, they could do much worse than to systematically employ this body of literature to show up conceptual failings in international relations coverage of international organisations and global governance.

The trend towards an international public policy does not mark a turning away from international relations. Weller and Xu have been determined to maintain their engagement with international relations, and their commitment to bringing other scholars into dialogue with public policy perspectives and concerns, which is greatly to their credit. As noted, they routinely position their work in between the poles of rational-choice principal–agent writings and constructivist scholarship (even if Weller and Xu tend to be closer to the latter than the former). Similarly, they relate their findings on IOs back to prevailing international-relations wisdom on how these institutions function and influence global policy-making. It could only be to the benefit of international-relations scholars if they were to take up this invitation and join the discussion.

REFERENCES

Avant, D.D., Finnemore, M. & Sell, S.K. (eds), 2010, *Who Governs the Globe?*, Cambridge: Cambridge University Press

Axelrod, R., 1984, *The Evolution of Co-operation*, New York: Basic Books

Barnett, M.N. & Finnemore, M. 1999, 'Politics, Power and Pathologies in International Organizations', *International Organization*, vol. 53, no. 4, pp. 699–732

—— 2004, *Rules for the World: International organization in global politics*, Ithaca: Cornell University Press

Bevir, M., Rhodes, R.A.W. & Weller, P., 2009, 'Traditions of Governance: History and diversity', *Public Administration*, vol. 81, no. 1, pp. 1–191

Claude, I.L., 1971, *Swords into Plowshares: The problems and progress of international organization*, 4th edn, New York: Random House

Cox, R.W. & Jacobson, H.K. (eds), 1973, *The Anatomy of Influence: Decision-making in international organizations*, New Haven: Yale University Press

Geertz, C., 1973, *The Interpretation of Cultures*, New York: Basic Books

Global Policy, <www.globalpolicyjournal.com/about/background>, accessed 10 December 2013

Haas, E.B., 1964, *Beyond the Nation-State: Functionalism and international organizations: Functionalism and international organization*, Stanford: Stanford University Press

Hawkins, D.G. et al. (eds), 2006, *Delegation and Agency in International Organizations*, New York: Cambridge University Press

Heclo, H. & Wildavsky, A., 1974, *The Public Government of Public Money*, London: Macmillan

Keohane, R.O., 1984, *After Hegemony: Co-operation and discord in the world political economy*, Princeton: Princeton University Press

March, J.G. & Olsen, J.P., 1989, *Rediscovering Institutions: The organizational basis of politics*, New York: Free Press

—— 1998, 'The Institutional Dynamics of International Political Orders', *International Organization*, vol. 52, no. 3, pp. 943–69

Nielson, D.L. & Tierney, M.J., 2003, 'Delegation to International Organizations: Agency theory and World Bank environmental reform', *International Organization*, vol. 57, no. 2, pp. 241–76

North, D.C., 1990, *Institutions, Institutional Change and Economic Performance*, Cambridge: Cambridge University Press

Oye, K.A. (ed.), 1986, *Co-operation under Anarchy*, Princeton: Princeton University Press

Rhodes, R.A.W., 2011, *Everyday Life in British Government*, Oxford: Oxford University Press

Weaver, C., 2008, *Hypocrisy Trap: The World Bank and the poverty of reform*, Princeton: Princeton University Press

Weller, P. & Xu, Y., 2010, 'Agents of Influence: Country directors at the World Bank', *Public Administration*, vol. 88, no. 1, pp. 211–31

Xu, Y. & Weller, P., 2004, *The Governance of World Trade: International civil servants and the GATT/WTO*, Cheltenham: Edward Elgar

—— 2008, '"To Be but not to Be Seen": Exploring the impact of international civil servants', *Public Administration*, vol. 86, no. 1, pp. 35–51

—— 2009a, *Inside the World Bank: Exploding the myth of the monolithic bank*, New York: Palgrave

—— 2009b, 'Chrik Poortman: A world bank professional', *Public Administration Review*, vol. 69, no. 5, pp. 868–75

10

LEARNING A NEW TRICK:
INTERNATIONAL CIVIL SERVANTS
Xu Yi-chong

My first encounter with Pat Weller in the late 1990s decreed that we both had to learn a new trick—I needed to learn about domestic civil servants, Pat needed to learn about international civil servants. Do civil servants have a role to play in international organisations (IOs)? Are they any different from domestic ones? What impact can they make on international decision-making? 'Of course, they make a difference', Pat asserted, without knowing much about IOs. 'They may do, but scholars in international relations (IR) do not talk about them', I responded. This started our journey, with constant debates and disagreement, examining IOs as institutions, especially the role of those who work at IOs: international civil servants (ICS).

Examining the role, behaviour and performance of international civil servants was new not only for Pat, but also for most IR scholars. 'International institutions that bring nation-states together in formal organisational structures are a prominent feature of the contemporary global political system' (Jacobson 2000: 149), which has been built on the well-established Westphalian system. Since the mid-twentieth century, the principle of the sovereign state has been further confirmed by many countries that traditionally had no such concept of 'sovereignty'.

IR scholars consequently have examined the nature of the Westphalian system, the rules and norms governing the system, and the behaviour of all states in this self-help anarchic system. They shied away from asking the question about 'some independent actors' other than states (Waltz 1979). Even those who did examine IOs were, understandably, never far away from building their analysis on states and state behaviour in multi-lateral cooperation under the Westphalian system. Yet, to argue that international institutions have no identity independent of their members seemed odd to those who study domestic politics. 'Organisations are created with purposive intent in consequence of the opportunity set resulting from the existing set of constraints . . . and in the course of attempts to accomplish their objectives are a major agent of institutional change' (North 1990: 5). Their objectives, governing rules, and operations have to be analysed independently from both the broader system structure and the strategies and behaviour of their individual members. With this understanding, Pat entered the field, learning a new trick.

This chapter has three parts. The first part discusses the background of the puzzle that Pat faced when he first entered the field—why international civil servants had escaped the attention of IR scholars and why they deserve examination. It looks at the history of IR studies on IOs and how it became necessary and a natural evolution for IR scholars to consider IOs, not as passive forums but as strategic actors, in their analysis in the past fifteen years or so.

The second part examines briefly the approaches to understanding civil servants, both domestic and international. Amazed, or more precisely, awed, by the endless debate on proper ways of studying politics—positivist, interpretivist, or qualitative methods (Lin 1998, Dahl et al. 2004; Bevir and Kedar 2008; Mearsheimer and Walt 2013)—Pat prefers to study politics, and more precisely, the 'art of governing', by taking advantage of his training as a historian—'to tell a story to send out a message'. Even though some new nuanced views about IOs have developed recently, they offer little insight into how international civil servants operate, what their views, strategies and behaviours are; how these are shaped by the organisation they work for; and how the organisation and its operation are affected by how these officials operate. All these questions about organisations and especially about those working in organisations ('organisational entrepreneurs', coined by Douglass C. North 1990) have long been taken for granted by Pat and many scholars of domestic politics. In the eyes of those who study domestic politics, 'people' working in organisations have to be taken seriously as they are integral parts of the organisations. Focusing on the civil servants and the head of IOs may 'not suffice to understand the performance' of IOs (Elsig 2010b: 346), but without including them in our analysis, we will never be able to provide an adequate explanation of why and how IOs operate the way they do. The best way of doing so is to talk to these officials, observe their actions, and analyse their behaviour with the insight of political science as a discipline. If this is regarded as 'descriptive anthropology' or 'story telling', and not scientific, so be it. Pat identifies his research by the subject under study rather than by an ideological school or a methodology. On the latter, he tends to ask how a methodology can assist and how useful it is.

The third part of this paper discusses specific issues that shape the behaviour of international civil servants. Some are about the organisation they work for: the organisational structure, the mission of the organisation, and the institutional culture, while some are about these officials, their career structure, their expertise and competence, and their legitimacy. Institutional and agent-based variables interact, affecting not only the operation of IOs but also the outcome of multi-lateral cooperation. The subject of the capacity, role and impact of international civil servants is little understood not only because insufficient work has been done, but, more importantly, because their status as faceless and nameless officials is often taken too literally by IR scholars. Those studying domestic politics take IOs as the prerogative of IR scholars. A pooled knowledge and effort of political scientists in various sub-fields, with a combination of approaches, may allow scholars to extract new ideas at close range (Collier 1999) about IOs in general and people working for them specifically.

BACKGROUND

Before the 1990s, studies on IOs were nearly all centred on their member states, and even then the focus was on a few powerful states. The most prevalent position among scholars of international politics was that IOs 'were tools that nation-states used as they desired and could, sometimes for cooperative purposes and sometimes for contestation' (Jacobson 2000: 150). As instruments of powerful states in a sovereignty-based Westphalian system, IOs had neither an identity nor a life of their own. Scholars had already developed 'a body of grand theories—or what are sometimes called the "isms"—that had long shaped the study of international politics' (Mearsheimer and Walt 2013: 3)—realism, liberalism, Marxism and constructivism. This view of a sovereignty-based system continued even though IOs had grown in number, size and coverage, and various scholars had developed much more sophisticated views about world politics. International institutions were, for example, able to 'enhance the likelihood of cooperation by reducing the costs of making transactions . . . create the conditions for orderly multi-lateral negotiations, legitimate and delegitimate different types of state action . . . help to bring governments into continuing interaction with one another . . . and create basis for decentralised enforcement founded on the principle of reciprocity' (Keohane 1984: 244–5). International institutions, therefore, were given a life of their own, not to mandate what governments must do, but to help governments pursue their own interests through cooperation. The new approaches to understanding IOs, such as regime theory (Keohane 1984; Krasner 1983) and new institutionalism (Ruggie 1998), opened the door for scholars to challenge the fundamental views that states were the only key players in international politics, and that IOs could only serve in passive roles or as inactive forums.

Starting in the 1990s, as an increasing number of IR scholars treated IOs as 'strategic actors' in world politics in their own right (Gilligan and Johns 2012: 240), it became necessary to examine IOs as organisations, especially their 'bureaucratic features'. In carrying out several key functions—authorising the use of force, manipulating domestic politics, developing bureaucratic expertise, and adjudicating disputes—IOs 'are creating their own systems of rules and identities' (March and Olsen 1998: 946), and their discretions and autonomy shape the actions of IOs and facilitate the process of multi-lateral cooperation. Pat got into the field at the time of this change, as the details of the Uruguay trade negotiation under the auspices of the General Agreement on Tariffs and Trade (GATT) gradually surfaced. The striking difference between the negotiations and their outcomes in two new policy areas—trade-related intellectual property rights (TRIPS) and trade in services—raised questions about the role played by the small yet highly professional secretariat of the GATT. To examine what role the GATT secretariat played and how it facilitated the negotiations, Pat adopted the method he had learned from Heclo and Wildavsky's study, *The Private Government of Public Money*— talking to officials and ambassadors who were involved in negotiations, including the former directors general, to find out 'the rules by which they live, the custom they observe, the incentives they perceive and act upon' (Heclo and Wildavsky 1974: xvii). A famous quote given by one official at the GATT/WTO, *Esse, non videri* (To be, but not to be seen), reveals a lot about international civil servants, something that had not been recognised by many in the study of IOs.

In the past decade or so, increasing numbers of scholars have shifted their attention and research focus to 'the unseen hand in treaty reform negotiations' (Beach 2004) and officials working in IOs in a 'straitjacket' behind the scene (Busch 2006). Some have come to the conclusion that 'the activities of treaty secretariats are not only noteworthy for scholars of international organisations but also central to gain a more comprehensive understanding of intergovernmental political processes' (Bauer 2006: 23). Others repeated what Robert McLaren said in 1980, that 'the findings of public administration, concerning the secretariats of national governments, are not applicable to the secretariats of international organizations' (McLaren 1980: 127), as it is the composition of IOs and their preferences that decide how IOs operate and function (Martin 2006; Thompson 2006). This is when Pat launched another effort to examine international civil servants in their own right. This time, it was the staff at the World Bank. Pat believed that no organisation, domestic or international, can be understood without an analysis of the people working within it: who they are, what they do, what their responsibilities are, what quality and skills they have, what their relationships are, what potential influence they may have, and how and when they may influence the decision-making process and policy implementation. All this was done again by talking to current and former World Bank officials, from its headquarters in Washington DC to capitals where the Bank has its offices, along the way building trust with the people under observation. In a similar experience to Heclo and Wildavsky, 'once this initial trust exists, officials are anything but faceless men' (Heclo and Wildavsky 1974: xviii), volunteering their versions of a real world, which Pat could analyse.

GETTING THERE: UNDERSTANDING ORGANISATIONS AND ORGANISATIONAL ENTREPRENEURS

To understand IOs, Pat believed he should appreciate other approaches that had at least given some attention to international civil servants, and to assess the degree to which they tackled the relevant issues. So he started examining the existing models through lens of domestic policy-making and asking if they could identify the contributions of different actors. He then could determine which parts of these theories he could build on.

Organisations, domestic and international, and people within them 'engage in purposive activity' (North 1990: 73) and therefore they should be analysed, both separately and jointly. Organisations have their own structures, missions, strategies and logic of behaviours; so have organisational entrepreneurs. International organisations are bound to achieve the common interests and shared objectives of their creators—the states. States, while pursuing their self-interest through multi-lateral cooperation at IOs, are also constrained by the rules, norms, interests, and logic of behaviour of organisations themselves.

To understand the behaviour of both organisations and organisational entrepreneurs, scholars have developed various approaches. For those who study domestic politics, one key issue is the relationship between 'political masters' and their civil servants: how can voters (principals) make politicians (agents) accountable for their actions; and how can elected politicians (principals) make bureaucrats (agents) accountable for their delegated authority and discretion (Alesina and Tabellini 2008; Bendor, Glazer and Hammond 2001)? These questions are asked simply because civil servants, especially those in the high echelons, can exert significant influence in politics. Pat's favourite conversation in the series, *Yes, Minister*, is a good illustration of this:

> Betty Oldham: Look, Sir Humphrey, whatever we ask the Minister, he says it is an administrative question for you, and whatever we ask you, you say is a policy question for the Minister. How do you suggest we find out what is going on?

> Sir Humphrey Appleby: Yes, yes, yes, I do see that there is a real dilemma here. In that, while it has been government policy to regard policy as a responsibility of Ministers and administration as a responsibility of Officials, the questions of administrative policy can cause confusion between the policy of administration and the administration of policy, especially when responsibility for the administration of the policy of administration conflicts, or overlaps with, responsibility for the policy of the administration of policy ('Yes, Minister: A Question of Loyalty, #2.7', 1981).

Delegation is inevitable and it also creates potential for agent slack in the form of *shirking*, 'where an agent minimises the effort it exerts on its principal's behalf, and *slippage*, 'when an agent shifts policy away from its principal's preferred outcome and towards its own preferences' (Hawkins et al. 2006: 8), as the result of information asymmetry, expertise gaps, and effective monitoring.

The principal–agent analysis was introduced to study IOs in the last decade as more and more scholars acknowledged that IOs should be treated 'as *actors* that implement policy decisions and pursue their own interests strategically' (Hawkins et al. 2006: 5). Scholars who have evoked the principal–agent analysis seek to explain the relationship between the principals (states), which have created and granted authority to IOs in the first place, and agents (IOs), who are expected to exercise the delegated authority and discretion but tend to create accountability issues (Pollack 1997; Nielson and Tierney 2003; Grant and Keohane 2005). Their studies ask: what authority and discretion do states delegate to IOs and when? What control mechanisms (ex-ante or ex-post) can be put in place to deter agent slack? How can, and how do, states through their representation at IOs monitor the agent's exercise of discretion to ensure agents do what their principals want them to do? In international politics, however, principals are willing to delegate and reluctant to monitor, while agents (IOs) pursue what they think their principals want them to do simply because the principals either cannot agree or do not care enough to impose specific instructions. More importantly, this set of literature often treats both the principal (states) and the agent (IO) as single entities to explain their relationship. Of course, neither is.

The simplified 'principals' and 'agents', however, allowed scholars to engage in positive model-building or hypothesis-testing exercises (Binmore 1998; Koremenos 2008; Johns 2007; Helfer 2008; Urpelainen 2012). For example, the cheap-talk model is sometimes adopted to explain this principal–agent relationship. Scholars have argued that international bureaucrats, as 'informational agents', have the opportunity to communicate their private information costlessly to two or more of their principals with heterogeneous preferences. Since all principals 'prefer a bureaucrat agent who is biased in favour of [themselves] with the outside option' (Johns 2007: 247), the result of the negotiations among the principals tends to 'make all IO member states better off' (Gilligan and Johns 2012: 236). Others are not as optimistic about delegation. They argue that even though states may find international delegation useful in addressing the challenges associated with increasing interdependence, states will do what they can to control the behaviour of IOs by exploring and employing a wide range of mechanisms to ensure their interests are being served, which include 'detailed rules, screening and selection, monitoring and reporting requirements, institutional checks and sanctions' (Hawkins and Jacoby 2006: 199).

The principal–agent analysis has shifted from claiming that IOs have no personality (the realists' view that IOs are merely a forum where states bargain) to acknowledging that both IOs as collective entities and international civil servants enjoy special types of authority beyond what is legally delegated to them, and they then apply these formal and informal authorities to pursue interests and objectives that may or may not align with those of specific individual states, including the powerful ones. This approach, nonetheless, tends to emphasise one side of this relationship—the states, and their calculation, strategies and decisions to select mechanisms to ensure IOs do what the states want them to do. The concerns of principal–agent scholars about international civil servants being too powerful and too influential may be misplaced because, as in domestic politics, 'outright bureaucratic sabotage, disobedience, or insubordination by top officials tends to be extremely rare' (Page 2012: vii). In practice, member states have no interest or inclination to exercise their oversight and control and often willingly defer decisions to international civil servants. When this occurs, the behaviour of international civil servants needs to be analysed.

The agent, international organisation and its organisational entrepreneurs behave not only under the constraints created by the formal and informal rules imposed on them by the principal, but also according to their own 'logic of expected consequences' and the 'logic of appropriateness' (March and Olsen 1998). Therefore, to understand the politics and dynamics of international organisations, we need to take into consideration both the principal and the agent, neither of which can be treated as single actors. For example, the Word Trade Organization (WTO) contains at least four sets of the principal–agent relationship: state missions to WTO and the ministries in charge of trade and other matters in the capital; state missions to WTO with the director-general of the WTO; state missions to the WTO with the WTO secretariat; and the WTO director-general and its professional staff.

Opening up the black box of the agent and examining its internal operations in a similar way as those who study domestic politics and public policy seems to be a step too far for many IR scholars. As Lisa Martin has admitted, assuming the executive board 'is the principal, and that the management and staff (treated as a unitary actor) is the agent' may have simplified the principal–agent relationship at the International Monetary Fund (IMF) (Martin 2006: 142; see similar acknowledgements in Gould 2006: 288). Yet, 'IOs gain autonomy as a result of intentional state decision, not through a careless process driven by staff' (Martin 2006: 141). Others echo the view: 'We need not focus on bureaucracies to understand IOs as agents . . . since many IOs have no meaningful staff, let alone autonomous bureaucracy' (Thompson 2006: 254). The question of whether or not staff have any independence or autonomy is thus a non-question. Randall Stone also argues that, to understand the behaviour of the IMF, one just needs to understand 'a borrowing country's importance to the IMF's leading board members', rather than its internal operation, because the IMF 'internalizes the interests of its principals, so there is no action on the principal–agent front' (Stone 2004: 579; 2002).

The view that the bureaucracies of IOs (regardless of their size) and their bureaucratic politics have no role to play in world politics clearly contradicts those studies that examine the operation of specific IOs and the reflections of those working in IOs (Gill and Pugatch 2005; Marshall 2008; Elsig 2010a; Chwieroth, 2013). IOs, large or small, political or economic, are complicated institutions that have their own distinct politics. Those politics concern not only their ultimate principals (states), but also their internal operations. More specifically, IOs as agents are aggregated entities of both executive leaders and staff. As organisational entrepreneurs, their interests and behaviour have to be analysed independently from their members. This realisation led to studies of the impact of an international bureaucracy that pursues interests that may or may not be exactly the ones of any individual member states. Questions are raised about the preferences of international bureaucracies and their civil servants: how do they define their interest; how do they influence the process of multi-lateral decision-making; and how do they work with member states in facilitating multi-lateral cooperation? Recently, increasing numbers of scholars have acknowledged that the performance of IOs may 'reflect the behaviour of two sets of actors, the member states and the staff [and] the causal influences on good or bad performance may come from within the IO or from external sources' (Gutner and Thompson 2010: 231). Focusing on the internal reasons for the successes or failures of IOs, scholars have introduced political sociology into IO studies.

Building on Weber's argument on domestic bureaucracy, Michael Barnett and Martha Finnemore examine IOs as 'social creatures' that do not necessarily follow the path planned by the states. They identify several key sources of 'bureaucratic dysfunctions' of IOs—formal and informal, delegated and non-delegated authority, knowledge (including expertise and information) and rules—that allow IOs and their entrepreneurs to follow the path that may not be planned, and act autonomously in ways that may or may not reflect the interests and mandates of their member states. Specifically, Barnett and Finnemore argue that international civil servants enjoy special types of authority beyond their rational-legal authority, such as political impartiality, moral stand on championing multilateral cooperation and/or global interests, and their special expertise in a particular area. They then apply these authorities in influential ways to classify and define the overall discourse in a given policy area, fix meaning in a social world, and actively guide norm diffusion (Barnett and Finnemore 2004: 21–4). While its attention may remain focused on the authority and discretion that states decide to delegate, and the control mechanisms they have developed and adopted to ensure the delegated authority would serve their interests, this approach nonetheless takes us some way towards understanding the discretion possessed and exercised by international bureaucracies. It treats IOs as bureaucracies and focuses on their 'authority and autonomy'. It argues that rational-legal or delegated authority, moral standing, and expertise allow IOs to develop independent roles; they can sometimes, as a consequence, become dysfunctional when they fail to carry out their specified (or designated) missions. In discussing 'the way they may fail and the ways they evolve', Barnett and Finnemore (2004: 16) highlight the internal culture, shared beliefs, and practices of bureaucracies, which are all defined and shaped by the organisational structure and the environment within which they operate. While Barnett and Finnemore argue that their empirical studies 'reveal the active processes of debate and contestation within these organisations' (Barnett and Finnemore 2004: 159), they admit that exploring the implications of these factors is not the objective of their study. Without disaggregating the exercise of discretion to see how an organisation works, these studies again treat IOs as single, undifferentiated composites and thereby emphasise the importance of the pathology of an organisation (Barnett and Finnemore 2004: 57, 63).

Building on the work of organisational sociology, Catherine Weaver, in her book, *Hypocrisy Trap*, explains why the World Bank does not live up to its grand visions. Her focus is on the 'culture of the Bank'—how the culture of the Bank reacts to new proposals, seeking to incorporate them into existing attitudes to resist external pressures for change. For Weaver, 'hypocrisy' (if the term is not regarded as pejorative) is both functionally useful and inevitable as the World Bank is subject to the same kinds of pressures and pathologies that plague all complex organisations. The gap between the external pressures with high expectations and international bureaucratic goals and the reality on the ground needs to be explained; however, the concept of culture, if partly persuasive as it undermines the rational choice assumptions in IR theory, does not enable the analyst to interpret why there are differences across regions and within sectors at the World Bank. Its empirical cases particularly show that the clash between external pressure and the Bank's bureaucratic goals is more about the clash among various stakeholders rather than between them and the Bank. When organisational culture is used to explain the gap, it presents a single view of an organisation, as some other analyses have done: the Bank and its activities have been explained either as theological zealotry (George and Sabelli 1994) or through an economist's intellectual rigidity (Woods 2006).

Pat came into the field from a different angle—paying attention to what 'people' do in any given IO. For those who study domestic politics, this is the way it is always done. Organisational culture, organisational incentives, professional (or normative factors, in neo-institutionalist parlance) and international bureaucratic pressures cannot be explained until organisational entrepreneurs are brought into the centre of discussion. International civil servants may be faceless and nameless; but they are in no way non-existent. The behaviour and operation of IOs need to be explained by examining not only the formal structure, rules, norms, and expectations, but also, more importantly, the players and their relationships—state representatives, the head of IOs and the staff.

March and Olsen argue that players act according to either 'the logic of consequential calculation' or 'the logic of appropriateness' (March and Olsen 1998). The first explains the behaviour of self-interested maximisers, while the latter sees 'political actors as acting in accordance with rules and practices that are socially constructed, publicly known, anticipated, and accepted' (March and Olsen 1998: 953). They are not necessarily mutually exclusive. For example, decisions made and actions taken by civil servants may conform to the rules and the structure of the organisation; they may also maximise personal interests. How to strike a balance between the two is at the core of how they behave and begs examination. To understand these questions, Pat believes we need to examine the actual processes of interaction between the 'masters' (states and the head of IOs) and international civil servants—how they 'cooperate, bargain and fight, both among themselves and between each other' (Heclo and Wildavsky 1974: xii). Once 'people' are included in the investigation of IO operations, the myth that one IO has one pathology, one culture, and one set of behaviour disappears.

Why and how do the staff of the IMF, World Intellectual Property Organization (WIPO) and the World Bank exercise 'informal governance' over the programs and sometimes even the negotiations, while those at other IOs, such as the WTO, are less able to do so? How and why do member states want the secretariat to develop a 'member-driven' process of reform at the World Health Organization (WHO)? How is the relationship between the in-house executive board and the staff at the IMF and the World Bank different from that at the WHO or the Food and Agriculture Organization (FAO)? The starting point to answer these questions is to examine the characteristics of the players, their roles, and the intra- and inter-institutional frameworks within which they act to change organisational behaviour, action capabilities, and outcomes (Olsen 2008).

INTERNATIONAL CIVIL SERVANTS IN ACTION

International organisations and their rules of good governance are 'empty boxes' without the essential dynamic of the *agents* who shape, implement and maintain them (or undermine or distort them). Likewise, effective IOs are largely, if not entirely, the product of interactions of key players (heads of IOs, state representatives and the staff). The processes by which these three sets of players both interact and work to strengthen (or undermine) institutions need to be understood as *political processes*. By 'political processes' we mean the activities of conflict, negotiation and cooperation involved in making and implementing decisions (or rules about how decisions are to be taken) about how resources are to be used, produced and distributed. Such activities seldom occur in a structural vacuum, but are always framed by (sometimes contradictory or conflicting) institutional arrangements (both formal and informal), cultural requirements and uneven distributions of often quite distinctive sources and forms of power and authority.

The literature that is most helpful in explaining IOs as organisations where a political process takes place is developed by political scientists who study domestic politics. Instead of asking whether IOs have autonomy or act as purposive actors, they take it for granted that IOs do. It is then important to understand how any organisation operates and why it operates the way it does by examining the process within which political masters (states) and bureaucrats (the international civil servants) interact with each other. Political masters are supposed to guide and control, rather than merely reflect and react to, what international civil servants do. States try to do so by defining the structure of the organisation, the general responsibilities, and the way things should be done. The behaviour of people at IOs and their relationships are shaped and restrained by the organisational structures, rules, procedures, norms, and culture. All these aspects of institutions are acknowledged by political scientists, such as March and Olsen, who try to explain the behaviour of 'individuals' in the context of an institution (March and Olsen 1998), by economists, such as North, who emphasises that human interactions are shaped by 'humanly devised constraints' which may be formal or informal (North 1990: 3), and by sociologists, such as Weber, whose ideal type of bureaucracy is often used as a benchmark to reform bureaucracies.

Structure

Formal organisations provide a codified and normative structure within which civil servants operate. The structure of IOs defines resource contribution and allocation, procedures in decision-making and power relationships. How is an organisational structure translated into behaviour? In some IOs, this structure is hierarchical while in others it tends to be more flat. In an IO with a hierarchical structure, the role and influence of the staff depend a lot on their leaders, whether it's the president, director-general or managing director. How leaders delegate power and authority and how they coordinate the exercise of influence are all important for the behaviour and performance of civil servants. An IO with a formal hierarchical structure can function in a flat way if its leader is willing to delegate and its senior officials are more willing to work in a collegial environment. How staff are selected affects their capacity to influence process and outcomes. In those IOs where staff are recruited through a combination of merit and geography, hierarchical control may not be as tight as in IOs where the staff are strictly recruited on the basis of merit (Taylor and Groom 1988). Where professional expertise is pre-eminent, discretion will be greater. In IOs with flat structures, international civil servants have more room to take initiative. A flat structure plus decentralised offices provide international civil servants with even more opportunities to exercise their bureaucratic entrepreneurship (Nay 2011). For example, country directors of the World Bank based in the field work closely with the governments of the client countries, and often see themselves as the representatives of the state to the Bank and the representative of the Bank to the state. This dual role enables country directors to engage in 'formulation of policies', 'determining an optional course of action', 'setting a strategic direction for the intended policy support program and steering it through the often treacherous waters in which policy is made' (Gill and Pugatch 2005: 7). Decentralisation at the WHO presents different challenges: six regional offices have their own governance arrangements, with directly elected regional directors and extensive country office networks, while the headquarters sends out its own field people to country offices too. This presents unique challenges not only to the director-general of the WHO but also to those working at the regional offices and the headquarters and country offices, the latter two of whom are supposed to be accountable to the director-general (Burci and Vignes 2004; Clift 2013).

Missions

The mission of IOs provides the collective responsibilities for the players, and the guidelines for what IOs are to achieve, and consequently affects not only the recruitment of staff but also the way they work. Meanwhile, 'ambiguous mandates are symptomatic of organisations' need to serve their constituents' (Babb 2003: 5). An ambiguous mission requires officials to define and redefine the mission. In so doing, they introduce new ideas, mechanisms and procedures to fill the content of ambitious and/or ambiguous missions. These ideas, mechanisms and procedures cannot be disassociated from the institution they work for, but they are the products of these officials.

In IOs that primarily deal with political and security issues, officials are more constrained in interpreting the mission as diplomats from member states tend to insert more control. In some such IOs, such as the International Atomic Energy Agency, even their officials tend to be seconded from governments of member states (Claude 1971; Taylor and Groom 1988; Perez 2005). In the more technical IOs, such as WIPO and WHO, professional staff often work with their counterparts from the capital cities on many technical issues, rather than state representatives in the UN missions. The responsibilities of these international civil servants then are less clearly delineated. At each stage of decision-making, wider initiative may be needed; state delegates often rely heavily on the technical expertise of highly qualified and widely dispersed staff to identify, develop and recommend proposals for action, and to evaluate and oversee their implementation, as explained by a senior official:

> When countries at a standing committee of the WIPO agree to discuss certain issues, the secretariat prepares a text. Following this, technical people from member states make their comments and put in their submissions. Then the secretariat prepares a revised text for the next meeting. The process may go for several years until you get a text which is just about right. Then you can call a diplomatic conference and hope to conclude the treaty. The secretariat therefore plays a quite active role in shaping the text and the treaty.

In IOs dealing with technical issues, 'the secretariat has to provide their own path, the guidance, and the objectives'. These professional experts can speak the language of their counterparts from capitals but they also need to learn the language of diplomats who 'may be at very junior level but love to show that they are powerful in making decisions on behalf of their states without really an appreciation about the knowledge and the subject matter.' Another added:

> Technical experts from capitals discuss and negotiate the issues based on the draft our staff had worked out, but political diplomats from the missions in Geneva started coming to meetings; they were frankly speaking, vastly superior in negotiating skills and know far better about the procedures than the technical experts even though they know little about the substance. Our staff are technical experts, working at the technical level, but have to learn the political skill, to steer and move the debate towards the centre and also to devise programs that try to strike a balance, sometimes in the face of rather difficult pressures coming from the different sides.

This explanation provides a much richer description of how people at IOs operate than those who only recognise the technical competence of international civil servants.

Competence

Organisational competence varies. How international civil servants exploit their expertise, experience and control of information is an empirical question that depends, to a large extent, on the trust and legitimacy they gain from their leaders and member states. This is not a small matter in the sense that the same group of highly recognised technical experts at one IO can have significant influence and impact on assisting member states and facilitating cooperation at one particular time, but not at another. It depends on their international identity, and the trust they can build with those who they are supposed to serve. Not every civil servant can become an international civil servant automatically, even though all international civil servants must express their explicit 'loyalty' to the international organisation. Comparing two senior officials, one director-general explained:

> One has the organisational interest at heart but can also provide a bridge to her own government; the other has never managed to switch from a national official to an international one. She would say, 'We would do things this way or that way'. The statement triggered immediate resentment as people would interpret *we* as her country and she never managed to shake off her national prejudices and become an international staff.

On 'trust', a senior official at the WTO, the most 'member-driven' organisation, explains:

> It is not that we are manipulators or anything; we do not think of ourselves as some Machiavellian puppet masters that can control destinies. We do not have power, but we do have influence if we use it carefully. What we can do is to facilitate people finding solutions, helping kick in ideas informally. Very often delegates come to us and ask for advice, quietly, off the record—about how they should pursue a certain issue. A lot of this comes down to trust and confidence between us and the delegates of member states.

Culture

An organisation develops its distinct culture, which over time creates expectations of the behaviour of those working at the organisation. 'Institutions are carriers of cultural prescriptions and expectations' (Olsen 2008: 15), and the behaviour of civil servants must be understood within this context. Two aspects of organisational culture are important in shaping the behaviour of international civil servants: one is philosophical and one is procedural. Development is the core philosophy of most staff at the World Bank. People may have different understandings of what development means and how to achieve development, but they believe in and often are committed to assisting developing countries to develop before they seek a career at the Bank. It is difficult to see how someone who is not a free-trader can work at the WTO.

The procedural aspect of organisational culture is 'the product of accumulated experience and tradition, created by the familiarities within a particular set of tasks and problems, and influenced perhaps by the personalities of leading administrators' (Self 1972: 92). It is also known as the collective personality of the organisation. New recruits are inducted into established ways of thinking and reasoning, and methods of doing things. 'The pursuit of purpose is associated with identities more than with interests, and with the selection of rules more than with individual rational expectations' (March and Olsen 1998: 951). One good example is the opening speeches of the directors general of three IOs, the WHO, WIPO and WTO, at a joint press conference on health, intellectual property and trade. The WHO director-general emphasised the importance of allowing generic drugs to enter the market, and extending the period of exemption for trade-related intellectual property. The WIPO director-general reiterated that proper protection of intellectual rights is at the heart of innovation and access to medicines and medical technologies. The WTO director-general repeated liberalisation of trade as the best way of promoting access to medical technologies and innovation (WTO 2013). The three speeches reflected what institutionalism calls the logic of appropriateness: their speeches were anticipated and accepted given their identity and the obligations of that identity.

Culture nonetheless is not static. New expectations are created as circumstances and demand mutate, while organisational culture tends to have long-lasting impact on behaviour. For example, the staff at IMF can debate various issues and policy options no less fiercely than those at the World Bank. Yet, the organisational culture at the IMF is that once a decision is made, the staff act as an army. This conversion process from 'anarchy of ideas to an army' is very different from the 'university-type' culture at the World Bank. At WIPO, senior staff tend to be more risk averse than those at the WHO, as lawyers tend to contemplate various aspects of a given issue. The culture of the WHO secretariat is medical, in the way that the language of the World Bank was engineering and later economics. They tend to work like medics: everything can be triaged and settled quickly; everything is possible and fast. As a senior official of an IO explained:

> It is a totally different ball game when working with the vast majority who were doctors at the WHO and when working with the vast majority who are lawyers at WIPO. Doctors are used to taking decisions because in an emergency room, there is one doctor in charge who is telling everyone what they have to do and nobody questions, you just get on with it. On the other side, lawyers are very risk-averse: they are all about on the one hand and on the other. So getting a decision point is much harder because everything is flogged to death in argumentation before you get there.

The formal structures and rules of IOs create an environment and incentive structures within which civil servants operate. Informal factors, such as norms, expectation, and organisational culture, and individual and collective capacities built on their expertise, competence and, most importantly, trust of their 'masters', all matter. The causal relationship between these formal and informal factors and the behaviour and performance of civil servants can be explained better by adopting an interpretative approach than hypothesis testing.

CONCLUSION: FUTURE STUDY OF INTERNATIONAL CIVIL SERVANTS

It is not sufficient to acknowledge that 'international organisations—intergovernmental bureaucracies, formally controlled by multi-lateral governmental mechanisms but operated by self-confident international civil servants—play [a role] in international governance' (Bauer 2006: 26). Nor is it enough to show that international civil servants in many IOs have the expertise that their member states lack. International civil servants, like their domestic counterparts, do not exist in an organisation alone. They interact with member states and the IO leaders, who come in all shapes and with all ideological and managerial orientations. It is this interaction that often forms the incentive structure within which international officials operate. A limited number of studies on the relationship tend to focus on a single IO (Beach 2004; Joachim, Reinalda and Verbeek 2007; Chwieroth, 2010). If international civil servants have their own identity and possess certain features that are different from state representatives at IOs or their domestic counterparts, comparative studies of different IOs are needed.

More than a decade into the field, Pat has not developed what is known as a grand theory 'ism' for international organisations and international civil servants. The empirical work and extensive and intensive interviews of officials have provided a relatively comprehensive understanding of how IOs operate, and especially the roles and impact of their officials. The most comforting reward, perhaps, is the comments made by senior officials at the IMF and the World Bank:

> Thank you for explaining these organisations in Geneva and Rome to us: they come across as quite different organisations from time to time and under different managements. They are even at odds in terms of what they want and what policies they are proposing. How do they really work? So can you just explain that a little bit because it seems to be going to the heart of the governance question?

After hearing the 'story' about the FAO, a former World Bank vice president said,

> The whole story seems to be one dysfunction after another dysfunction at FAO. We know agriculture's going to get tougher, we know it's going to get more important and so you have this disconnect between an important sector with real needs and the way the institution's being treated and the way the institution's being run is completely dysfunctional.

Officials from other IOs also raise the question: 'So you have a very large highly competent staff; how can they tolerate to see their organisation coming down year after year? Has there been any internal kind of revolt or at least reflection on how can we revamp our institution?' Being able to identify the patterns of behaviour of players and explain how IOs actually operate is more important to Pat than finding a fancy label to identify a sub-set of political science or a methodology to describe his research. Studies with extensive and intensive interviews might not lead to the creation of grand theories, but they can explain actions. As Heclo and Wildavsky explained in their work: 'The participant is the expert on what he does; the observer's task is to make himself expert on why he does it' (Heclo and Wildavsky 1974: xvii). Indeed, in conducting these interviews, Pat was wisely advised by a long-serving retired senior official at an IO:

> So I always say—when you especially as academics examine the governance issue, do go behind the structures, the systems, the processes and the procedures. They are meaningful only when you examine how people function in these organisations and what relationship they have built over the years that shape the operation of these IOs.

In the recent changing of the guard at the WTO, the director-general and three of his four deputies all jumped the fence: they had been ambassadors; now they are international officials of the secretariat. The switch is a good example of 'where you stand depends on where you sit'. Before the switching, a typical comment from ambassadors was: 'The secretariat is only a secretary and has no role to play in this'. After the switch, the new director-general could state: 'I have started, with the chairman of the General Council and the secretariat, internal technical work with a view to identify the options available . . . and so please be ready for that conversation'. So after all, IO leaders do have a view and a position, as do international civil servants. Those who study domestic politics will not be surprised by the switch of the attitude and the ensuing statement, while those in IR might be horrified to hear that states may actually have to discuss something presented to them that developed at the secretariat. But it was ever thus. The future of IO study clearly needs an integration of some of the work done in other sub-fields of political science to understand the intricate operation of organisations, and especially the dynamic relationships among those involved.

REFERENCES

Alesina, A. & Tabellini, G., 2008, 'Bureaucrats or Politicians?', *Journal of Public Economics*, vol. 92, no. 3–4, pp. 426–47

Babb, S., 2003, 'The IMF in Sociological Perspective', *Studies in Comparative International Development*, vol. 38, no. 2, pp. 3–27

Barnett, M. & Finnemore, M., 2004, *Rules for the World*, Ithaca, NY: Cornell University Press

Bauer, S., 2006, 'Does Bureaucracy Really Matter?', *Global Environmental Politics*, vol. 6, no. 1, pp. 23–49

Beach, D., 2004, 'The Unseen Hand in Treaty Reform Negotiations', *Journal of European Public Policy*, vol. 11, no. 3, pp. 408–39

Bendor, J., Glazer, A. & Hammond, T., 2001, 'Theories of Delegation', *Annual Review of Political Science*, vol. 4, pp. 235–60

Bevir, M. & Kedar, A., 2008, 'Concept Formation in Political Science,' *Perspectives on Politics*, vol. 6, no. 3, pp. 503–17

Binmore, K., 1998, 'Review of Robert Axelrod, "The Complexity of Cooperation"', *Journal of Artificial Societies and Social Simulation*, vol. 1, no. 1, at http://jasss.soc.surrey.ac.uk/1/1/review1.html

Burci, G.L. & Vignes, C.H., 2004, *World Health Organisation*, The Hague: Kluwer Law International

Busch, P.O., 2006, 'The Secretariat of the Climate Convention,' Global Governance Working Paper, no. 22, October, <www.glogov.org>

Chwieroth, J.M., 2010, *Capital Ideas*, Princeton, NJ: Princeton University Press

—— 2013, 'The Silent Revolution', *Review of International Organisations*, vol. 8, no. 2, pp. 265–90

Claude, I.L., 1971, *Swords into Plowshares*, New York, NY: Random House

Clift, C., 2013, 'The Role of the World Health Organisation in the International System', Chatham House, Centre on Global Health Security Working Group Papers, February

Collier, D., 1999, 'Letter from the President', *APSA-CP—Newsletter of the Organised Section in Comparative Politics of the American Political Science Association*, vol. 10, no. 1, pp. 1–6

Dahl, R.A., Bewley, T.F., Rudolph, S.H. & Mearsheimer, J., 2004, 'What Have We Learned?' in I. Shapiro et al. (eds), *Problems and Methods in the Study of Politics*, Cambridge: Cambridge University Press

Elsig, M., 2010a, 'Principal–Agent Theory and the World Trade Organisation', *European Journal of International Relations*, vol. 17, no. 3, pp. 495–517

—— 2010b, 'The World Trade Organisation at Work', *Review of International Organisations*, vol. 5, no. 3, pp. 345–63

George, S. & Sabelli, F., 1994, *Faith and Credit*, London: Penguin

Gill, I. & Pugatch, T. (eds), 2005, *At the Frontlines of Development*, Washington, DC: The World Bank

Gilligan, M.J. & Johns, L., 2012, 'Formal Models of International Institutions', *Annual Review of Political Science*, vol. 15, pp. 221–43

Gould, E., 2006, *Money Talks*, Stanford, CA: Stanford University Press

Grant, R.W. & Keohane, R.O., 2005, 'Accountability and Abuses of Power in World Politics', *American Political Science Review*, vol. 99, no. 1, pp. 29–43

Gutner, T. & Thompson, A., 2010, 'The Politics of IO Performance', *Review of International Organisations*, vol. 5, no. 3, pp. 227–48

Hawkins, D.G. & Jacoby, W., 2006, 'How Agents Matter', in D.G. Hawkins et al. (eds), *Delegation and Agency in International Organisations*, New York: Cambridge University Press, pp. 199–228

Hawkins, D.G. et al. (eds), 2006, *Delegation and Agency in International Organisations*, New York: Cambridge University Press

Heclo, H. & Wildavsky, A., 1974, *The Private Government of Public Money*, London: Macmillan

Helfer, L.R., 2008, 'Monitoring Compliance with Unratified Treaties', *Law and Contemporary Problems*, vol. 71, no. 1, pp. 193–218

Jacobson, H.K., 2000, 'International Institutions and System Transformation', *Annual Review of Political Science*, vol. 3, pp. 149–66

Joachim, J., Reinalda, B. & Verbeek, B. (eds), 2007, *International Organisations and Implementation*, New York: Routledge

Johns, L., 2007, 'A Servant of Two Masters', *International Organisation*, vol. 61, no. 2, pp. 245–75

Keohane, R.O., 1984, *After Hegemony*, Princeton, NJ: Princeton University Press

Koremenos, Barbara, 2008, 'When, What, and Why Do States Choose to Delegate', *Law and Contemporary Problems*, vol. 71, no. 1, pp. 151–92

Krasner, S. (ed.), 1983, *International Regime*, Ithaca, NY: Cornell University Press

Lin, A.C., 1998, 'Bridging Positivist and Interpretivist Approaches to Qualitative Methods', *Policy Studies Journal*, vol. 26, no. 1, pp. 162–80

McLaren, R.I., 1980, *Civil Servants and Public Policy*, Toronto: Wilfred Laurier University Press

March, J.G. & Olsen, J.O., 1998, 'The Institutional Dynamics of International Political Orders', *International Organisation*, vol. 52, no. 4, pp. 943–69

Marshall, K., 2008, *The World Bank*, London: Routledge

Martin, L.L., 2006, 'Distribution, Information, and Delegation to International Organisations', in D.G. Hawkins et al. (eds), *Delegation and Agency in International Organisations*, New York, NY: Cambridge University Press, pp. 140–64

Mearsheimer, J.J. & Walt, S.M., 2013, 'Leaving Theory Behind: Why hypothesis testing has become bad for IR', Harvard Kennedy School Faculty Research Working Paper series, RW13–001, January

Nay, O., 2011, 'What Drives Reform in International Organisations?', *Governance*, vol. 24, no. 4, pp. 689–712

Nielson, D.L. & Tierney, M.J., 2003, 'Delegation to International Organisations', *International Organisation*, vol. 57, no. 2, pp. 241–76

North, D.C., 1990, *Institutions, Institutional Change, and Economic Performance*, Cambridge: Cambridge University Press

Olsen, J.P., 2008, 'The Ups and Downs of Bureaucratic Organisation', *Annual Review of Political Science*, vol. 11, pp. 13–37

Page, E.C., 2012, *Policy Without Politicians*, Oxford, UK: Oxford University Press

Perez, A.F., 2005, 'The International Atomic Energy Agency in the Changing Structure of International Organisation Law', The Catholic University of America, Columbus School of Law, Legal Studies Series, no. 2007-4

Pollack, M.A., 1997, 'Delegation, Agency, and Agenda Setting in the European Community', *International Organisation*, vol. 51, no. 1, pp. 99–134

Ruggie, J.G., 1998, *Constructing the World Polity*, London: Routledge

Self, P., 1972, *Administrative Theory and Politics*, London: George Allen & Unwin

Stone, R.W., 2002, *Lending Credibility*, Princeton, NJ: Princeton University Press

—— 2004, 'The Political Economy of IMF Lending in Africa', *American Political Science Review*, vol. 98, no. 4, pp. 577–91

Taylor, P.G. & Groom, A.J.R. (eds), 1988, *International Organizations at Work*, London: Pinter

Thompson, A., 2006, 'Screening Power,' in D.G. Hawkins et al. (eds), *Delegation and Agency in International Organisations*, New York, NY: Cambridge University Press, pp. 229–54

Urpelainen, J., 2012, 'Unilateral Influence on International Bureaucrats', *Journal of Conflict Resolution*, vol. 56, no. 4, pp. 704–35

Waltz, K.N., 1979, *Theory of International Politics*, Reading, MA: Addison-Wesley Publishing Company

Weaver, C., 2008, *Hypocrisy Trap: The World Bank and the poverty of reform*, Princeton, NJ: Princeton University Press

Woods, N., 2006, *The Globalizers*, Ithaca, NY: Cornell University Press

WTO, 2013, 'Conference between Health, Intellectual Property and Trade Key to Access to Medicines', <www.wto.org/english/news_e/sppl_e/sppl266_e.htm>, 5 February

PART 6

COMPARATIVE GOVERNMENT

11

WHO RULES? DEMOCRATIC VERSUS BUREAUCRATIC LEADERSHIP

John Kane and Haig Patapan

On joining Griffith University's Department of Politics and Public Policy (as it was then called) a couple of decades ago, we were naturally keen to learn about the demands of university life and, over the occasional coffee, benefited greatly from the advice, experience and wise counsel of Pat Weller. Pat was not only one of Australia's premier scholars of politics and administration, but also a successful administrator in his own right. One wry observation of his we have never forgotten: 'Universities', he said, 'hire for teaching, promote for research, and reward for administration'. This, we were to learn, was indeed the 'iron law' of the modern academy.

That an institution dedicated to teaching and research would end up rewarding its administrators disproportionately was no surprise to a man thoroughly familiar with theories of organisational behaviour. Pat's pithy statement effectively encapsulated the findings of Philip Selznick's classic 1949 study of the Tennessee Valley Authority, a 'grass-roots democracy' organisation devised to strengthen individual choice and local institutions, and to counter the trend towards bureaucratic centralisation. It soon emerged that the needs of the administration were at tension with the ideal of democratic participation, resulting in an administrative co-optation of power in a process that Selznick said revealed the 'tyranny of means and the impotence of ends' (Selznick 1984a [1949]). However well-meaning an organisation's members, 'organisational imperatives' sooner or later produced an organisational 'character' with a tendency to undermine the organisation's original purposes and goals.

Selznick (1984b [1957]) went on to write *Leadership in Administration*, an influential book on leadership, another important theme in Pat's scholarship. Pat is an authority on Australian politics and Westminster government, and much of his work has focused on the core executive of cabinet and prime minister. His famous biographies of major political figures include Malcolm Fraser and John Button, and have brought to life the challenges faced by political leaders. He is equally well known, however, for his extensive scholarship on public administration and public-sector reform. These two strands of scholarship have intersected in important works such as his exemplary and much-discussed case study of the 'children overboard' affair in *Don't Tell the Prime Minister*. This best-selling monograph detailed how the politicisation of the public service and consequent compromise of its independence prevented its effective handling of a politically charged affair (on which Pat provided expert testimony to a Senate committee hearing).

In this chapter we take a leaf from Pat's book to look again at the themes of leadership and administration, re-engaging a question that first arose when democratic governments began to adopt the bureaucratic form and which we call the challenge of bureaucratic leadership. In the past, even to talk of something called 'bureaucratic leadership' (rather than the discreet public service of administrative 'mandarins') smacked somewhat of undemocratic usurpation. Yet it was always difficult to deny that senior bureaucrats, entrusted with considerable latitude in the determination of often ambiguous and complex policies, inevitably exercised the kind of judgement that implied a form of leadership. But what exactly was (or should be) the nature of this leadership, and what sort of challenges did it present to democratic leaders?

Selznick, despite his awareness of organisational dangers, nevertheless believed that a 'creative' and 'responsible' leadership could safely accommodate democratic concerns (Selznick 1984b). Some claimed that this bureaucratic leadership was better seen as a form of public entrepreneurship (Lewis 1980; Doig and Hargrove 1987; Moore 1995). Larry Terry, drawing on Selznick's insights, argued that it was time to 'put leadership back into the administration of public bureaucracies' and that bureaucratic leadership is essential for good governance (Terry

(2002) [1995]: 169). Though he acknowledged that bureaucratic leaders may pose a threat to the public good, he also thought that instruments of administrative accountability, normative constraints and public scrutiny in the American system provided sufficient safeguards. He therefore advocated that public managers assume a legitimate role in governance while avoiding short-sighted reforms that compromised the long-term integrity of public institutions. Terry called this 'administrative conservatorship', bureaucratic leadership that was a form of 'statesmanship guided by a moral commitment to preserve the constitutional balance of power in support of individual rights'. For Terry, 'bureaucratic leaders are protectors of our Republic and democratic way of life' (Terry 2002: 169).

Others have argued, however, that a dynamic 'change-agent' style of leadership was inappropriate for the public sector. Frederickson and Matkin (2007) proposed public leadership as 'gardening' (rather than architecture or engineering), where possibilities are limited by soil and climate, and accomplishment is slow. The 'gardener' who works with available resources, who recognises the nature of an administrative culture and appreciates the need for incrementalism, becomes for them the model for good bureaucratic leadership.

These debates indicate an important and still unresolved question concerning the proper bases of bureaucratic leadership and its implications for democratic legitimacy. Following our research into the nature of democratic leadership, we revisit the issue by approaching it from the perspective of elected leaders, for whom it poses especially acute difficulties.

Democratic leaders make policy decisions ostensibly for the public good, but must rely on a competent public service to ensure that policies are properly implemented. They are therefore critically judged not only as policies themselves, but also on the way the public sector fulfils expectations of 'service delivery', with the result that leaders are often severely blamed for administrative failures. The Federal Emergency Management Agency's mishandling of the Katrina disaster in New Orleans in 2005 was, notoriously, rapidly sheeted from senior managers to President George W. Bush to his lasting damage. Indeed, democratic leaders are even held responsible for the adverse actions of private companies over whom they have regulative responsibility but little direct control, as the Obama administration discovered in dealing with the BP oil spill in the Gulf of Mexico. Yet democratic leaders may feel equally challenged when public-sector managers act perfectly competently but too independently. The latter need a degree of discretionary freedom in order to act for the public good, but if their exercise of freedom seems contrary to the wishes or intentions of elected leaders, it inevitably challenges the authority of the elected government.

The problem is no doubt amplified by the sheer size of modern bureaucracies, itself a response to ever-rising public demands that mandate an ever more expansive and sophisticated administration. Expectations regarding policies in traditional areas such as health, employment and education grow more burdensome even as democratic leaders try to grapple with new and unfamiliar threats to financial systems, the environment and national security. Despite the sincere desire of some to 'roll back' government, it is safe to wager that large and complex bureaucracies are here to stay as an inevitable aspect of modern life.

Certainly, managing the great administrative behemoths presents peculiar challenges, and indeed over the last several decades, leaders in nearly every developed democracy have undertaken vigorous, so-called managerialist reforms to achieve two separate but connected goals: to make the public sector more efficient and effective by making it less hierarchical and bureaucratic; and to exert firmer control over agencies by neutralising the independent power of senior bureaucrats. And yet the bureaucratic challenge for democratic leaders is not merely one of effective control (which CEOs of all large companies face), but one of legitimacy. More precisely, it involves a competition over authority between protagonists appealing to differing bases of legitimacy: one to democratic election and the other to expertise and an ethic of public service. Although elected leaders are notionally in authoritative command of their ever-expanding bureaucracies, the reality has always been much more complicated, as we will try to show.

The very fact that we qualify our modern democracies with the adjective 'liberal' attests to the fact that the bases of legitimacy in such regimes are too complex to be reduced to any simple conception of a sovereign democratic will embodied in elected representatives. The democratic will is constrained by constitutions and laws and by the judicial systems that safeguard them, which has meant that some effectual (though never final) balance has had to be achieved over time between their competing principles. Professionalised bureaucracies may be less well anchored theoretically than, for example, the judiciary due to modern constitutionalism, but they too form an indispensible part of the system. Moreover they appeal to moral sources of legitimacy that, like law, are always in potential conflict with purely democratic authority.

Kenneth Meier and Laurence O'Toole (2006: ix) posed the central issue in general terms at the start of their book, *Bureaucracy in a Democratic State*: 'Can the imperatives of an administrative system be reconciled with the norms of democratic government? Or is bureaucracy, with its expertise, insulation, and byzantine procedures, the enemy of popular control?' (Meier and O'Toole 2006: ix). Here we will answer this with an equivocal 'Yes and no', and try to show why such equivocation is unavoidable.

We will begin by outlining and clarifying the central challenge that bureaucracies present to democratic leadership and will then deepen the analysis by examining the history of the adoption of continental bureaucratic administrations by democratic leaders, explaining what was perceived as being at stake—in the sense of significant advantages and risks—in doing so. We will then look at the way democratic leaders in recent decades took up the challenge of achieving a balance of authority and control, which was perceived as having gotten seriously out of kilter; in particular, by trying to explain some of the unintended consequences of the managerialist reforms. Finally we will conclude by explaining why the tension between bureaucratic and democratic authority must be perennially managed but can never be definitively resolved.

DEMOCRATIC VERSUS BUREAUCRATIC AUTHORITY

Democratic leaders are, in theory, servants of the sovereign people, and liable to be sharply reminded of this when they forget or over-reach. This makes the public bureaucracy, in effect, the servant's servant. The democratic legitimacy of the elected leaders, which the bureaucracy lacks, gives them undoubted authority over the administrative machine. The bureaucratic instruments of the civil service are meant to serve the public principally through obedience to the elected leadership. Yet democratic leaders often find that their administrations, far from being pliant tools, have become unwieldy and impenetrable. Leaders can feel helplessly squeezed between the unrelenting pressure of the sovereign people's demands and their own incapacity to meet them satisfactorily with instruments that are under imperfect political control. In their frustration they are prone to view bureaucratic inertia or obstruction as usurpation of legitimate democratic authority.

Making the case for their own superior authority is, however, more complicated than might be imagined. Leaders are, for one thing, bedevilled by the typically ambivalent attitude of a democratic people towards its leaders, a generally under-explored problem of democratic leadership (Dahl 1985; Ruscio 2004).[1] The egalitarian democratic ideal—most famously formulated as 'government of the people, by the people, for the people'—leaves only a small and largely undefined theoretical space for leaders. The more democratic a regime becomes, the less may any individual or group claim any natural, God-given or inherited right to govern, which is a right that can be granted only by the sovereign people to its (temporary) representatives. The concept of popular sovereignty carries with it the implication that democratic leaders, however necessary they are and however securely elected, enjoy only the most provisional legitimacy. Indeed, they must often suffer and accept humiliations that leaders in other regimes would never tolerate, because the hope that democrats invest in their leaders is always tempered by a ready instinct to mistrust and a preparedness to dismiss from office.

This problem is compounded if the bureaucracy, the servant's servant, is able to draw on an independent source of legitimate authority derived from a notion of unmediated service to the democratic populace, turning its relationship with elected leaders into one of potential contest rather than subservience. The civil service does not, after all, *belong* in any real sense to democratic leaders, who are merely its temporary custodians. The true principal of the civil service is the sovereign people, whom it serves under a higher ethos of public service, always in principle distinguishable from service to transient politicians, whatever their electoral credentials. The central role of public bureaucracies has always been service to and guardianship of the public interest, conceived as separable from purely private interests. Such a role, however, can only with difficulty be harmonised with the idea of serving the public through non-partisan obedience to the will of democratic representatives. What happens when an expert bureaucracy's views of what constitutes the true public interest differs from those of the elected government?

There is a simple and standard democratic answer to this, of course—bureaucratic deference to the elected leadership—but this hardly exhausts either the practical or theoretical tensions involved. There is a permanent possibility of such clashes because of the inevitably different perspectives of professional career administrators, with their technocratic expertise and long experience, and democratic leaders, with their particular policy and ideological agendas, and special sensitivities to urgent public demands arising from their need to be re-elected. In cases of conflict, it is tempting for bureaucrats to see themselves as the embodiment of Jean-Jacques Rousseau's rational 'general will', a will that must necessarily oppose, for the good of all, the merely transient and arbitrary will of the majority as embodied in the elected government (Rousseau 1978: iii). Moreover, democratic politics are usually fractious or chaotic, while permanent bureaucracies may appear relatively stable and therefore more able to deliver essential public services reliably. In some polities at some times, people have held their bureaucracies in great respect while regarding their elected representatives with utter contempt (for example, in France on occasion, or in Japan until the bursting of the economic bubble).

Yet the contest between bureaucratic and democratic authority is seldom clearly decided in favour of one rather than the other. It is instructive to contrast the bureaucratic challenge to democratic leaders to the challenges presented by judiciaries, which were made independent by the separation-of-powers doctrine. In addition to this doctrine, judges in any policy controversy can draw, implicitly or explicitly, on the august and independent authority of law itself. This derives not only from a traditional view of law as immemorial and transcendent, but also from the fact that liberal-constitutionalism asserts so adamantly the principle of democratic government *under the rule of law*. Elected executives and legislatures may control the creation of statute law, but the rule-of-law principle inevitably grants special authority to those whose solemn task is to equitably administer, interpret and safeguard the law, whether its origin is a constitution, a statute, or an accumulated body of 'common' law. Asserting any equivalent non-democratic authority on behalf of the bureaucracy is more problematic. In most developed countries law has gradually arrived at an uneasy but generally stable modus vivendi with democracy. The same cannot be said for bureaucracy. The precise boundaries of any independent authority to which public-sector leaders may lay claim are far from clear, though it is generally articulated in terms of an ethos of the public good, public service or, in the United States especially, constitutionalism (Bertelli and Lynn 2006).

B. Guy Peters (1987) describes a continuum of possibilities for the politics–administration relationship from, at one end, formal separation within a hierarchical system dominated by political officeholders to, at the other, government by bureaucracy that marginalises the influence of politicians. The former, though often venerated in theory, is never observed in reality, while the latter would clearly constitute a formidable challenge to democracy. Some have argued that the French administration, with its elite corps of professionally trained directors and strong 'statist' tradition, constitutes a case of bureaucratic government, though others argue the reality is more complex (Elgie and Griggs 2000; Elgie 2001). Relationships in most democratic countries are, in fact, located at some intermediate position along the continuum, and may be characterised by either mutual accommodation or competition between elected and administrative leaders for control over policy. The American system is certainly especially prone to adversarialism, but even the Netherlands—a 'consensual' democracy with a bureaucracy founded on values of loyalty, merit and political neutrality—witnessed a series of highly public confrontations between ministers and senior civil servants in the 1990s, which some thought suggested a dangerous trend towards bureaucratic autonomy or even hegemony ('t Hart and Wille 2006). Westminster systems can be equally combative. Margaret Thatcher's reforms of the British civil service when she was prime minister were provoked by her previous experience as secretary of state for education, which had made her hostile to powerful and unresponsive public service 'mandarins' with strong policy preferences of their own (Peele 2004: 178).

Thatcher believed that the old-style bureaucracy, although trained in discreet subservience, actually possessed an independent will capable of opposing a democratic leader's authority. And indeed, the upper layer of the old service was peopled by powerful lifetime bureaucrats with the experience, knowledge and discretionary authority to significantly shape and influence policy. These were brilliant, relatively anonymous figures who, as Rhodes and Weller put it, 'worked in the shadows, advising, managing and influencing the direction of their respective countries. They were the mandarins, recognised as the real rulers, the providers of continuity' (Rhodes and Weller 2001: 1). Such hidden rulers inevitably challenged the authority of here-today-gone-tomorrow elected leaders. The managerialist reform movement of the 1980s sought, among other things, to reduce their power and disperse their functions more widely throughout the service.

It is important to note, however, that this potential for mutual suspicion and conflict between democratic leaders and administrators has existed ever since democratic governments first adopted bureaucratic forms of administration. Indeed, democratic leaders originally took up bureaucracy with a mixture of hope and fear—hope that 'rational', meritocratic, bureaucratic government would provide improved governmental outcomes for public benefit, and fear that it might become a rival centre of power, and of undemocratic power at that. A brief excursion into the history of democratic-bureaucratic development will help us to appreciate the depths and dimensions of the problem.

THE HISTORICAL THREAT AND PROMISE OF BUREAUCRACY

The modern bureaucratic form of administration was developed in Prussia and France under monarchical or imperial regimes, based originally on the example of hierarchically ordered military organisation (Karl 1987: 27). The 'continental model' became that of a powerfully autonomous, highly prestigious organisation serving an impersonal state (the so-called *Rechtsstaat* founded on legal norms rather than personal rule; see Kickert 2005). The democratising Anglo-American states of the nineteenth century sought to reform their own amateurish, patronage-ridden, inefficient administrative organisations to bring them in line with the impressively professional, impartial, public-service oriented continental bureaucracies on the Continent, particularly that of Germany, but feared that bureaucracies developed by illiberal regimes might prove fatal for systems of popular government (Karl 1987: 28; Heper 1985). Both French and German models nurtured an ethos of professional 'public service' quite divorced from any notion of serving the popular will as expressed through electoral politics (Caplan 1988: 4–5). The point of continental bureaucracy was not to give the people what they wanted, but to provide what was good for 'the nation'.[2]

Woodrow Wilson, most famously, believed it necessary to 'Americanise' this system in order to 'get the bureaucratic fever out of its vein', yet recognised the dangers in having a 'corps of civil servants prepared by a special schooling and drilled, after appointment, into a perfected organisation, with appropriate hierarchy and characteristic discipline' (Wilson 1887: 202, 210, 217–19). Would such officials not become a 'government within government', an 'offensive class' prone to 'domineering, illiberal officialism'? (Wilson 1887: 216, 221).[3] Wilson suggested a number of ways to counter such dangers, the principal one being, most famously, the separation of the political from the administrative sphere. Democratic leaders would set the tasks for a non-partisan administration that would be an efficient instrument 'removed from the hurry and strife of politics'.

This politics–administration distinction was also observed by continental administrators deeply involved in setting policy directions for society, who wished to pursue 'rational-scientific' policy untroubled by the fractious politicking of civil society. By contrast, the validation of the distinction in the Anglophone world, where civil society dominated the state rather than vice versa, in part reflected a determination to adopt the bureaucratic model without diluting the authority of democratically elected leaders. Nevertheless, the desire to shield 'rational' administration from the biasing or corrupting effects of selfish politics was also evident in Anglo-American reforms. The famous 'Northcote-Trevelyan Report' of 1854 envisaged a British civil service staffed by permanent officials of generalist education who would be non-partisan and politically neutral, ensuring a professional administration insulated from corrupting political influences (Northcote and Trevelyan 1954).[4] In the United States, President Andrew Jackson (1829–1837) had, on the contrary, tried to democratise official posts and make participation in government more accessible to the common man (Wilentz 2005: 315), but his good intentions were submerged by a 'spoils system' in which appointments were made on the basis of political loyalty rather than competence (Hoogenboom 1959). The Pendleton Act of 1883 tried to strike a balance between the professional elitism of Northcote-Trevelyan and Jackson's democratically inclusive spirit (van Riper 1997), but Wilson believed this did not go far enough towards full professionalisation.

Wilson's wish would be more or less realised as civil services of Anglophone nations everywhere became increasingly bureaucratised. The typical modern civil service in advanced democracies featured the familiar hierarchy of interlocking offices governed by prescriptive rules and authoritative command, safeguarded by strict documentation, staffed by career bureaucrats possessed of technical expertise, and undergirded by an ethos of non-partisan public service. The democratic version of the politics–administration distinction was emphasised, with the political sphere of elected leaders clearly distinguished from an administration staffed by 'neutral' bureaucrats, thus apparently solving the issue in democracy's favour while promising efficient government.

The problem with this 'neutralisation' of the service was that the politics–administration distinction could not be realistically maintained (Waldo 1948), at least not if 'distinction' were taken to mean 'dichotomy'. 'Dichotomy' implied a strict separation in which administrators had no voice in policy matters, and politicians no hand in administration.

But as James Svara argued, the dichotomy idea was a mythical artefact of a 1958 article by Wallace Sayre that reinterpreted the history of the politics–administration distinction in absolutist terms, derailing discussions about the proper interaction of politics and administration, and promoting a model that was 'patently untenable' (Svara 2001: 178). The real distinction to be made, as Patrick Overeem (2005) pointed out, was not one between administration and politics per se, but between 'partisan politics' and 'policy politics'—one might say between *interested* and *disinterested* politics. Public administration was to be shielded from malign partisan, sectoral, or personal interests while professionally cooperating with elected leaders in creating policy. Neutrality did not imply passive instrumentality, as is so often assumed.[5]

This view recalled the stated intention of 'The Northcote-Trevelyan Report', which was to create 'an efficient body of permanent officers, occupying a position duly subordinate to that of Ministers . . . yet possessing sufficient independence, character, ability, and experience to be able to advise, assist, and, to some extent, influence, those who are from time to time set over them' (Northcote and Trevelyan 1954: 3). Svara contended indeed that a return to Wilson and other founders provided a better theoretical basis for contemporary public service under a principle of 'complementarity'.

> Complementarity entails separate parts, but parts that come together in a mutually supportive way . . . Complementarity stresses interdependence along with distinct roles; compliance along with independence; respect for political control along with a commitment to shape and implement policy in ways that promote the public interest; deference to elected incumbents along with adherence to the law and support for fair electoral competition; and appreciation of politics along with support for professional standards. (Svara 2001: 177)[6]

Conjoining of the 'separate parts' demands mutual respect for the legitimate but distinct demands of democratic politics and service-oriented professional administration, even if 'deference' must in the end require that the administration bow to the democracy.

Many senior public servants would say, of course, that this is exactly how they have always understood their role, which raises the question of why democratic leaders have so often suspected them of larger ambitions. The central fear of democratic leaders is that insulating expert administrators from partisan influence, even if it ensures professionalism, also vouchsafes them an independence that enables them to flout, subtly or overtly, the leader's democratic authority. Wilson was quite aware of this danger but noted that all sovereigns, and the people, were suspicious of their servants, a problem that could not be overcome by dividing powers: 'If it be divided, dealt out in shares to many, it is obscured; and if obscured, it is made irresponsible'. On the contrary, Wilson advocated trust, with larger powers and unhampered discretion invested in the heads of the service where it may be 'easily watched and brought to book' (Wilson 1887: 214).

Such a view of action and discretion obviously implied, even if it was never clearly stated, genuine leadership in the civil service. The *type* of leadership required could also be seen in the responsibilities of civil servants who were supposed to act with frankness, vigour and impartiality while remaining sensitive to their subordination to elected superiors within a democratic system. As administrations everywhere were steadily bureaucratised along continental lines, installing rule-governed systems of strict command and control, such leadership naturally accumulated, as Wilson foresaw, at the top.

DEMOCRATIC LEADERS TAKE ON THE BUREAUCRATS

In Westminster-style governments, the civil service mandarins are permanent career bureaucrats strategically located at the critical boundary between political and administrative spheres, able to influence the shape and direction of almost all public policy. Below them are layers of administrators, theoretically obedient to the will of the mandarins; above them were political masters who had to be discreetly instructed, advised, guided but finally (and again, theoretically) obeyed. The mandarins' strength and shield, from a democratic perspective, was that their important leadership role was conducted under a screen of public invisibility, safeguarded in the Westminster system by the doctrine of ministerial responsibility (under which ministers accepted public praise or blame for all the actions of their departments).

In the United States, senior bureaucrats are much less shielded from democratic pressures than their Westminster counterparts. Their leadership is perennially challenged by the continuing practice of rotation, which blatantly 'politicises' the service and creates an enduring division between political appointees and members of what became known as 'the permanent government'.[7] Barry Karl notes that, 'the embedding of the conflict between mass democracy and elite professionalism in the American political structure is what . . . shapes the American meaning of bureaucracy and American attitudes toward it' (Karl 1987: 27). In a liberal political culture that already harbours deep suspicions of government as such, 'bureaucrat bashing' by elected leaders became a favourite means of deflecting blame for political failures, producing a characteristically American hostility towards bureaucracy and professional bureaucrats. The latter, for their part, always felt themselves unfairly maligned and derided, but nevertheless clung to a vision of public-service leadership that, when exposed, was in permanent tension with the popular sovereignty principle embodied in democratic leadership.

Democratic leaders are never without resources for asserting themselves against the bureaucrats, for they possess the authority to reorder radically the shape of bureaucracy and to alter the rules and conditions within which it operates. Sooner or later, bold leaders were bound to cash in this advantage and try to assert firmer control. In the United States, such attempts had been under way since Franklin Roosevelt argued that full democratisation required tying the presidency to an 'enlightened administration' capable of meeting them (Milkis 1993; Cook 1996).

Most postwar studies, however, emphasised the limits of presidential influence over the bureaucracy (Cronin 1980; Hooton 1997; Cronin and Genovese 2004).[8] Career officials, it seemed, had numerous ways of resisting presidents and their appointees, and worked in environments where many competitive pressures came to bear besides those of the executive. Moreover, they often harboured personal goals that were in conflict with those of the presidency. Worse, according to Theodore Lowi (1979), policy was now effectively determined by 'iron triangles' of special-interest lobbyists, appointed bureaucratic officials, and narrowly self-interested congressional sub-committees. The bureaucracy was no longer a faithful servant of elected democratic leaders, but exercised its own leadership as an independent player in a closeted game that essentially suborned the larger public interest.

By the late 1970s, bureaucracy had become a byword for obstinate stupidity and incompetence. The proliferation of rules mindlessly applied, and of documented procedures blindly followed, produced the nightmare of endless 'red tape'. The entrenchment of seniority systems (the cardinal sin for Northcote and Trevelyan, who had emphasised selection and promotion based on proven merit) ensured that bureaucracies turned into sclerotic, inefficient and process-obsessed organisations.[9] Democratic leaders around the world recognised the need to regain political control of administrations that had allegedly become laws unto themselves, to ensure more reliable and more efficient outcomes. They drew on these long-standing complaints against bureaucracies to mount an assault.

A set of reforms defining the so-called 'new public management' became familiar in liberal democracies everywhere; their aim was to create a more flexible and efficient 'entrepreneurial' organisation capable of delivering enhanced services at lower unit cost (Pollitt 2003: 27–8). The old sites of public leadership in the higher reaches of the service were dismantled by the removal of tenure and the introduction of fixed-term, performance-based contracts. The independence of senior public servants was purposely destroyed, and their policy role altered to one mostly of management, their task now being to make the bureaucracy more consistently obedient to the will of elected ministers. The general hope was that responsiveness to public demands could be improved and more effective outcomes gained for tax monies spent if a new kind of public servant could be created. This would be someone with qualities of flexibility, innovation, entrepreneurialism, capacity for independent and discretionary judgement, ethical competence, policy awareness, sensitivity to political factors and managerial competence. Policy roles, meanwhile, were increasingly passed into the hands of non-administrative advisers whose personal loyalty was to the democratically elected leader who had hired them.

The genuine appeal of these reforms was that they aimed to replace a blind, blundering bureaucratic machine with an intelligent and adaptive organisation more serviceable to overstretched governments. The anticipated rationality of the old bureaucracy had proved (at least to the satisfaction of the reformers) highly irrational, and a different, less mechanistic conception of reason was now advanced. Conditions would be created in which responsible individuals could act with discretionary intelligence to the demands encountered in their work, thereby abandoning the familiar safety of mechanical rule-following. What was demanded, in effect, was the exercise throughout the entire service of the kind of political prudence formerly expected only of senior officials.[10] Public servants at lower levels were now asked to understand policy and to take some responsibility for it—analysing, costing, formulating, advising, implementing and evaluating. Initiative was expected, and initiative implied leadership, which was now explicitly demanded of nearly every public servant. Even as leadership was intentionally weakened at the top, efforts were made to disperse it throughout the whole service. Leadership consultants were employed, leadership training courses ordered, leadership techniques explored, and leadership retreats undertaken.

Laudable as this ambition seemed, the effect was also to disperse the dilemma of democratic leadership versus bureaucratic independence throughout the bureaucracy. The problem of democratic legitimacy would now arise, at least potentially, every time a relatively junior public servant exercised his or her discretion. Democratic leaders were aware that distributing discretionary freedom raised the problem of maintaining control from above, a control that could not be forfeited without grave political risk. Blame for any bureaucratic initiative that created public opposition or scandal would inevitably be sheeted back to the responsible elected representative.[11] It was hoped that marketisation, or quasi-marketisation, of public services would introduce the automatic discipline and allocative efficiency believed to characterise the private sphere—the market would, in other words, substitute, to some extent, for old-fashioned rule-ordered control. But such rationality as genuine markets may induce in individual entrepreneurs (a matter of some doubt after the Global Financial Crisis) is narrowly calculating and instrumentally geared to profit. Such discipline did not even begin to address, let alone exhaust, many of the demands placed on the reasoning powers of public servants—for example, of equity, justice, protection, defence of rights, and environmental preservation.

The type of leadership demanded was no longer purely bureaucratic. Like that of the senior officials of old, it had become inherently political, and was thus exposed to all the perils and uncertainties of the democratic realm. Public policy is, by its very nature, political, and therefore subject to all the vagaries, pressures and perplexities of democratic politics. Modern bureaucratic reforms, having effectively neutered the political power of senior managers, tended to distribute their political responsibilities throughout the whole bureaucratic organisation, but the management of policy demands skills that can be developed only through long experience. Some of this experience is inevitably painful, and the pain is not simply that of a penalty imposed for breach of protocol or neglect of proper procedure. It is pain of an altogether different quality, more profound for touching on political matters and having political consequences that may reverberate up through the bureaucratic apparatus into the democratic leader's office. The demand that public servants be 'apolitical' in their professional lives became nonsensical under these new conditions. They could no longer ignore politics once significant policy responsibility had been devolved into their hands. To properly fulfil their new role they had to inhabit the mental universe of their democratic political masters, while remaining their subordinate servants, cultivating acute political sensitivities, and prudentially calculating the political dimensions of all their plans and actions.

ACHIEVING A BALANCE

The dual needs of democratic leaders to control the bureaucracy (rather than be controlled by it) and to ensure improved public outcomes were separately perfectly comprehensible. But it was not perhaps foreseen that the combination of these, if determinedly pursued, would result in a thoroughly politicised bureaucracy. Private-sector rhetoric of enterprise, risk-taking and bold vision was undoubtedly very dangerous in this regard, for it encouraged just the sort of independent action that might, at any instance, threaten to usurp the popular will and arouse public ire. Public servants are not private agents and cannot behave as if they are.

Yet public administrations, like all organisations, need good leadership if they are to perform adequately. To achieve this requires a persuasive model of the form of leadership appropriate in the public sector, perhaps something akin to Frederickson and Matkin's (2007) unheroic image of the public-sector leader as careful 'gardener'. Effective leadership in the public sector certainly requires an imbued ethic of professional public service that combines integrity and technical competency—this is the bedrock of legitimacy upon which any decent civil service must build. But it also demands more; it requires a particular sensitivity to the constraints imposed by a democratic political environment and an ability to act prudently within it. It is confusing, for example, for professional civil servants to be told that they are legally required to be 'apolitical', but are then required to perform efficiently in a role that demands the most acutely political appreciation of the democratic-bureaucratic nexus.

This is to recall Overeen's prescriptive advice to observe a distinction between partisan politics (to be avoided by public servants) and policy politics (which cannot be avoided). In combination with Svara's idea of complementarity of effort between political masters and public servants, this may seem to solve the bureaucratic-democratic dilemma. We must, however, enter a realistic cautionary note here. The problem of bureaucratic versus democratic authority cannot be definitively solved, but must, by the nature of things, be perennially managed.

It is true that all policy is inherently political, for policies set the political values and directions for a whole society. It is therefore impossible for public servants to be seriously involved in policy, as they must be, without being involved in politics. Yet it is also impossible that they be altogether shielded from partisan politics, for the very 'neutrality' that is demanded of them requires that they be partisan according to the ideological stripe of the government of the day—or, if they cannot, to resign. This is what it means to accept the supremacy of the democratic element among the competing bases of legitimacy—legal, bureaucratic-technocratic and political. And yet the very dependency of liberal-democratic regimes on strongly functioning bureaucracies inevitably qualifies the strength and meaning of that supremacy. The judicial sphere, for its part, is protected by the doctrine of the separation of powers as the bureaucracy is not, but the bureaucracy nevertheless finds moral legitimacy in a conception of public service (implying some broad understanding of the public good) that is almost never simply reducible to, or identical with, the ideological and policy predilections of the elected government. Given the interdependencies involved, it is inevitable that policy contests occur, not just between political parties, but within administrations and between them and their professional administrative machines. The trumping power of democratic legitimacy is genuine, but in practice it will seldom be straightforwardly deployed or inevitably victorious.

One may accept that it is neither possible nor desirable to return to the old-style bureaucracy, but the necessary dependence of elected leaders on the good performance of the administrative apparatus indicates the employment of experts with a strong professional ethos, which will inevitably be a public-service ethos. Yet the very existence of such a strong-minded class implies the ever-present possibility of resistance to leadership directives, based on differences from what the public interest requires, as much as on accommodation and compliance. The democratic leader, as the people's elected representative, may seem to have greater legitimacy and therefore authority over the bureaucracy, but the ethic of public service represents a claim that the people's bureaucracy can always deploy to counter it. The relationship between leader and administration will always be a complicated and somewhat contested one, but one that works best when built on relations of trust, mutual respect, and a willingness to negotiate differences.

The permanent challenge that bureaucracy presents to democratic leaders can be managed more or less well. It is important to note that Svara's complementarity requires a certain mutuality of understanding between democratic and bureaucratic leaders, and failures can occur on either side. Well-meaning administrators deeply imbued with an ethos of public service will achieve little without the willing cooperation of the elected democratic leadership, and ideologically committed democratic leaders will likewise not achieve much without the willing cooperation of an amenable bureaucracy.

CONCLUDING REMARKS

Prudent public managers are those who are capable of acting and leading effectively without endangering democratic legitimacy. But their elected political masters must reciprocate, or effective governance becomes impossible. Democratic leaders who fail to appreciate the ethos of public service risk embracing the kind of failures that may be fatal to their political fortunes. There is, however, no possible formula or prioritisation of principles that can guarantee an optimum balance. This is a matter of historical contingency regarding the people and forces involved. The source of the problem lies in the partly competing, partly interdependent bases of legitimacy within liberal democratic regimes that give rise to the need for complementarity without ever being able to guarantee its accomplishment.

We started by reflecting on Pat's sage counsel on the challenges faced by scholars in the academy. We conclude these thoughts with a tribute to Pat Weller, not just for the example of his scholarship, but just as importantly for the leadership he has shown over many years within our school and in the various centres he has led. We are both personally indebted to him and to his capacity to foster and maintain a scholarly community characterised by serious rigour, collegiality, mutual recognition and, of course, a great deal of fun. We thank him sincerely, and thank the editors of this volume for the opportunity to pay him proper respect.

NOTES

1. For a detailed account of the problem of democratic leadership and more specifically, its implication for bureaucracy see Kane and Patapan (2012).
2. A remarkable feature of the *Rechtsstaat* tradition has been its capacity to weather extreme political crises and vast socio-economic changes over centuries, not to mention the waves of managerialist reform of recent years. Rhodes and Weller note with regard to French administration that, 'It is scarcely surprising that the nostrums of the private sector recycled by the new public management failed to strike a responsive chord. The powerful officials of a strong state were unmoved and the moving finger of the new public management writ and then moved on with nary a mark to show for its pains' (Rhodes and Weller 2001: 248).
3. Wilson added: 'We can borrow the science of administration with safety and profit if only we read all fundamental differences of conditions into its essential tenets. We have only to filter it through our constitutions, only to put it over a slow fire of criticism and distil away its foreign gases' (Wilson 1887: 219).
4. The 'generalist' education (usually in the classics) of the British was in marked contrast to the specialist education provided in the French *Grandes Ecoles*, a network of elite technical and administrative schools reformed and expanded by Napoleon (Silberman 1993: 114–16). It was also in contrast to the Benthamite school, which requires specialist systems of administration, staffed by experts, who would deal with the problems of an industrialising and urbanising society (Greenaway 2004: 6).
5. Brian J. Cook (1996) argues that two conceptions of public administration have coexisted in American politics from the beginning, the 'instrumental' and the 'constitutive', though the instrumental has always dominated, unfortunately in Cook's view. In the constitutive vision, bureaucracy helps shape public policy and thus the character of the political community, a responsibility that requires classical 'practical wisdom' rather than technical expertise.
6. The observations of a Wisconsin state senator, from an active politician's perspective, lend practical support to Svara's principle. Mordecai Lee (2001) argued that, in his experience, elected officials interacted with administrators on the basis of political common sense rather than according to any ruling norm defining their relationship (though political decision-making implicitly cast administrators in a subordinate role).
7. The perennial nature of their relationship can be judged from the title of Maranto (2005): *Beyond a Government of Strangers: How career executives and political appointees can turn conflict into cooperation*.
8. Most such studies followed Richard Neustadt's classic (1960) report on the presidency, which argued that presidents had the power to persuade more than to command.
9. Some critics claimed that bureaucracy also worked to preserve entrenched bureaucratic interests rather than serve the public interest. Niskanen (1973), for example, argued that bureaucrats had a rational interest in increasing the size of their budgets independently of public need or demand.

10 For the importance of the idea of prudence in public service see: Formaini (1990); Cooper (1991, 2001); Hart (1984); Cook (1996); Kane and Patapan (2006).
11 It was a telling sign of the times that, in Westminster systems, the ancient rule of ministerial responsibility was in fact relaxed or in some instances repudiated under the new regime. Public servants were sometimes publicly 'unmasked' when it suited ministers to shift blame for some scandal away from themselves. Whatever the short-term expediency of such a course, it hardly seemed to indicate an adequate general solution to the problem of democratic accountability that the new public management had created.

REFERENCES

Bertelli, A.M. & Lynn Jr, L.E., 2006, *Madison's Managers: Public administration and the Constitution*, Baltimore: Johns Hopkins University Press

Caplan, J., 1988, *Government without Administration: State and civil society in Weimar and Nazi Germany*, Oxford: Clarendon Press

Cook, B.J., 1996, *Bureaucracy and Self-Government: Reconsidering the role of public administration in American government*, Baltimore: Johns Hopkins University Press

Cooper, T.L., 1991, *An Ethic of Citizenship for Public Administration*, Englewood Cliffs, New Jersey: Prentice-Hall

—— (ed.), 2001, *Handbook of Administrative Ethics*, 2nd edn, New York: Marcel Dekker

Cronin, T.E., 1980, *The State of the Presidency*, Boston: Little, Brown & Co.

Cronin, T.E. & Genovese, M.A., 2004, *The Paradoxes of the American Presidency*, 2nd edn, New York: Oxford University Press

Dahl, R.A., 1985, *A Preface to Economic Democracy*, Polity Press, Cambridge

Doig, J. & Hargrove, E.C. (eds), 1987, *Leadership and Innovation: A biographical perspective on entrepreneurs in government*, Baltimore: Johns Hopkins University Press

Elgie, R., 2001, 'France: "Dual structure, shared dilemma"', in R.A.W. Rhodes & P. Weller (eds), *The Changing World of Top Officials: Mandarins or valets?*, Buckingham: Open University Press, pp. 11–40

Elgie, R. & Griggs, S., 2000, *French Politics: Debates and controversies*, London: Routledge

Formaini, R., 1990, *The Myth of Scientific Public Policy*, New Brunswick, USA: Transaction Publishers and the Social Philosophy and Policy Center

Frederickson, H.G. & Matkin, D.S.T., 2007, 'Public Leadership as Gardening', in R.S. More, T.F. Buss & C.M. Kinghorn (eds), *Transforming Leadership for the 21st Century*, Armonk, NY: M.E. Sharpe, pp. 34–45

Greenaway, J., 2004, 'Celebrating Northcote/Trevelyan: Dispelling the myths', *Public Policy and Administration*, vol. 19, no. 1, pp. 1–14

Hart, David K., 1984, 'The Virtuous Citizen, the Honourable Bureaucrat, and Public Administration', *Public Administration Review*, vol. 44 (Special Issue), pp. 111–20

Henderson, Keith M., 2004, 'Characterising American Public Administration: The concept of administrative culture', *The International Journal of Public Sector Management*, vol. 17, no. 3, pp. 234–50

Heper, M., 1985, 'The State and Public Bureaucracies: A comparative and historical perspective', *Comparative Studies in Society and History*, vol. 27, no. 1, pp. 86–110

Hoogenboom, A., 1959, 'The Pendleton Act and the Civil Service', *The American Historical Review*, vol. 64, no. 2

Hooton, Cornell G., 1997, *Executive Governance: Presidential administrations and policy change in the federal bureaucracy*, Armonk, NY: M.E. Sharpe

Kane, J. & Patapan, H., 2006, 'In Search of Prudence: The hidden problem of managerial reform', *Public Administration Review*, vol. 66, pp. 711–24

—— 2012, *The Democratic Leader: How democracy defines, empowers and limits its leaders*, Oxford: Oxford University Press

Karl, B.D., 1987, 'The American Bureaucrat: A history of sheep in wolves' clothing', *Public Administration Review*, vol. 47, no. 1, pp. 26–34

Kickert, W.J.M., 2005, 'Distinctiveness in the Study of Public Management in Europe', *Public Management Review*, vol. 7, no. 4, pp. 537–83

Krigier, Martin, 2012, *Philip Selznick: Ideals in the world*, Stanford; Stanford University Press

Lee, Mordecai, 2001, 'Looking at the Politics–Administration Dichotomy from the Other Direction: Participant observation by a State Senator,' *International Journal of Public Administration*, vol. 24, pp. 363–84

Leonnig, C.D., 2008. Widespread Complaints about a Rudderless Government, *Washington Post*, 6 November, <www.washingtonpost.com/wp-dyn/content/article/2008/11/06/AR2008110602572.html>, viewed 7 November 2010

Lewis, E., 1980, *Public Entrepreneurship: Toward a theory of bureaucratic power*, Bloomington: Indiana University Press

Lowi, T., 1979, *The End of Liberalism: The second republic of the United States*, New York: W.W. Norton & Company

Maranto, R., 2005, *Beyond a Government of Strangers: How career executives and political appointees can turn conflict into cooperation*, Lanham, MD: Lexington Books

Meier, K.J. & O'Toole, L.J., 2006, *Bureaucracy in a Democratic State: A governance perspective*, Baltimore: Johns Hopkins University Press

Milkis, S.M., 1993, *The President and the Parties: The transformation of the American party system since the new deal*, New York: Oxford University Press

Moore, M.H., 1995, *Creating Public Value: Strategic management in government*, Cambridge, MA: Harvard University Press

Neustadt, R., 1960, *Presidential Power and the Modern Presidents: The politics of leadership*, New York: Macmillan

Niskanen, W.A., 1973, *Bureaucracy: Servant or master?*, Chicago: Aldine-Atherton

Northcote, S.H. & Trevelyan, C.E., 1954 [first published 1853], 'The Northcote-Trevelyan Report', *Public Administration*, vol. 32, no. 1, pp. 1–16

Overeem, P., 2005, 'The Value of the Dichotomy: Politics, administration, and the political neutrality of administrators', *Administrative Theory & Praxis*, vol. 27, no. 2, pp. 311–29

Peele, G., 2004, *Governing the UK: British politics in the 21st century*, Oxford: Blackwell

Peters, B.G., 1987, *The Politics of Bureaucracy*, New York: Longman
Pollitt, C., 2003, *The Essential Public Manager*, Maidenhead: Open University Press
Rhodes, R.A.W. & Weller, P. (eds), 2001, *The Changing World of Top Officials: Mandarins or valets?*, Buckingham: Open University Press
Rousseau, J-J., 1978 [first published 1762], *On the Social Contract with Geneva Manuscript and Discourse on Political Economy*, ed. and trans. R. Masters & J. Masters, New York: St Martin's Press
Ruscio, K.P., 2004, *The Leadership Dilemma in Modern Democracy*, Cheltenham, England: Edward Elgar
Selznick, P., 1984a [1949], *TVA and the Grass Roots: A study of politics and organization*, Berkeley: University of California Press
—— 1984b [1957], *Leadership in Administration: A sociological interpretation*, Berkeley: University of California Press
Silberman, B., 1993, *Cages of Reason: The rise of the rational state in France, Japan, the United States and Great Britain*, Chicago: The University of Chicago Press
—— 2001, 'The Myth of Dichotomy: Complementarity of politics and administration in the past and future of public administration', *Public Adminstration Review*, vol. 61, no. 2, pp. 176–83
Svara, James H., 2001, 'The Myth of Dichotomy: Complementarity of politics and administration in the past and future of public adminstration', *Public Administration Review*, vol. 61, no. 2, pp. 176–83
't Hart, P. & Wille, A., 2006, 'Politicians and Bureaucrats in the Netherlands: A delicate relationship', *Public Administration*, vol. 84, no. 1, pp. 121–46
Terry, Larry D., 2002 [1995], *Leadership in Public Bureaucracies: The administrator as conservator*, 2nd edn, Thousand Oaks, CA: Sage
van Riper, P., 1997, 'The Pendleton Act of 1883 and the Professionalism of the US Public Service', in A. Farazmand (ed.), *Modern Systems of Government: Exploring the role of bureaucrats and politicians*, Thousand Oaks, California: Sage, pp. 196–211
Waldo, D., 1948, *The Administrative State: A study of the political theory of American public administration*, New York: Ronald Press
Wilentz, S., 2005, *The Rise of American Democracy: Jefferson to Lincoln*, New York: W.W. Norton & Co
Wilson, W., 1887, 'The Study of Administration', *Political Science Quarterly*, vol. 2, no. 2, pp. 197–222

12

WESTMINSTER FUTURES: AUSTRALIA, CANADA, NEW ZEALAND AND THE UNITED KINGDOM IN COMPARATIVE PERSPECTIVE

Robert J. Jackson

Professor Patrick Weller's contributions to comparative government are widely known, especially his work on the public service and prime ministers of Australia, Canada, New Zealand and the United Kingdom. Less well known, perhaps, are his outstanding contributions to general studies of the Westminster form of government. In this chapter I focus on this aspect of Dr Weller's work, discussing the past, the present, and future of Westminster systems, with emphasis on both the 'internal' challenges in Australia, Canada, New Zealand, and the United Kingdom, and the 'external', global variables that are likely to affect all countries, including those that follow the Westminster system of governance. This essay about Westminster-style government and its future comes at a unique time of transition in the nature and role of government everywhere.

THE ESTABLISHMENT OF WESTMINSTER

Led by Weller, experts have explored the duelling vocabularies that define the myths about Westminster government. They have done an excellent job of dissecting and explaining the topic. They have grappled with the role of tradition, showing the timeless impact of Westminster in different cultural and historical settings. They have confronted the issue of how societies and governments adapt to the future without losing their past. Their analysis in *Comparing Westminster* explores how governmental elites in Australia, Britain, Canada, New Zealand, and South Africa interpret and adapt their Westminster systems (Rhodes, Wanna and Weller 2009). The volume examines in detail the interrelated features of Westminster systems and identifies five meanings of—or narratives about—them. First, they examine 'Westminster as heritage'—elite actors' shared governmental narratives understood as both precedent and nostalgia. Second, they describe 'Westminster as a political tool'—the expedient cloak worn by governments and politicians to defend themselves and criticise their opponents. Third, they analyse 'Westminster as a legitimising tradition'—providing context for elite actions and serving as a justifiable point of reference for navigating an uncertain world. Fourth, they summarise 'Westminster as an institutional category'—a useful descriptor of a loose family of governments with shared origins and characteristics. Fifth, they enquire if 'Westminster is an effective political system'—asking whether it is a more effective and efficient political system than consensual parliamentary government.

In its early stages, the Westminster system was simply regarded as a form of government modelled after the United Kingdom. The term came from the Palace of Westminster. When the system stabilised in the UK, it was exported to Commonwealth states after they received responsible government, beginning in the mid-nineteenth century with the first of the Canadian provinces and the former Australian colonies, and eventually continuing as other British colonies became independent at the end of the nineteenth and beginning of the twentieth centuries. Everywhere they were *sui generis*, one-off situations that could only be understood as individual cases, or by cross-state comparison of their particular institutions of government. In most of these countries the new Westminster systems were embedded in a set of written constitutions and codified federal institutions.

In theory, and for some years in practice, the Westminster parliamentary system provided a fairly clear-cut system of governance and accountability. A party or coalition of parties formed a government after an election, and was in a position to put much of its program in place. While a minority party (or parties) might aggressively attack the government, it could not permanently delay its program or defeat it. When the next election occurred, the public knew which party to hold accountable for the programs, and could reward or punish them at the ballot box.

The practice of Westminster government outside the UK reached its zenith around the turn of the twentieth century when Australia, Canada, and New Zealand became truly independent countries. Deeply held myths about the UK governing style penetrated these societies and served to justify a system of government imbued with the trappings of a monarchical form of government.

AFTER EMPIRE AND THE WANING OF WESTMINSTER

The waning of Westminster did not begin until after World War I, when the empire began to disintegrate. World War II amplified the effect—ending with the collapse of the colonial system around the world. After those two wars some countries withdrew from the British Empire while others became independent. Officially, the new organisation became the British Commonwealth of Nations in 1931, and in 1949 it was reduced to the Commonwealth of Nations with no mention whatsoever of Britain in the title. Around two billion people and 54 states continue to be members of the new Commonwealth, almost three dozen of which use variations of the Westminster system. Unlike the United Kingdom, almost all of them codified their constitutions in a written form—even if they continued to be influenced to a great extent by the conventions, practices, and precedents of the Parliament of the United Kingdom.[1] There were both strengths and weaknesses in these hybrid forms of government, but Britain was no longer the centrepiece of an empire. Belief in the superiority of the British government declined and the values associated with its superiority slowly withered. The idea of state equality, and to a lesser extent human equality, gained a solid footing throughout the countries once governed by the Crown and British government. Today, the strength of conviction once so prominent in the British Commonwealth is no longer present. The magnetic attraction in things British has been going, going, and perhaps is even gone.

Even Westminster language has become quaint—outside parliamentary premises few are familiar with such terms as 'the usual channels', 'whips', 'nodding through', 'pairing', and 'hung parliament'. At the academic level, scholars have even become sceptical about how much governments actually govern, hemmed in as they are by larger economic and global factors. The idealised Westminster model has been found to be based on certain conditions and assumptions not currently present. The characteristics of Westminster have become weak or tenuous even in the UK. Moreover, and possibly more importantly, the UK and some Commonwealth countries have become accustomed to living without majority governments. The changing nature of demographics, electorates, electoral systems, party structures, and culture has led to more divisions and even more minority governments throughout the Commonwealth. There has been a rise in the number and significance of 'veto actors' in every country (on veto actors see Jackson 1995, Tsebelis 2002).

Let us, therefore, examine the situation directly with reference to four countries: first, from *within* and then from *outside*. Of course, it is difficult to generalise about their futures. I can provide only limited guidance regarding what will happen the next time these governments confront stalemates or look to other countries for advice on how to govern themselves.

CHALLENGES TO WESTMINSTER FROM WITHIN

Primary domestic conditions for Westminster systems and its contemporary challenges include an independent sovereign country; majority government; centralised government; cabinet government; collective and individual responsibility; and electoral systems, fixed election dates and the party system.

An independent sovereign country

Few states today are truly independent, if they ever were. The United Kingdom's membership in the European Union (EU), the European Convention of Human Rights, and the European Court reduces its independence to a large extent in several fields. Some directives of the EU Commission and the Council of Ministers can become community law without ratification by the Parliaments of member states. The EC institutions are extremely complex and deserve more space than this chapter allows, but clearly the future of the UK's relationship and membership in the EU is hotly debated in the country, and however it turns out will have a significant impact on Westminster institutions. All federal systems such as those in Australia and Canada also agree to some limitations on central state authority. Novel and modern trade arrangements such as the North American Free Trade Agreement (NAFTA) go so far as to provide bi-national panels that can make binding decisions on Canada, the USA and Mexico—even perhaps against the wishes of their governments. Only New Zealand, perhaps, breaks this pattern of reliance on federal or federal-like institutions.

Majority government

At one time, adherence to this principle was clear and unequivocal. A prime minster would have the support of a majority in the appropriate house of parliament, or at least be able to ensure that there was no opposing absolute majority in the responsible institution. In this majority government model, no separation of executive and legislative bodies existed. Authority was fused in the cabinet which, along with the prime minister, was answerable to Parliament. Such single-party majority government prevailed for much of the last two centuries, but it is becoming apparent that majority governments no longer dominate, and coalition, minority and hybrid governments are becoming much more the norm than the exception.

United Kingdom

According to the most recent UK Cabinet Manual,[2] a UK minority Parliament takes one of three forms—a single-party minority government, a formal inter-party agreement or a formal coalition government (United Kingdom Cabinet Office 2011: 15). After the 2010 general election, the Conservatives and Liberal Democrats under the leadership of David Cameron and Nick Clegg chose a formal coalition government. Despite internal party differences over some major policies, the government is committed to 'hanging together' until the next election. But it is in a precarious and perhaps losing position. Despite agreement on fundamental economic principles, the coalition is based on a hodgepodge of mixed philosophies and policy commitments. The Conservatives maintain their ideals of less governmental interference in society, but the Liberal Democrats, although decidedly for human rights, want greater state intrusion and control in specific policy fields such as lifestyle issues of smoking, drinking, and the right to read magazines with air-brushed photos of nude models. At the 2010 general election, Clegg's popularity was plus 72 per cent; by mid-2013 it had dropped to minus 59 per cent.

The attacks on David Cameron are savage. His time spent promoting the 'Big Society' (whatever that is!) has been wasted, as most people claim not to understand it. He is in damage control over preventing a tax allowance for married couples, stopping grammar schools from being set up, back-tracking on abolishing an inheritance tax, and promising not to re-organise the National Health system but then going ahead with reforms. Division continues over the electoral system and there is full-scale Conservative revolt over legislation to give voters the power to sack their own members of parliament (MPs) in a recall.

The most difficult issue for the coalition concerns Europe. On this topic, the prime minister cannot control his backbenchers. In the summer of 2013, 114 voted against him in a ballot for an immediate referendum on the EU, thereby opposing the coalition and Cameron's legislative program of a referendum *after* the next election. Although defeated 277 to 130, the vote on the amendment to the Queen's Speech was the largest backbench revolt Cameron had faced since the 2010 election. Of course, party officials downplayed the issue as being a free vote and said it was within party policy to have a referendum anyway.

The coalition has never experienced smooth sailing, and recently there has been a rise in fringe parties. There is a significant possibility that no party will win a majority government in the next election. Clegg has not made it easy for the coalition. As he put it, 'the absolute worst thing to do would be to give the keys to Number 10 to a single party government—Labour or Conservative' (*Economist* 2013).

The results of the April 2013 local elections gave sceptics of the Cameron–Clegg coalition a new weapon. The United Kingdom Independence Party (UKIP) has been experiencing an increase in popularity. Led by Nigel Farage, the UKIP (which Cameron initially disparaged as made up of 'fruit-cakes, loonies, and closet racists') obtained more than 23 per cent of the vote. The party, which is indeed anti-intellectual and increasingly racist, is unlikely to win any or many seats in a general election, but it could take as much as 6 or 7 per cent of the Tory vote, which could destroy the Conservative hold on government. Fear of this possibility is partially why MPs from marginal seats oppose coalition policy on Europe as well as other conservative issues that Farage supporters propose. The prime minister and other Tory grandees have stopped calling UKIP rude names, and seem prepared to treat it with respect in order to head off losses in next year's European election, and in the following UK general election.

The UKIP reflects a broader attack on established parties throughout the democratic world. The Tea Party in the US is the most obvious example, but many others exist. Many people resent the impact of forces such as globalisation that are outside their control. In the UK, these factors include immigration and the power of Brussels. Anti-politics and splinter parties are on the rise and will make it difficult for many parties to win majorities. Of course, the closer marginal parties get to power the more they will tend to act like regular parties.

Australia
Coalition governments are common in Australia. The Liberal/National parties have governed for much of this century. However, the overall political structure is regarded as a two-party system because of the nature of the Labor/anti-Labor contest. The alternative-vote electoral system allows Liberal and National parties to contest disputed seats without losing them to Labor, and both parties are more opposed to Labor than each other. Such coalitions may sometimes require elaborate and difficult negotiations to achieve understandings between their members, but as long as they keep Labor out of government both parties tend to be satisfied with coalition arrangements.

The House of Representatives is dissolved and elections are called by the Governor-General on the advice of the PM. In Labor, power is paramount. When Prime Minister Kevin Rudd realised that he did not have the numbers to confront Julia Gillard in a vote in June 2010, he withdrew as party leader and prime minister without a formal contest. Gillard was then sworn in as Australia's 27th prime minister. But in the ensuing election on 21 August 2010, Labor achieved only a minority government—Labor and the Coalition each won 72 seats in the 150-seat House of Representatives. Six crossbench MPs held the balance of power. The one Green and three independents sided with Gillard, declaring they would support her on confidence and supply issues. She became prime minister of the first hung Parliament since 1940.

On 24 June 2013, the tables were turned. Rudd won a vote of Labor members of parliament by 57 to 45. Gillard resigned and Rudd once again became prime minister of Australia, albeit with a minority government reliant on independents in the House of Representatives. These events show that in the Labor Party, at least, prime ministers have to be vigilant of caucus dissent. The minority government issue in Australia was resolved in the 7 September 2013 election when Tony Abbott's Liberal/National Coalition won 90 seats, giving them an immense majority in the House of Representatives. Kevin Rudd's outgoing Labor government gained only 55 seats.

The Australian Senate has 76 seats; 40 were up for re-election in 2013. Unlike the House of Representatives, which uses a preferential ballot system in single-member constituencies, Senators are chosen by a single, transferable vote system across the six states and two territories. Due to an extraordinary swapping of preferences, several micro-parties were elected. The Coalition government controls only 33 seats in the Senate, and Labor controls 26. Seventeen Senator seats are now held by small parities—nine Greens, three Palmer United, and five independents and micro-parties. The Coalition will need the support of at least six non-Coalition Senators to pass any legislation through parliament.

In other words, the blockage possibilities have now moved to the upper house from the lower house, as has often been the case before. Prime Minister Abbott will be forced to negotiate with a host of micro-parties in the Senate. A study of executive-legislative relations across several periods in the Commonwealth Parliament and in the six states and two territories illustrates that this circumstance holds over time, and is not contingent on particular policies, issues or personalities (Jackson 1995). The role of 'veto actors' (which occurs when the government does not control an absolute majority) has approximately the same importance and the same effect in all periods. In some situations, 'veto actors' come from the lower house and in other cases they come from opposition parties or independents in significant numbers in the upper house. The role of veto actor in Australia has now shifted from the House of Representatives to the Senate. A few states at any particular time have deviated from this basic pattern, but overall the contention holds—Australia often blends majoritarian and consensus forms of government. The net result is a form of democracy in which majority rule is allowed to function, although somewhat tempered by compromise, with veto action in some policy fields in most legislatures and over time.

But is Australian democracy majoritarian, consensual, or in recent years has it followed 'Aussie Rules?' Australian democracy is unique. It slavishly follows neither the traditional majoritarian British model of democracy nor the consensus principles of consociational European democracy. If there is any consistent principle it is that Australian democracy is essentially utilitarian or pragmatic, as politicians ask basically two questions—'Will it work?' and 'Do we have the numbers?' I have referred to this revision of the Westminster model elsewhere as 'Aussie Rules Democracy' (Jackson 1995).

New Zealand

Currently, New Zealand has a minority government. In fact, in the House of Representatives, minority or coalition governments are now the norm. In 1993, a binding referendum changed the country's electoral system from the traditional first-past-the-post rules to a new mixed-member proportional representation system (MMP), and this was reaffirmed in 2011. The new system was used first in 1996 and elections are held about every three years, based on the prime minister's request to the governor-general to dissolve the house.

Under the leadership of John Key, the National party won the 2008 election, ending nine years of Labour government. But it was a minority government. The National government required the support of the Association of Consumers and Taxpayers (ACT), the United Future Party, and the Maori Party. The leaders of these three parties were given ministerial posts—i.e. were paid—but remained outside the cabinet, while their parties supported the government on supply and confidence issues. (The New Zealand government calls this arrangement a coalition government, not a minority government or hung parliament.) Four parties were in opposition—Labour, Greens, New Zealand First, and Mana Party. After the 2011 election, which Key won again (but found himself two seats short of a majority), ACT, United Future, and Maori parties joined the so-called coalition and the former system was continued. The next election will be in December 2014 if there is not a dissolution sooner.

The New Zealand political system provides another new twist on Westminster-style government, and it could become a new norm elsewhere. If two-party dominance continues to diminish, through the persistence of changing voting patterns, the rise of third or splintered parties, and/or the adoption of proportional representation, many assumptions of Westminster majority government will need to be examined. Permanently hung parliaments will certainly require constitutionalists to go back to the drawing board about the utility of many precedents and conventions. A second vital question will arise: how effective will minority governments be over the next few years in running state institutions, especially in times of major economic difficulty?

Canada

With a coalition government in the UK and minority governments in Australia and New Zealand, only Canada seems to disturb the contemporary pattern with its majority government. The 2 May 2011 election gave a strong mandate to the Conservatives, and in July 2013 Prime Minister Harper put in place one of the largest cabinets in Canadian history. This majority situation may be short-lived.[3] While Canada had a clear government majority in every election but one from 1877 to 1953, the percentage of minority governments has increased steadily since World War II, along with the rise of the multi-party system. Eleven elections resulted in no party winning an absolute majority in the House of Commons.

There were three minority governments in a row directly before Harper got his majority. In Canada, such minority governments usually (but not always) have been short-lived and tend to pass less legislation than majority governments. The Canadian Parliament is a volatile and less predictable place during minority governments. In minority situations, minor parties may even have more influence on policy than their support in the country warrants. Until the 2011 election, the House of Commons witnessed this tumultuous effect in three minority governments. At times, legislation was amended by the opposition; at other times the government taunted the opposition to amend or defeat its legislation and force an election. In order to remain in office, Harper was forced by the Bloc, Liberals and NDP to compromise on significant legislation.

Centralised government

In the original United Kingdom unitary model, all government was centralised in London, but that was never true in Australia or Canada as each began as a federal system of government.[4] Even in the United Kingdom, the relatively recent devolution to Northern Ireland, Wales, and Scotland has moved considerable governmental power to Belfast, Cardiff and Edinburgh. A Scottish vote on independence will be called by autumn 2014. It could pass, but even if it fails, it may still lead to greater decentralisation. Although not representing a federal state, the UK prime minister has even used data from the Welsh Parliament to condemn the Labour Party about social policy because it controls the Welsh assembly as well as forming the opposition in London. Is the condition of centralised government of the Westminster system even plausible today in federalised or highly decentralised unitary systems?

Cabinet government

In the standard Westminster model, all final authority resides in cabinet, where in theory decisions are to be made collectively. But even in the UK this model is now invalid as Patrick Weller demonstrated in his distinguished article on 'Cabinet Government: An elusive ideal' (Weller 2003). In Australia, Canada, New Zealand and the UK, prime ministers alone and also sub-committees of the cabinet have been known to make decisions independent of the whole cabinet. Bicameralism—two houses of parliament—also weakens the premise of majority government control, and most Westminster governments have upper houses (although not all; New Zealand is a prime example). In the UK and Canada, the respective prime minister appoints most members of the British House of Lords and all members of the Canadian Senate, while in Australia, members of the upper house are directly elected by the people. In Canada, the Senate can delay and even prevent legislation from passing—witness the example of its 1988 blockage of the Free Trade deal with the United States. The Australian Senate is remarkably significant as it is required for passing government legislation and budgets, and this has sometimes proved difficult.[5]

Collective and individual responsibility

There has been erosion in the acceptance of these two principles. Many modern governments have accepted defeats in Parliament that at one time would have been treated as matters of confidence and triggered resignations or elections. In other circumstances, governments have chosen to let the people decide divisive issues in referendums. In 1975, for example, the UK cabinet divided over joining Europe, and the matter had to be sent to the people in a referendum. Moreover, the increasing size of government has sometimes led ministers to evade responsibility for their departments or make scapegoats of their civil servants. The latter is possible because civil servants are now visible, appearing more in public and before committees of parliament.

If this present trend of coalition and minority governments continues, the principles of collective and individual responsibility cannot be sustained. If more than one party forms a government, the cabinet's collective responsibility and even secrecy will be subject to several altered conditions. Governments will not be able to treat crucial decisions as votes of confidence. There may even be a tendency to propose more free votes so that decisions can be left open to ad hoc majorities in parliament. Party politics will also be affected, as relations between the party masses and their leadership are likely to become more contentious. Internal party revolts should be expected to increase and become more public. Party manifestos and election promises will undoubtedly become even less reliable as guides to government decision-making. As elections approach, coalition partners or fair-weather friends in minority governments may agitate for more influence. In the UK coalition and perhaps even some minority governments, as in New Zealand, individual ministers may find they are paired in government with members of another party and need to compromise on their electoral commitments. There will be an increase in the number of governments with coalitions that have explicit agreements about shared authority, and minority parliaments under pressure from small or even crossbench parties.

Parliament's power should be expected to increase as Westminster principles wane or vanish, while cabinet's power may diminish. Also, as collective and individual ministerial power decreases, more power will move to outside forces—such as party officials, journalists, and especially interest or pressure groups. The approach to policy-making may change—perhaps becoming more open and transparent but also less effective and disciplined. In this case, experience from the US and other presidential systems may provide an instructive, but perhaps disturbing, comparison.

Electoral systems, fixed election dates and the party system

There are major new challenges to the standard system of voting in the UK and Canada, with constant pressures for proportional representation. The UK case is obvious because of the terms of the Conservative–Liberal Democrat coalition. In both the UK and Canada there has also been a move to fixed election dates, which limit the power of prime ministers to call elections at their pleasure. So far, the short-term result of these changes remains more nuanced than the public understands, and the long-term, unintended consequences of fixed-election laws are unknown. There is uncertainty because the monarch's reserve powers had diminished over time in both the UK and Canada long before the new laws were enacted.

The *Fixed Term Parliaments Act 2011* in the UK fundamentally altered the Crown's prerogative on the dissolution of parliament, while retaining the reserve powers over prorogation and summoning Parliament. Election dates in the UK are now determined in three ways—they may be triggered automatically five years after the day a Parliament is elected (i.e. the next time will be in May 2015), by the loss of a confidence vote in the House, or by MPs passing a motion for an earlier election date by a two-thirds vote.

In Canada, Bill C-16 amended the Canada Elections Act. It requires that an election takes place on the third Monday in October, four years after the preceding election—in the present situation, on 19 October 2015. Unlike in the UK, although there is a fixed election date, the Canadian law does not prevent early dissolutions being approved by the governor-general on the advice of the prime minister. Despite all the 'chit-chat' to the contrary, as Canada has a written constitution, only an amendment to the *Constitution Act 1982* could have eliminated the Crown's right to agree to a dissolution, and even the law about five-year parliaments is questionable.

Conclusion on internal forces

In summary, the existence of veto actors (hung parliaments, coalition governments, minority governments, bicameral impacts, federal and decentralised government structures) is growing in all four Westminster countries. In the real world, there are consequences of change and the nature of governing is one of them. In order to govern their countries, Westminster-style governments often have to negotiate with some political institution(s) other than their own party. What characteristics or props need to disappear in these countries before they are no longer Westminster systems? It is crucial to understand that once one pulls the major props out from under a tradition of government, a question remains outstanding: when do such systems end or new ones begin? The grouper family of fish includes species that are born female and become male later in life (protogynous hermaphrodites). What should we call an ever-changing species of government?

CHALLENGES TO WESTMINSTER FUTURES FROM WITHOUT

Scholars of Westminster have a daunting task. The model is in retreat, not only being torn asunder from within, but being challenged from below, sideways and above (Jackson 2013; Weller, Bakvis and Rhodes 1997). How broad changes in the wider political environment will affect the institutions of all types of governments, including the various Westminster varieties, is difficult to predict. What is certain is that Westminster systems will evolve as strains on them intensify.

Perfect prediction is not possible, of course. Forecasting is always inexact, and plans for the future are always questionable. Proverbially, predictions are fine as long as they are not applied towards the future and are not remembered when events prove them faulty! Much that is unpredicted and unpredictable can and will happen. Here are a few not so enlightening predictions that have been made by top professionals over the years:

- Heavier-than-air flying machines are impossible.
- There is not the slightest indication that nuclear energy will ever be attainable.
- There is a world market for about five computers.

Challenges to Westminster from below

New forms of mass communications are affecting all governing systems. Westminster is no exception. The new media models provide little straightforward coverage of news and public affairs, but rather biased commentary and disjointed images of violence and chaos. Journalists profit from the bombast. They provide ghoulish perspectives about what can be done about the problems of government, without reflecting on the fact that there are many ways to think about politics, and that there is more than one side to each story. Aggressive and personalised journalism is undermining the legitimacy of political institutions and leaders in almost all countries. The daily news is little more than a series of video clips so slowed down that one gets to view only one issue at a time, as if events are not connected through history and society. We never get to see the complete story, just fragments or disjointed events. In democracies, continually we hope that the media will lead discussions of public affairs, but they rarely do so. The media is not concerned with what is in the public interest, but in what interests the public.

The internet and social networking have amplified these corrosive effects. State documents are regularly leaked by WikiLeaks and others. Facebook and instant messaging allow individuals and groups to hijack and control agendas, and blacken or extol public figures. How is the public supposed to judge whether the blurbs, bits, and bytes of current news are fact or opinion? Despite the vital importance of a free press, it still presents difficulties for governance. Journalists tend to have little comprehensive knowledge or respect for democracy. They tend to disparage institutions and politicians everywhere. In the simplest terms, they never get it straight that to decide means to divide!

Challenges to Westminster from sideways

The initial euphoria that followed the end of the Cold War is gone, and the reality that replaced it has created uncertainties over the best forms of government, from presidential to parliamentarian, and from consensual to majoritarian. The new world order is messy and becoming more dangerous. There is a new landscape for governance, with new and mounting pressures against liberal democratic regimes from autocracies. While the dream of expanding economic opportunity is fading from much of the West, opposition from 'state capitalism' is on the rise. There has been a shift in global economic power, and to some extent autocracies are filling the void left by the democratic ideal (Jackson 2013).

The most pertinent example comes from China. In 1989 China was on the brink of collapse, but then the Communist Party changed its economic strategy, putting in place the so-called Beijing Consensus, a mixture of communism and free market capitalism.[6] Many countries have begun to emulate this approach, casting off the ideals that are linked to liberal democracy such as the rule of law, independent courts, transparency, and a free media.

Today, China is peddling its Beijing Consensus in Africa, the Middle East and South-East Asia. And many developing countries are now accepting the need for state control of public wealth, investment and enterprise. China is training judges, police and other judicial officials around the world. The implications for Westminster systems are not absolutely clear, but these new circumstances provide a forceful challenge to all democracies, and state capitalism appears to be gaining in strength.

Challenges to Westminster from above: Globalisation and security issues

As the world grows more interdependent, global politics wields a growing influence on the decision-making of political leaders in all countries. No country, however powerful, is totally self-sufficient or independent. The actions of one state have repercussions for others, and globalisation—the integration of states through increasing contact, communication, and trade that binds people together—continues to increase rapidly. Whether we sarcastically call it *globaloney* or *globalphobia*, there is no denying the impact of the global economy on the governance of Australia, Canada, New Zealand, and the United Kingdom.

Many political issues are intermestic; that is, simultaneously domestic and transnational or global. Individual states are no longer totally self-sufficient: economic, environmental, social, and political interdependence has become a salient feature of modern life. The flow of goods, services, technology, capital and even terrorism around the world has changed how governments operate. The interdependence of states is affecting levels of investment, prosperity, and banking failures, and to some extent taking away the ability of individual governments to control their own economies. Can divided liberal-democratic Westminster governments, and multi-level governments such as federations, function effectively in the new globalised environment?

Revolutions in science and technology have dramatically changed the world economy. Scientific knowledge more than doubled in each of the four decades following World War II, and the pace of technological change continues to accelerate at an ever quicker pace. The speed of change is best illustrated by a few examples. In the nineteenth century when the Australian, Canadian and New Zealand states were basically structured, the world was dominated by colonial empires; today those empires no longer exist, and the United States stands alone as a military superpower. In 1867, the only way to circle the globe—either for travel or for communication—was by ship. Today, sea travel has been eclipsed by vast aviation networks. Communications systems have entered the space age, making use of fibre optics, microwaves and satellites for instant global communication.

Business corporations are increasingly transnational. Ownership and control of global activities are becoming 'stateless', without particular links to any specific country. Because of this, a state's competitive advantage is no longer as identified with its own particular group of companies as it was in 1867. Many multinational corporations exceed the economic strength of most states. And the flow of capital also illustrates the point. Each day the flow of capital around the world twice exceeds the combined GDPs of all the OECD countries.

The idea that the world has become more interdependent is commonplace today. Indeed, the argument that the world was reducing in size was mentioned in Jules Verne's book *Around the World in Eighty Days*, published in 1873 at the zenith of the British Empire and acceptance of Westminster forms of government. In recent years, academics and policy-makers have adopted the term globalisation as if it were something completely novel, but the process has deep roots. Patterns of migration, trade, finance, intercultural influence, and even international systems have been developing and undergoing constant change from the beginning of history.

But there is something different about today's globalisation. It is connecting people in novel ways. The new issues concern not only the process of globalisation, but also its extremely rapid development and its impact on state power. This new form of globalisation has both critics and supporters. Some theorists believe that globalisation has taken on a life of its own—that it creates new institutions and problems—while others more optimistically think that globalisation is a positive force, creating a world society and culture. Many issues that historically mobilised individuals, groups and states now possess an international dimension. However, globalisation and the march towards one global system do not mean that all states and people will be affected in a similar manner. The process has, and will continue to have, divergent effects—both good and bad—in countries throughout the Commonwealth.

The new security issues will also impact on the future of Westminster government. The old security issues referred basically to state security and how states maintained their vitality in the world. The new security issues and dilemmas are about how states and societies are affected, and perhaps afflicted, by non-state actors such as networks of terrorists and others who would harm people around the world. They also include issues of human security that are posed by economic inequalities, illness and environmental degradation. The old concept of security is well established in the study of international relations. While the new security issues are not as developed and do not constitute uniform concepts or theories in the discipline, they nevertheless are central to an understanding of global politics today because of the way they are affecting state institutions and policies.

Historically, the security dilemma meant that each state had to decide whether to increase its military strength and risk provoking others *or* not to arm and leave itself vulnerable to attack. Today, however, security also includes how states can protect themselves against transnational challenges, and how they can aid weaker, failing and underdeveloped states. Dangers generally arise not from strong states, but from those that are divided and disintegrating. Almost all of the violent conflicts since the Cold War have been internal, not international. It was a weak state that harboured Osama bin Laden, not a strong one. A new security dilemma therefore arises from the fact that an increase in a country's military strength may not provide a corresponding increase in its security. The state is under challenge, and while its security is not obsolete and will not disappear, it can no longer be based entirely on weapons and soldiers.

At a minimum, strategic and military planning is extraordinarily difficult in a world with no clear enemy and many dangers. The new security issues arise from the implications of ubiquitous insecurity—violent threats coming from a number of places and non-state sources all at the same time.

Stable states possess not only shared interests but also shared identities. While there are 193 states, there are closer to 10,000 nations or societies spread around the globe. The 'state', 'nation', and 'people' do not coincide in most countries. There are many millions of overseas Chinese, Russians, Hungarians, Romanians and Turks living outside of their home countries; millions of Kurds, Palestinians, Tamils, Ibos, Zulus and Tibetans are without a state; and millions of Muslims, Hindus and Sikhs are living in Asia, searching for new homes as refugees in the developed world. Many don't acknowledge the 'state' in which they find themselves as their 'nation'. Such diversity also exists in America and Europe: with very few exceptions, most of the states of Europe have sizable ethnic minorities, and inside many of them there are what we would call nations (i.e. culturally linked groupings of people). In Australia, Canada, New Zealand and the United Kingdom, immigration issues have become flash points that will affect the survivability of the Westminster systems. The clashes make it mandatory to consider the paradox of how to make the world safe for such diversity, and diversity safe for the world.

Is the modern state, and therefore Westminster, being diminished in importance because of globalisation and new security concerns? As individuals, we experience the importance of the state when we pay our taxes and line up for security checks at airports. It is by far the most powerful force in our lives, but it is changing with the times. Many new problems related to health, the environment, terrorists, and even pirates cannot be handled by individual states, but this does not mean that the state is now insignificant, as some contend. In fact, one could argue that modern forms of surveillance, data processing, and information control are actually increasing the power of individual states. The idea that the state might be in demise is premature, and tied to an idealised and abstract notion of the state and the Commonwealth members that never existed in history.

Many of the new problems the world faces are difficult to address because they exist inside the protective shells of extant states, or are transnational in nature, and also because existing concepts and the institutions based on them are structured on earlier state-to-state relations and the East–West conflict in general. As the world becomes more connected—with global economics, global technology, global communications and global weapons—what will remain of the notion of sovereignty and its notion of a hard-shelled state? Sovereignty is being reduced in importance. But at this time in the 21st century, the most important politics continue to be *within* and *among* sovereign states, despite that fact that security and prosperity increasingly depend on international cooperation.

Conclusion on outside forces

The state is clearly under challenge, but it is not obsolete, and will not disappear. Essentially, there are no alternatives with which to replace it. It is adapting. In 2013 there are about seven billion people on earth—projected to reach more than eight billion by 2025. Every second, the world population grows by more than two human beings. They are governed by 193 states, many of them following principles of government formulated more than a century ago. Our question is simple: will Westminster institutions be up to the challenges from both internal forces and the new globalised world? As the world globalises further and changes the nature of state organisations and their economies, is the Westminster system the most effective for confronting these changes? Can this be proven? Or merely asserted?

NOTES

1   A point to remember is that precedents themselves are examples of the application of conventions that have resulted from the adjustment of earlier precedents and norms to current problems. As such, however, they provide normative justifications for constitutional decisions.
2   Robert Hazell, et al., 2009, *Making Minority Parliament Work: Hung Parliaments and the Challenges for Westminster and Whitehall*, London: University College, Institute of Government, the Constitution Unit.
3   Note as well that for the first time ever, in 2011 the position of Leader of the Official Opposition was taken by the New Democratic Party—with the Liberals confined to a third and humiliating place in the House of Commons. But the rise of young Quebecker Justin Trudeau as leader of the Liberal Party may upset early predictions about the continuation of recent Conservative successes.
4   Federal systems possess legal powers that are divided constitutionally between a central and regional government, such as states or provinces. There are many more unitary than federal systems. See Robert J. Jackson and Doreen Jackson,

2008, *Comparative and World Politics*, 5th edn, Toronto: Pearson, chapter 10 on constitutional frameworks.
5 See the 1975 case when Governor-General Sir John Kerr dismissed Prime Minister Gough Whitlam, using his reserve power, and replaced him with the Opposition Leader Malcolm Fraser.
6 The term 'Beijing Consensus' was first used in Joshua Ramos, 2004, *The Beijing Consensus*, London: Foreign Policy Center. There is an extensive bibliography of books on China and its new global role.

REFERENCES

Economist, 21 September 2013

Jackson, R.J., 1995, 'Foreign Models and Aussie Rules: Executive-legislative relations in Australia', *Political Theory Newsletter*, vol. 7, no. 1, pp. 1–18

—— 2013, *Global Politics in the 21st Century*, Cambridge: Cambridge University Press

Rhodes, R.A.W., Wanna, J. & Weller, P., 2009, *Comparing Westminster*, Oxford: Oxford University Press

Tsebelis, G., 2002, *Veto Players: How political institutions work*, Princeton: Princeton University Press and Russell Sage Foundation

United Kingdom Cabinet Office, 2011, *The Cabinet Manual: A guide to laws, conventions and rules on the operation of government*, London: United Kingdom Cabinet Office, October

Weller, P., 2003, 'Cabinet Government: An elusive ideal', *Public Administration*, vol. 81, no. 4, pp. 701–22

Weller, P., Bakvis, H. & Rhodes, R.A.W. (eds), 1997, *The Hollow Crown: Countervailing trends in core executives*, London: Macmillan

13

POLITICS AS WORK: A CREDO
Patrick Weller

We go to work. Our leaders govern. We wonder why they do not behave logically, adopting polices we see as sensible. They puzzle over what to do, trying to integrate the different demands. We expect much, receive less and complain. They struggle constantly.

Yet this distinction between what most people do—work—and what leaders of government do is essentially false. Being prime minister is a job, perhaps not quite like any other, but still a job that has to be tackled, day in, day out. There may be times when days are hectic, unpredictable, harrowing; when forces, both internal and external, combine into paroxysms of terror; when careers end suddenly (even if never quite so terminally as they did for Tudor politicians). But it has its routines, its constant demands, its expectations and its rhythms.

To understand how we are governed, we need to strip away the glamour of the position and make sense of those routines, to understand how our leaders tackle the daily challenges. Onto the foundation of those routines, expectations and perceptions of the job we need to erect the reactions to events, the new plans and initiatives.

We often create narratives to explain history that describe the unusual, the novel and the unexpected. We make sense of history by simplifying the process, by tracing the steps through which policy-makers travel on a particular occasion, or by pursuing a single policy through its initiation to its delivery. The story is at the centre of our focus. Sometimes we spend more time explaining why decisions were made than the decision-makers spent on making them, for the decisions are often part of a complex torrent of issues. We fillet history to tell a good story of unusual events. We make it sound logical, sensible and explicable, when it may have been the rushed consequence of misunderstood circumstances.

We need to put crises and dramas in the context of the daily life, to show how the excitement occurs within the routines. Looking back with the benefit of hindsight, that is what I think I have tried to do, although I could not claim at the time that this was what I thought or what I was trying to explain. Retrospect gives an air of logic to what, at the time, seemed to be a series of random choices. In making those choices, what I read mattered. We are the product of our accumulated knowledge.

BOOKS AND THE 'WOW' FACTOR

Do books change lives? Of course they do. Do we realise that they are doing so at the time? Perhaps less often. However, I argue that, for me, four books would fit that description and that I was aware of it when I had finished reading them. Most, again in retrospect, touch on the issue of politics as work.

The first did not but was nonetheless the most important: *King Richard III* by Philip Lindsay (1933), read in 1956 when I was twelve. Suddenly history lived. From being a series of dates that had to be memorised, history became contested, disputed, passionate and exciting. From that day in 1956, I planned to read history at university and I never wavered for a moment. That's influence. It mattered to me that Richard III had been maligned by history for a crime he probably did not commit. I still care; I was fascinated when he was dug up from the Leicester car park in 2012 and then identified, 500 years after he was killed in battle, betrayed and fighting bravely. Only in 2013 did I discover that Lindsay, usually a novelist and script writer, found his love of history at Churchie School in Brisbane where his mother lived after separating from his father, Norman Lindsay. Richard III stayed with me. At Oxford, I helped found the Oxford University Fellowship of the White Boar to hold dinners and meetings in his honour. It did not survive for long. However, I look at his portrait every working day. It has hung over my desk for the last 50 years.

The second direct influence was Peter Loveday and Allan Martin's *Parliament Factions and Parties* (1966). I had arrived as a history tutor in

Tasmania in 1967. Professor Gordon Rimmer gave me the book with the comment that it debated the origins of political parties in Australia. The book was about political management in NSW before 1890, about how factions were organised, and about political organisation long before the Labor Party, thus challenging Labor's claim, espoused then particularly by Bede Nairn, to be the first political party in Australia. Rimmer thought I should apply the methods to Tasmania. I found it fascinating. The excitement took me to Canberra to meet Nairn and then to Melbourne to meet the authors. It led to a PhD scholarship in the ANU and a seamless switch from history to political science.

The third book was Hugh Heclo and Aaron Wildavsky's *The Private Government of Public Money* (1974), a study of the Treasury in Britain. It coincided with the Royal Commission into Australian Government Administration (RCAGA), created by the Whitlam government and led by Herbert Cole 'Nugget' Coombs. I was asked to write a report of financial controls under the Australian Treasury. I knew little about the subject to start with, but then no one else did either. Heclo and Wildavsky had provided insights into the informal rules, routines and procedures by which the British Treasury maintained its dominance, and became a blueprint for the study. With a team of colleagues from RCAGA, I attended our first interview with Treasury officials. Many of my colleagues thought the Treasury had told us nothing. With the benefit drawn from reading Heclo and Wildavsky, I knew the Treasury officers had revealed a lot of insights, if little hard information, into the way they operated, and into the culture and assumptions the officers took to their work. As long as no one else had read it (a condition that did not apply for long), I had an advantage. Heclo and Wildavsky were strong on method but mercifully light on theory; they anticipated much of the new institutionalist and interpretivist literatures that emerged two decades later. They taught me how to study working lives.

The fourth inspiration was Robert Caro's first volume of his amazing biography of Lyndon Johnson (Caro 1982). It took LBJ from his poor background to Congress to his first senatorial election, where his opponents stole the election by stuffing ballot boxes. LBJ would not let that happen again. More importantly, it told the story of how LBJ organised his rise; he calculated whom he needed to meet, and whom he needed as patron. He worked all the hours needed, and then some more. The basis of his rise was hard work, calculated sycophancy, an ability to engender loyalty in those who worked for him that lasted a lifetime and, never to be underestimated, the commitment to deliver what he promised. The story of how he brought electrical power to the Hill country of Texas is a triumphant story of political effectiveness and a touching account of the poor boy from the area receiving the grateful thanks of his constituents. The chapter on life for farmers' wives in the torrid Texas climate without benefit of electricity, as late as the 1930s, is a wonderful study of the hardships that LBJ alleviated. At times, Caro seems to hate LBJ's more nauseous crawling; at times he admires his sheer drive. The first volume was published in 1982. Three more followed at decade-long intervals. It remains the best political biography I have read. I await volume five with great anticipation.

Caro's study had an immediate impact on my choice of subjects. I had just completed a comparative study of prime ministers, and I wondered if it was possible to do for an Australian prime minister what Caro had done for LBJ: identify the organisational and routine basis of power. If power is exercised in crisis, the foundations are laid by the processes and structures that have been carefully put in place and become almost second nature. I wanted to see if it was possible to define how a prime minister worked on a day-to-day basis. Malcolm Fraser, prime minister from 1975 to 1983, had just lost power. I asked to see him, explained what I wanted, and he generously agreed. He also arranged access to the cabinet records of his government for me; that access started a year after his government fell. It was a privilege, and it was fascinating. The data has never been as good since!

There is one other book that was influential for me, but not with the thunderclap of these four. In those cases, I realised immediately that the books provided me with a model of how to develop a research strategy. The other book was Richard Neustadt's *Presidential Power*, published in 1960. Its impact was more gradual and insidious.

There are two particular insights that live with me. The first is the comment: 'The power of the president is the power to persuade' (Neustadt 1960: 11). Neustadt directs attention away from the idea that in politics command is all; he proposes that in real politics, persuasion and consent are the more important. The other insight was an issue of approach. In the introduction Neustadt explains how he set out to write the book:

> To analyse the problem of obtaining personal power one must try to view the Presidency from over the President's shoulder, looking out and down with the perspective of *his* place. This

> is not the way we conventionally view the office; ordinarily we stand outside it, looking in. From outside, or from below, a president is 'many men' or one man wearing many 'hats', or playing many 'roles' . . . For present purposes, [this framework] becomes a block to insight. The President himself plays every role, wears every hat at once . . . To analyse this aspect of his job we need a frame of reference as unlike the usual category as the view from inside out is unlike that from outside in. (Neustadt 1960: ii)

Understanding how actors see the world is a crucial prerequisite to understanding why they act the way they do.

All my principal influences were books. I like books, both reading and writing them. Books allow the development of an argument, the presentation of information, the accumulation of evidence and, often, a good story elegantly told. Journal articles can make a point, but must be abbreviated in approach.

Good commercial publishers used to be the outlets for many of the great political scientists of the past who could thus take their messages far beyond their peers. Wildavsky (1979), Neustadt (1960), Charles Lindblom (1977) Peter Self (1972), March and Olsen (1988) (to name some of those from whom I learnt most) published with Little Brown, John Wiley, Basic Books, Allen & Unwin and the Free Press respectively. University presses were often for the books that were academically good but which might not have a market, rather than their modern function of acting as a proxy for quality. Books were judged as much by their long-lasting impact as their publisher.

It is interesting to note that it remains respectable, and quite common to cite books written 30 or more years ago, while articles from the same time are far more rarely referenced. I suspect most of our leading figures, including those listed above, will be remembered too for the books they wrote: the *magnum opus* or two that define a career. There is something persuasive about the long, carefully constructed arguments that books present, and something timeless about the weight of evidence that few articles, designed to participate in continuing and current debates, can contain.

UNDERSTANDING POLITICS

Definitions of politics abound. Perhaps the ones we find most persuasive are the ones that reflect our understandings of the activity and its challenges. When I took over teaching first-year Political Science from David Adams at the ANU in 1981, he had an opening lecture that included a number of definitions of politics to show the students the different ways of understanding it. I added a few more. I am not sure now if they were his or mine, but all this time later, two stand out, one about politics generally, the other about the challenge of governing.

The first comes from a work on political education, first published in 1951 by the conservative philosopher, Michael Oakeshott.

> Politics I take to be the activity of attending to the general arrangements of a set of people whom chance or choice have brought together. In this sense, families, clubs and learned societies have their 'politics'. But the communities in which this manner of activity is pre-eminent are the cooperative hereditary groups, many of them of ancient lineage, all aware of a past, a present, and a future, which we call 'states' . . . I speak of this activity as 'attending to the arrangements', rather than as 'making arrangements', because in these hereditary co-operative groups the activity is never offered the blank sheet of infinite opportunity. (Oakeshott 1991: 45–6)
>
> In political activity, then, men sail a boundless and bottomless sea; there is neither harbour for shelter nor appointed destination. The enterprise is to keep afloat on an even keel; the sea is both friend and foe; and the seamanship consists in using the resources of a traditional manner of behaviour in order to make a friend of every hostile occasion. (Oakeshott 1991: 60)

I love the language and the imagery. The phrase, 'never offered the blank sheet of infinite opportunity' haunts me. We have a history that shapes what we do, a present to survive, and a future to prepare for. Governing is for the long term; there are no permanent solutions to most social problems. Governments can, at best, manage the pressures and try to put into effect policies that ameliorate the future conditions. Most problems today are a consequence of policies that were once seen as solutions; the answers to one problem have themselves become problems for later governments to solve. Treasurers manage the economy because they can never solve it. New forces emerge. There can never be an end to history.

Instinctively, conservative politicians see themselves in these terms. New Zealand Prime Minister Robert Muldoon, when asked his ambition, hoped he would leave the country no worse off than when he found it. (He probably failed!) Malcolm Fraser told me:

> Government is not really about a series of unrelated events. There is a continuous job of administration to be undertaken . . . if somebody was prepared to make the judgement that the Commonwealth was administered well during those years, without defining any particular achievement or area of government, I think it would be as much as anyone could expect. To me that would be better, or mean more, than one particular event. There is always one thing that somebody can do or that will be well done in terms of government; that might also mean a lot of things have been done very badly. (Weller 1989: 405)

There is a common sense to that conclusion that may reflect the speaker but resonates when governments try to point to moments of glory amid a devastated political landscape. Beware policy monuments.

My second definition was taken from Hugh Heclo:

> Politics finds its sources not only in power but also in uncertainty: men collectively wondering what to do . . . Governments not only power . . . they also puzzle. Policy making is a form of collective puzzlement on society's behalf; it entails both deciding and knowing. (Heclo 1974: 305)

The more I watch politicians and observe them in action, the wiser this concept of politics seems. There almost certainly can be no other way of operating. So much is unknown that governments must govern even while they learn. I like the comment of a Treasury secretary who argued 30 years ago:

> There were those who believed in econometric forecasting; it was held to be the ultimate in precision. So far as I am concerned, it was all a lot of bullshit. The plain fact was we tried to thrust in the right direction, the right direction being the direction your hunches led you to adopt. (Weller 1989: 215)

That might be seen as heresy in this quantitative world, but as advice it has an essential modesty and realism.

Contingency, doubt, uncertainty: these are the defining concepts for the study of politics. People matter. It can be called situated agency, or agents in context. Men and women make their own history, if not entirely as they please. They are constrained by history, expectations and institutions. The political scientist's job is to explain why. Our tools are our imagination, our research, and our judgement. We seek to tell a story, a narrative that is organised in a way that is persuasive and talks to the patterns of behaviour. For me, the task of political science is to better understand the workings of politics. If what I write has no connection with the way it works, with the lived experience, then the failure is mine. In this enterprise, theory is a crucial tool to shape the questions, to order the argument, to assess the evidence and to direct the findings. It is, for me, a means to that end, not an end in itself.

Of course, that may put me at odds with the majority of political scientists who see contributions to theory as the lodestone for research. Positivist, often quantitative, political science seeks patterns of explanations. While I want to understand politics—the historian manqué—they want to make the study of politics akin to a natural science.

Politics is not, and cannot be, a natural science, because the core of our subject is the uncertainty and contingency that pervades political life. If the prime ministers and departmental secretaries have problems explaining, from day to day, precisely what happened and why, and if the officials of international organisations give very different versions of the workings of their institutions, how can we reconstruct and explain those events except as a post hoc rationalisation? For me, that often raises questions about the usefulness of statistical analysis, where the data must be forced into categories that are themselves artificial, where models are simplified to provide explanations, but where contingency and uncertainty are often excluded. Yet we know that any one account of the event will be challenged by those with different values, different perspectives, and different views of what occurred. Even the motives of an individual will be challenged. Spin—less pejoratively, the alternative interpretation—is always present. How can we view our subject except with a pinch of scepticism, perhaps interspersed with moments of naive hope?

But what else would anyone expect from a person who found the disciplines of history and politics interesting *because* their stories were contested and meanings disputed? Richard III was an early victim of spin, woven by his Tudor enemies after he could not answer back. The stories of his crimes were initially peddled by his enemy Archbishop Morton, the chancellor of King Henry VII. They were popularised by Thomas More, not as pleasant a man as suggested by Robert Bolt in *A Man for all Seasons*, but cruel and vengeful. (Interestingly Bolt's play persuaded two very different young Australians to pursue political careers. Peter Costello and Kevin Rudd found the play inspiring. If we are to be educated through fiction, I find the nastier, narrow-minded, somewhat priggish character portrayed in Hilary Mantel's *Wolf Hall* more persuasive; just read More's *Utopia* to see why.) Then Richard III suffered the ultimate indignity: to be presented by the greatest writer of all time as a scheming and vicious villain. Who cares if the history is invented? No one could survive Shakespeare's brilliant portrait, not even a brave young man. These were Tudor spin doctors one and all. The victors write the history.

History, too, warns against normative readings of political life. There is a body of literature that suggests there are things prime ministers should and should not do. There are proposals that prime ministers should limit their own power; 'self-restraint' is one suggestion (Rose 1980: 340). The basis of the argument is a set of unstated constitutional conventions that are assumed to guide the way that governments should work. Richard French (1979) calls these writers the theorists; they assume that there is a set of suitable principles that define government. The problem is that any practices and conventions, even those sanctified by time, were themselves calculated responses to a political dilemma and settled upon for reasons of political benefit, whether for one or many parties. As the practice becomes settled, it gains credibility. The practical becomes the normative, the description of what actors should do. I can understand why observers demand that politicians abide by convention and practice; it has the value of predictability and often consensus. My problem is that, when the origins of conventions are uncovered, they are about political advantage. Most normative demands on governments require that they give up political advantage to satisfy a set of vague practices. The advocate then is no more than an historically informed participant using history to explain why a government action, while legal, is improper.

There is a second school that French (1979) calls the pragmatists. They see government as it is, messy, often based on compromise. Prime ministers and ministers do what they can; they make judgements about what they want and what they need to do. Decisions are based on calculations about the forces that surround them. Tactics are determined by what works, rather than by some unwritten constitutional provisions of what should be. Faced with a convention they will ask whether the costs of breaking it outweigh the benefits of keeping it. Given the continuity of governments, conventions often stand as expressions of mutual benefit, but not always.

It will be no surprise that I find the latter school far more convincing. 'Westminster' principles are always open to interpretation and use. They are far from irrelevant, but they do not prescribe particular actions or require specific responses (Rhodes, Wanna and Weller 2009: 219–33). Nor can we ascribe to ourselves as academics the right to take the moral high ground just because we are well informed. We can use history to explain our choices. We can provide examples of when governments worked well. We can provide strategies for action. Our propositions should be more historically informed, more carefully calibrated, more sensitive to the perils of contingency, than many other rushed proposals. In that sense they should be better. But, I would suggest, they do not have any greater moral suasion or weight just because of that. Political tactics will be determined as much by values and advantage as by historical accuracy.

DOES OUR RESEARCH MATTER?

We are threatened with impact studies. Our research funding can be affected by our capacity to have an impact, even if that impact is not as direct as university managers and governments would like. I remember a PhD student writing a thesis on Iran who said that he assumed the CIA had a unit dedicated to reading theses like his. *La jeunesse!* Of course, even a minimal understanding of policy-making illustrates the contingency, the need for policy entrepreneurs and champions, for windows of opportunity, even when an idea is only in the early stage of formulation. Virtually no academic idea is adopted for its own sake, whatever the protestations of self-importance in impact case studies. Time, place and opportunity all matter. The best ideas may be lost. We cannot predict when and where new perspectives are needed.

At an International Studies Association conference in San Francisco in 2008, Stephen Krasner talked about his experience in government. At risk of oversimplification, he proposed that nothing he had read as a political scientist was useful to him in government, except perhaps John Kingdon's idea of windows of opportunity, and nothing he had written was of interest to his new colleagues. They inhabited different worlds. Krasner argued that even if the general critiques of Graham Allison's (1971) work on the Cuban missile crisis were correct (and, as he said, he had written one himself), that still did not remove the requirement for officials to develop more precise strategies. It was not a message many in the audience wanted to hear as they insisted they knew how governments worked.

From outside the decision-making process, political scientists may have an influence, but it will be at best low-key. When doing research on government files, I have found the occasional copy of my work or my name as a reference for a point being made. It was used as an authority, but doubtless to bolster, not initiate, a case.

The author of an official history of the British civil service, Rodney Lowe (2011), passed on to me a copy of an article I wrote on the benefits of prime ministers' departments that he had found in Margaret Thatcher's papers. It was underscored in straight lines, a sign, her biographer writes (Moore 2013: 456), of approval. Disapproval was indicated by wavy lines. In the files with the article was an exchange of memos from September 1982, where her principal private secretary and the head of the Cabinet Office considered the Australian experience (badly misrepresented, in my view) and considered possible options. The principal memo started:

> I promised to send you a note about the ideas for strengthening and extending the role of the Cabinet Office in the direction of a 'Prime Minister's Department' which the Prime Minister mentioned at our meeting last week.

The paper, too, was annotated by Thatcher. 'No (underlined twice) I haven't made myself clear. This system would produce a strengthened bureaucracy. I want a strengthened strategy (underlined) section. Totally different.' So she pursued the ideas but did not adopt the Australian model. At least she thought about it and debated it with her staff. Whether there is a connection is hard to prove. Is that enough to claim impact?

I have written reports, for the Coombs commission, and for the Queensland government, and been on a prime minister's taskforce on public-service reform. I spent two years as chair of the Board of the Queensland Corrective Services Commission, a citizens' body that oversaw the operation of Queensland prisons. It was designed to take the politics out of prisons. Of course, it didn't. In most cases it was not something explicit I wrote that led to my involvement, rather the reputation drawn from what I had written, and the people I had met in the process: location and connection as much as any scholarship.

At times it is possible to push a process along. Cabinet handbooks used to be confidential documents, available only to those who needed to know. In 1982 I complained about the unnecessary secrecy in a lecture at the ANU; the next week a student walked up, said, 'You might be interested in this', and handed me a copy. I have no idea who she was. As I was editor of *Politics* (the forerunner of the *Australian Journal of Political Science*) I published the handbook as the first of an Occasional Document Series. (There never was a second.) I had asked a deputy secretary of the Department of Prime Minister and Cabinet what the department would do if I published it. He said it was a breach of copyright. I said I knew that. But, of course, they did nothing. When it was being revised, a public servant pointed out that as it was now public, the department may as well publish a version through the Australian Government Printing Service. It did, and the handbook has been public ever since, at no cost to anyone.

In the late 1980s I used to send copies of the cabinet handbook to Peter Hennessy in London; he would send them on to No. 10, asking when the UK would follow the Australian example. He regularly got the brush off. Then in 1992, he was told to wait. The release of *Questions of Procedure for Ministers* was promised in the election campaign and John Major duly released it in 1994. (For the wider story, see Baker 2000: 68.)

A link in the chain perhaps; influence possibly, but how to prove it; I have no idea. We nudge here, inform there, make sense of an issue, enter the debate, raise ideas, get cited, seek to persuade, sensitise, provoke, interest or encourage. We contribute. But decisions are not ours to make.

And we can do it only if we make sense and write clearly. We should write for the everyman in language they can understand because it makes sense. There is little validity in the claim that our writing should be obtuse because it is only intended for an inner circle talking to itself. We write about politics, not chemistry; we write about what people do in institutions. Yet the growing private language of the discipline, a sign, it seems to be argued, of professionalism, makes our meaning and findings obscure. If we want to be taken seriously by those who do make policy, and by no means all political scientists either want to or can, then we need to write to be understood. We cannot write in our own impenetrable jargon *and* complain when we are ignored.

UNDERSTANDING HOW WE ARE GOVERNED

The remit to understand how we are governed provides a number of challenges. Perhaps the best description of what I try to do is the explanation of Heclo and Wildavsky:

> To understand how political administrators work, we must begin by seeing the world through their eyes . . . We tell our tale largely from the viewpoint of participants, then, not to signify our agreement, but to explain their actions. The participant is the expert on what he does; the observer's task is to make himself expert on why he does it. (Heclo and Wildavsky 1974: xvii)

If they first offer a method, they then provide an encapsulation of the core issue when they replay Heclo's notion of contingency and struggle:

> Politics proceeds not only by powerful men [This was pre-Thatcher!] bargaining but also puzzled men learning to adapt their minds and operations to emerging problems. (Heclo and Wildavsky 1974: xix)

Bargaining and puzzling; power and thought; dealing and agonising; compromise and commitment. These are two sides of political practitioners whether politician, public servant or campaigner. Understand the interplay and we can, just sometimes, make sense of the real world we seek to interpret.

These are the themes that, in retrospect, I can identify as my concerns. I have argued that cabinets must maintain political support while they deliver policy cohesion; that prime ministers must constantly use their potential capacity to move policy; that civil servants must calculate where and how they can influence decisions; and that international civil servants work often informally to explain, nudge and inform. All need to appreciate the opportunities, the levers and the dangers.

There are many ways we can try to conceptualise the interplay of forces, all applicable to domestic and international organisations. In the two editions of *Public Policy in Australia*, my colleagues and I made a couple of suggestions. First, we proposed to adopt Richard Simeon's funnel of causality. We identified the different levels of explanations. At the broadest was the socio-economic environment, then there were questions of power, culture, ideology and institutions; narrower still were the policy-making processes and finally the specific public policy. The idea was to embrace institutional, process and case studies, with each explanation looking at a different level of the policy under consideration (Davis et al. 1988: 9). In the second edition, we saw public policy as an interaction of values, interests and resources, mediated through institutions and determined by politics (Davis et al. 1993: 7).

Neither approach seeks simple answers. Policy problems are the consequence of history, they must be tackled through existing institutions, they will be complicated by different interests, they will be made under pressure of time and limited resources, and they will be shaped by the temperaments and intellects of individuals. Change any of these factors, (and they will most likely *all* be contested) and the result is different. While policy-makers may be captives of their environment, such as the booming Chinese economy, there is someone out there making decisions that matter, even if not the proximate decision-makers.

Australian politics has been the subject of much of my work. Political scientists everywhere have some responsibility to understand how their own countries are governed. National politics is, and should be, at the core of the discipline. It is quite acceptable to publish in Australian journals if the audience is intended to be primarily Australian. After all, we should write to be read, not to get our work published in international journals. Many of the leading political science journals are, in effect, US domestic journals, with 80 to 90 per cent of the authors living in the USA (Sharman and Weller 2009). That may be because the US contains the great majority of the world's political scientists, or because it has methodological expectations that other countries do not, and do not want to, fulfil. Publishing there should not be the principal indication of quality for writing on Australian politics.

However, it is still necessary to keep the study of Australian politics theoretically acute and for the research to be done well. Poor political science anywhere is just that: poor. If we want other countries to pay attention to our writing on Australia, then we either need to use our cases to identify some broader points of general significance, or to use our data for comparative analysis. We cannot claim there is any intrinsic reason why scholars elsewhere should be interested in Australia; we have to make the way we do things relevant and interesting to them.

What works for trying to understand national policy-making, also works when applied to the study of international organisations.

Xu Yi-chong and I started to explore international organisations after a discussion about the potential impact of the secretariat staff on the outputs of the agency (Xu and Weller 2004, 2009). Why were findings about the bureaucratic influence of national civil services not applicable to international organisations too? We can trace their history, the formulation of the mission, and the changing roles they have played. We can identify the institutional rules, both formal and informal, in Douglass North's (1990) formulation of the concept of institution. We can identify the expectations that members, leaders and secretariats have and the way that those roles are interpreted, contested and changed. Their diverse interests and interpretations shape their choices. Then we can explain the how and the why of international organisations: what drives them, where they hit gridlock, the impact on their activities that institutional form, discipline, financing and decentralisation might have. Here is an agenda that seeks to challenge the orthodoxy, espoused fervently by member states (even while they often admit the opposite) that the member states are always in control and secretariats lack influence and are subservient. They are not. That is what makes them interesting.

Political scientists often face that inevitable question: 'You are claiming to be the experts, so what will happen?' We can often give an answer, not necessarily with precise odds and figures, but by using a combination of history, theory and an appreciation of the unique circumstance. Often we are right and it is not just a matter of good fortune. We can understand the dynamics of policy-making and political life. But we can never predict with assurance because we must be aware of the impact of contingency, personality and the unknown unknowns. In 2001, a *Tampa*-type incident could always be seen as a possibility; it was a predictable step in the escalating debate on boat arrivals. But no one, absolutely no one, could have anticipated the combination of *Tampa* and September 11.

LOOKING BACK

Our lives depend on fortune. I can only empathise with Alice.

> One day Alice came to a fork in the road and saw a Cheshire cat in a tree. 'Which road do I take?' she asked. 'Where do you want to go?' was his response. 'I don't know', Alice responded. 'Then', said the cat, 'it doesn't matter.' (Carroll 1865)

The road led to political science, to academe and to Brisbane. None of those would I have predicted just 50 years ago as I started at university.

REFERENCES

Allison, G., 1971, *Essence of Decision: Explaining the Cuban Missile Crisis*, Boston: Little Brown
Baker, A., 2000, *Prime Ministers and the Rule Book*, London: Politico's
Caro, R.A, 1982, *The Years of Lyndon Johnson: The path to power*, London: Collins
Carroll, Lewis, 1865, *Alice's Adventures in Wonderland*, London: Macmillan
Davis, G., Wanna, J., Warhurst, J. & Weller, P., 1988, *Public Policy in Australia*, Sydney: Allen & Unwin
—— 1993, *Public Policy in Australia*, 2nd edn, Sydney: Allen & Unwin
French, R., 1979, 'The Privy Council Office: Support for cabinet decision making', in R. Schultz et al. (eds), *The Canadian Political Process*, 3rd edn, Toronto: Holt Rhinehart & Winston
Heclo, H., 1974, *Modern Social Politics in Britain and Sweden*, New Haven: Yale University Press
Heclo, H. & Wildavsky, A., 1974, *The Private Government of Public Money*, Houndmills: Macmillan
Lindblom, C.E., 1977, *Politics and Markets*, New York: Basic Books
Lindsay, P., 1933, *King Richard III: A chronicle*, London: Ivor Nicolson & Watson
Loveday, P. & Martin, A., 1966, *Parliament Factions and Parties*, Melbourne: Melbourne University Press
Lowe, R., 2011, *The Official History of the British Civil Service, Volume 1*, London: Routledge
March, J.G. & Olsen, J.P., 1988, *Rediscovering Institutions*, New York: The Free Press
Moore, C., 2013, *Margaret Thatcher: The authorized biography, Volume 1: Not for Turning*, London: Allen Lane
Neustadt, R., 1960, *Presidential Power: The politics of leadership*, New York: John Wiley & Sons
North, D.C., 1990, *Institutions, Institutional Change and Economic Performance*, New York: Cambridge University Press
Oakeshott, M., 1991 [1962], *Rationalism in Politics and Other Essays*, Indianapolis: Liberty Fund
Rhodes, R.A.W., Wanna, J. & Weller, P., 2009, *Westminster Compared*, Oxford: Oxford University Press
Rose, R., 1980, 'Governments against Sub-Governments: A European perspective', in R. Rose & E. Suleiman (eds), *Presidents and Prime Ministers*, Washington: American Enterprise Institute
Self, P., 1972, *Administrative Theories and Politics*, London: Allen & Unwin
Sharman, J. & Weller, P., 2009, 'Where is the Quality? Political Science Scholarship in Australia', *Australian Journal of Political Science*, vol. 44, no. 4, pp. 597–612

Weller, P., 1989, *Malcolm Fraser PM: A study in prime ministerial power*, Melbourne: Penguin
Wildavsky, A., 1979, *Speaking Truth to Power: The art and craft of policy analysis*, Boston: Little Brown
Xu, Y. & Weller, P., 2004, *The Governance of World Trade*, Cheltenham: Edward Elgar
—— 2009, *Inside the World Bank*, New York: Palgrave

PAT WELLER'S BIBLIOGRAPHY

PUBLICATIONS, REPORTS AND GRANTS: 1971–2013

1971
'The Organisation of Early Non-Labour Parties in Tasmania', *Tasmanian Historical Research Association Papers and Proceedings*, vol. 18, no. 4, October 1971, pp. 137–48

'Disciplined Party Voting: A Labor innovation?', *Labour History*, vol. 21, November 1971, pp. 17–23

1973
'Meetings of the Early Australian Non-Labor Parliamentary Parties', *Political Science*, vol. 25, no. 2, December 1973, pp. 121–30

1974
'The Relationship Between Groups and Early Parties: Campbell reconsidered', *Politics*, vol. 9, no. 1, May 1974, pp. 41–5

'The Labor Party and the Defeat of Reid: A reassessment', *Labour History*, vol. 26, May 1974, pp. 14–18

'Groups, Parliament and Elections: Tasmanian politics in the 1890s', *Tasmanian Historical Research Association Papers and Proceedings*, vol. 21, no. 2, June 1974, pp. 89–103 (with G.N. Hawker) 'Pre-election Consultations: A proposal and its problems', *Australian Quarterly*, vol. 46, no. 2, June 1974, pp. 100–4

'From Faction to Party: The role and authority of the leader', *Political Science*, vol. 26, no. 2, December 1974, pp. 41–7

'Caucus Control of Cabinet, Myth or Reality?', *Public Administration*, vol. 33, no. 4, December 1974, pp. 300–6

1975

(edited & introduced) *Caucus Minutes 1901–1949: The minutes of the meetings of the federal parliamentary Labor Party: Volume I, 1901–1917*, Melbourne: Melbourne University Press, 1975

(edited & introduced) *Caucus Minutes 1901–1949: The minutes of the meetings of the federal parliamentary Labor Party: Volume II, 1917–1931*, Melbourne: Melbourne University Press, 1975

(edited & introduced) *Caucus Minutes 1901–1949: The minutes of the meetings of the federal parliamentary Labor Party: Volume III, 1932–1949*, Melbourne: Melbourne University Press, 1975

'Pre-selection and Local Support: An explanation of the methods and development of early non-Labor Parties in New South Wales', *Australian Journal of Politics and History*, vol. 21, no. 1, April 1975, pp. 22–30

(with R.F.I. Smith) 'Royal Commission: A chance for change?', *Contemporary Australian Management*, vol. 1, July 1975, pp. 22–6

1976

(with R.F.I. Smith) *Public Servants, Interest Groups and Public Policy: Two case studies*, Occasional Paper No. 12, Department of Political Science, RSSS, ANU, 1976

(with J. Cutt) *Treasury Control in Australia: A study in bureaucratic politics*, Sydney: Ian Novak, 1976

(edited & introduced with B. Stevens) *The Australian Labor Party and Federal Politics: A documentary survey*, Melbourne: Melbourne University Press, 1976

(with R.F.I. Smith) 'The Bureaucracy: Plus Ca Change . . .', *Politics*, vol. 11, no. 1, May 1976, pp. 53–7; reprinted in *Australian Politics: A new ball game?*, APSA Monograph 16, Sydney, 1976

'The Power and Influence of Party Meetings', in H. Mayer & H. Nelson (eds), *Australian Politics: A fourth reader*, Melbourne: Cheshire, 1976, pp. 387–90

(with R.F.I. Smith) 'Setting National Priorities: The role of the Australian government in public policy', in R.L. Mathews (ed.), *Making Federalism Work*, Canberra: Centre for Research on Federal Financial Relations, 1976, pp. 81–96

'The Schools Commission, Political Resources and Federal–State Relations', in R.M. Burns et al. (eds), *Political and Administrative Federalism*, Research Monograph No. 14, Canberra: Centre for Research on Federal Financial Relations, 1976, pp. 71–82

1977

(edited with J. North) *Labor: Directions for the eighties*, Sydney: Ian Novak, 1980

(edited with D. Jaensch) *Responsible Government in Australia*, Melbourne: Drummond, 1980

'Public Servants and the Briefing of Party Committees', *Australian Journal of Public Administration*, vol. 36, no. 2, June 1977, pp. 186–96

(with R.F.I. Smith) 'Learning to Govern: The Australian Labor Party and the institutions of government', *Journal of Commonwealth and Comparative Politics*, vol. 15, no. 1, March 1977, pp. 39–54

'Splitting the Treasury: Old habits in new structures?', *Australian Quarterly*, vol. 49, no. 1, March 1977, pp. 29–39

(with R.F.I. Smith) 'Inside the Inquiry: Problems of organising a public service review', C. Hazelhurst & J.R. Nethercote (eds), in *Reforming Australian Government: The Coombs Report and beyond*, Canberra: Australian National University Press, 1977, pp. 5–26

'Tasmania', in P. Loveday, A.W. Martin & R.S. Parker (eds), *The Emergence of the Australian Party System*, Sydney: Hale & Iremonger, 1977, pp. 355–82

(with P. Loveday & A.W. Martin) 'New South Wales', in P. Loveday, A.W. Martin & R.S. Parker (eds), *The Emergence of the Australian Party System*, Sydney: Hale & Iremonger, 1977, pp. 172–248

(with R.F.I. Smith) 'The Rise and Fall of Whitlam Labor: The political context of the 1975 elections', in H. Penniman (ed.), *Australia at the Polls 1975*, Washington D.C.: American Enterprise Institute, 1977, pp. 49–76

'The Establishment of the Schools Commission: A case study in the politics of education', in I.K.F. Birch & D. Smart (eds), *The Commonwealth Government and Education 1964–1974: Political initiatives and development*, Melbourne: Drummond, 1977, pp. 48–70 (reprint)

(with B. Lloyd & B. Stevens) 'State Power and Federal Intervention', in H. Radi & P. Spearitt (eds), *Jack Lang*, Sydney: Hale & Iremonger, 1977, pp. 212–26

1978

(edited with R.F.I. Smith) *Public Service Inquiries in Australia*, St Lucia, Qld: University of Queensland Press, 1978

(with R.F.I. Smith) 'Introduction', in R.F.I. Smith & P. Weller (eds), *Public Service Inquiries in Australia*, St Lucia, Qld: University of Queensland Press, 1978, pp. 1–13

'Forward Estimates and the Allocation of Resources' in R.F.I. Smith & P. Weller (eds), *Public Service Inquiries in Australia*, St Lucia, Qld: University of Queensland Press, 1978

(edited & introduced with B. Lloyd) *Federal Executive Minutes 1916–1955*, Melbourne: Melbourne University Press, 1978

'Caucus: A case for reform', *Politics*, vol. 13, no. 1, May 1978, pp. 182–5

1979

(with G. Hawker & R.F.I. Smith) *Politics and Policy in Australia*, St Lucia, Qld: University of Queensland Press, 1979

'The Labor Party and the 1977 Campaign', in H. Penniman (ed.), *The Australian National Election of 1977*, Washington D.C.: American Enterprise Institute, 1979, pp. 65–91

'By Their Works: . . . Parliamentary committees and their reports', in *Working Papers on Parliament*, Canberra Series in Administrative Studies, 5, Canberra: Canberra College of Advanced Education, 1979, pp. 59–64

1980

(edited with J. North) *Labor: Directions for the eighties*, Sydney: Ian Novak, 1980

(edited with D. Jaensch) *Responsible Government in Australia*, Melbourne: Drummond, 1980

'A State of Stability: Political parties in 1980', *Australian Quarterly*, vol. 52, no. 1, March 1980, pp. 20–31

(with A. Smart & A.M. Georges) 'Mobility in the Australian Public Service', *Australian Journal of Public Administration*, vol. 39, no. 1, March 1980, pp. 18–29; also published as *Public Service Board Research Paper No 3*, Canberra: AGPS, 1980

'Inner Cabinets and Outer Ministers: Lessons from Australia and Britain', *Canadian Public Administration*, vol. 23, no. 4, Winter 1980, pp. 598–615

(with J. North) 'Challenges, Constraints and Commitments', in J. North & P. Weller (eds), *Labor: Directions for the eighties*, Sydney: Ian Novak, 1980, pp. 1–8

'Implementation: Cabinet and the Bureaucracy', in J. North & P. Weller (eds), *Labor: Directions for the eighties*, Sydney: Ian Novak, 1980, pp. 60–72

'Controlling the Structure of the Public Service', in P. Weller & D. Jaensch (eds), *Responsible Government in Australia*, Melbourne: Drummond, 1980, pp. 196–203

1981

(with M. Grattan) *Can Ministers Cope? Australian Federal Ministers at Work*, Melbourne: Hutchinson, 1981

'The Study of Public Policy', *Australian Journal of Public Administration*, vol. 39, no. 3/4, September/December 1980, pp. 499–507; also published in G.R. Curnow & R.L. Wettenhall (eds), *Understanding Public Administration*, Sydney: Allen & Unwin, 1981, pp. 246–53

1982

(with W. Sanders) *The Team at the Top: Ministers in the Northern Territory*, Darwin: North Australia Research Unit Monograph, 1982

'Reforming Parliament', in G. Evans & J. Reeves (eds), *Labor Essays 1982: Socialist principles and parliamentary government*, Melbourne: Drummond, 1982, pp. 99–117

'The Commonwealth Budget System: An evaluation', in D. Shand (ed.), *Making Government Budgets Work: Canberra and the states*, Canberra: Canberra College of Advanced Education in association with the Australian Institute of Public Administration (ACT

Group), 1982, pp. 19–27; reprinted in D.J. Hardmen (ed.), *Government Accounting and Budgeting*, Sydney: Prentice-Hall of Australia, 1982, pp. 77–85

1983

'The Vulnerability of Prime Ministers: A comparative analysis', *Parliamentary Affairs*, vol. 36, no. 1, Winter 1983, pp. 96–117

'Do Prime Minister's Departments really Create Problems?', *Public Administration*, vol. 61, no. 1, Spring 1983, pp. 59–78

'Transition: Taking Over Power in 1983', *Australian Journal of Public Administration*, vol. 42, no. 3, September 1983, pp. 303–19

'Political Parties 1983: The battle to control the agenda', *Current Affairs Bulletin*, vol. 60, no. 7, December 1983, pp. 3–11

'Labor in 1980', in H.R. Penniman (ed.), *Australia at the Polls: The national elections of 1980 and 1983*, Washington, D.C.: George Allen & Unwin Australia for American Enterprise Institute, 1983, pp. 55–78

'The Anatomy of a Grievous Miscalculation: 3 February 1983', in H.R. Penniman (ed.), *Australia at the Polls: The national elections of 1980 and 1983*, Washington, D.C.: George Allen & Unwin Australia for American Enterprise Institute, 1983, pp. 248–80

1985

First Among Equals: Prime ministers in Westminster systems, Sydney: George Allen & Unwin, 1985, p. 228

'Strategic Leadership in Government', *Canberra Bulletin of Public Administration*, vol. 12, no. 2, Winter 1985, pp. 77–80

'The Cabinet and the Prime Minister', in A. Parkin, J. Summers & D. Woodward (eds), *Government, Politics and Power in Australia: An introductory reader*, 3rd edn, Melbourne: Longman Cheshire, 1985, pp. 28–39

'The Vulnerability of Prime Ministers in Canada and Britain', in R.G. Landes (ed.), *Canadian Politics: A comparative reader*, Scarborough, Ontario: Prentice-Hall of Canada, 1985, pp. 62–81 (revised and shortened reprint)

'Cabinet Committees in Australia and New Zealand', in T.T. Mackie & B. Hogwood (eds), *Unlocking the Cabinet: Cabinet committees in comparative perspective*, London: Sage for the European Consortium for Political Research, 1985, pp. 86–113

'Hawke Government: Collective or Responsible?', *Australian Quarterly*, vol. 57, no. 4, Summer, 1985, pp. 333–44

1987

'Assistant Ministers and Mega-departments', *Canberra Bulletin of Public Administration*, no. 52, October 1987, pp. 18–23

(with S. Fraser) 'The Younging of Australian Politics, or Politics as First Career', *Politics*, vol. 22, no. 2, November 1987, pp. 76–83

(with G. Davis) '"Negotiated Policy or Metanonsense?" A response to the prescriptions of Murray Frazer', *Australian Journal of Public Administration*, vol. 46, no. 4, December 1987, pp. 380–7

'Australia', in W. Plowden (ed.), *Advising the Rulers*, Oxford: Basil Blackwell, 1987, pp. 28–35

'Types of Advice' in W. Plowden (ed.), *Advising the Rulers*, Oxford: Basil Blackwell, 1987, pp. 149–57

'The Australian Labor Party', in G. Aplin, S.G. Foster & M. McKernon (eds), *Australians: An historical dictionary*, Sydney: Fairfax, Syme & Weldon Associates, 1987, pp. 31–2

'Prime Minister/Prime Ministerial Government', pp. 498–9; 'Cabinet/Cabinet Government', pp. 46–9, in V. Bogdanor (ed.), *The Blackwell Encyclopedia of Political Institutions*, Oxford: Basil Blackwell, 1987

1988

(with G. Davis, J. Wanna & J. Warhurst) *Public Policy in Australia*, Sydney: George Allen & Unwin, 1988, p. 229

1989

Malcolm Fraser PM: A study in prime ministerial power in Australia, Melbourne: Penguin, 1989

(edited with G. Davis & C. Lewis) *Corporate Management in Australian Government*, Sydney: Macmillan, 1989

'Politicisation and the Australian Public Service', *Australian Journal of Public Administration*, vol. 48, no. 4, December 1989, pp. 369–81

'Federalism and the Office of Prime Minister', in B. Hodgins et al. (eds), *Federalism in Canada and Australia*, Trent, Peterborough: Frost Centre for Canadian Heritage and Development, 1989, pp. 147–57

(with C. Lewis) 'Corporate Management: Background and Dilemmas', in G. Davis, P. Weller & C. Lewis (eds), *Corporate Management in Australian Government*, Sydney: Macmillan, 1989, pp. 1–16

1990

'Cabinet and the Prime Minister', in A. Parkin, J. Summers & D. Woodward (eds), *Government, Politics & Power in Australia*, 4th edn, Melbourne: Longman, 1990, pp. 28–42

'Reflections on the Cabinet Process', in B. Galligan, J.R. Nethercote & C. Walsh (eds), *The Cabinet and Budget Processes*, Canberra: Centre for Research on Federal Financial Relations, 1990, pp. 29–33

'Cabinet', in C. Jennett & R. Stewart (eds), *Consensus and Restructuring: Hawke and Australian public policy*, Sydney: Macmillan, 1990, pp. 16–26

1991

'Prime Ministers, Political Leadership and Cabinet Government', *Australian Journal of Public Administration*, vol. 50, no. 3, June 1991, pp. 137–44

'Amalgamated Departments—Integrated or Confederated—Establishing Criteria for Evaluating Machinery of Government Changes', *Canberra Bulletin of Public Administration*, vol. 65, 1991, pp. 41–7

'Political Science and Political Practice', *Australian Journal of Political Science*, vol. 26, no. 3, November 1991, pp. 395–408

'Support for Prime Ministers: A comparative perspective', in C. Campbell & M.J. Wyszomirski (eds), *Executive Leadership in Anglo-American Systems*, Pittsburg: Pittsburg University Press, pp. 365–83

'Transition to Government', in C.A. Hughes & R. Whip (eds), *Political Crossroads: The Queensland election of 1989*, St Lucia, Qld: University of Queensland Press, 1991, pp. 191–206

1992

(with J. Wanna & C. O'Faircheallaigh) *Public Sector Management in Australia*, Sydney: Macmillan, 1992

(edited) *Menzies to Keating: The development of the Australian prime ministership*, London: C. Hurst, and Melbourne: Melbourne University Press, 1992

'Prime Ministers and Cabinet', in P. Weller (ed.), *Menzies to Keating: The development of the Australian prime ministership*, London: C. Hurst, and Melbourne: Melbourne University Press, 1992, pp. 5–27

'The Development of the Australian Prime Ministership', in P. Weller (ed.), *Menzies to Keating: The development of the Australian prime ministership*, London: C. Hurst, and Melbourne: Melbourne University Press, 1992, pp. 202–11

'Financial Management Reforms in Government: A comparative perspective', *Canberra Bulletin of Public Administration*, vol. 67, no. 2, 1991, pp. 9–17

1993

(with G. Davis, J. Wanna & J. Warhurst) *Public Policy in Australia*, 2nd edn, Sydney: Allen & Unwin, 1993

(edited with J. Forster & G. Davis) *Reforming the Public Service: Lessons for recent experience*, Sydney: Macmillan, 1993

(with M. Gardner, N. Ryan & B. Stevens) 'The Role of the Public Sector: Implications for the Australian Public Service', *Canberra Bulletin of Public Administration*, vol. 72, 1993, pp. 1–23

'Party Rules and the Dismissal of Leaders: A comparative perspective', *Parliamentary Affairs*, vol. 47, no. 1, January 1994, pp. 133–43

'Reforming the Public Service: What has been achieved and how can it be evaluated', in P. Weller, J. Forster & G. Davis (eds), *Reforming the Public Service: Lessons from recent experience*, Sydney: Macmillan 1993, pp. 222–36

'Evaluating the State Governments, Reform is in the Eye of the Beholder', B. Stevens & J. Wanna (eds), *The Goss Government: Promise and performance*, Sydney: Macmillan, 1993, pp. 12–22

1994

(edited) *Royal Commissions & the Making of Public Policy*, Sydney: Macmillan, 1994

'Royal Commissions and the Governmental System in Australia', in P. Weller (ed.), *Royal Commissions and the Making of Public Policy*, Sydney: Macmillan, 1994, pp. 259–66

'The Role of the Public Sector: International Trends and Challenges', in I. Scott & I. Thynne (eds), *Public Sector Reform: Critical issues and perspectives*, Hong Kong: AJPA, 1994, pp. 31–58

1995

(with J. Wanna) 'Structuring Influence: Executive governance at the local level', in J. Caulfield & J. Wanna (eds), *Power and Politics in the City*, Sydney: Macmillan, 1995, pp. 58–71

(with E. Craswell) 'Accountability and Policy Delivery in Home and Community Care', in J. Caulfield & J. Wanna (eds), *Power and Politics in the City*, Sydney: Macmillan, 1995

1996

(edited with G. Davis) *New Ideas, Better Government*, Sydney: Allen & Unwin, 1996

'Commonwealth State Reform Processes: A policy management review', *Australian Journal of Public Administration*, vol. 31, no. 1, 1996, pp. 95–110

'The Universality of Public Sector Reform: Ideas, meanings, strategies', in G. Davis & P. Weller (eds), *New Ideas, Better Government*, Sydney: Allen & Unwin, 1996, pp. 1–10

'Explaining the Machinery of Government: A model for analysis', in J. Halligan (ed.), *Public Administration Under Scrutiny*, Canberra: University of Canberra/IPAA, 1996, pp. 165–88

(co-author) 'Democracy', in A. Milner (ed.), *Australia in Asia: Comparing cultures*, Melbourne: Oxford University Press, 1996, pp. 132–64

1997

(edited with H. Bakvis & R.A.W. Rhodes) *The Hollow Crown: Countervailing trends in core executives*, London: Macmillan, 1997

'Are Prisoners Clients?', *Australian Journal of Public Administration*, vol. 56, no. 1, 1997, pp. 125–7

(with J. Wanna) 'Departmental Secretaries: Appointment, termination and their impact', *Australian Journal of Public Administration*, vol. 56, no. 4, pp. 13–25

(with H. Bakvis) 'The Hollow Crown: Coherence and capacity in central government', in P. Weller, H. Bakvis & R.A.W. Rhodes (eds), *The Hollow Crown: Countervailing trends in core executives*, London: Macmillan, 1997, pp. 1–15

Political Parties and the Core Executive', in P. Weller, H. Bakvis & R.A.W. Rhodes (eds), *The Hollow Crown: Countervailing trends in core executives*, London: Macmillan, 1997, pp. 37–57

1998

(with B. Stevens) 'Evaluating Policy Advice: The Australian experience', *Public Administration*, vol. 76, no. 3, Autumn 1998, pp. 579–89

'Prisons, the Private Sector and the Market: Some Queensland lessons', *Australian Journal of Public Administration*, vol. 57, no. 4, 1998, pp. 111–17 (with J. Wanna) 'When Winners are Losers: The stalemate of Australian politics, *Asia-Pacific Review*, vol. 5, no. 3, Fall/Winter 1998, pp. 87–103

'Cabinet Government', entry in J.M. Shafritz (ed.), *International Encyclopaedia for Public Policy and Administration*, Boulder: Westview Press 1998, pp. 319–20

1999

Dodging Raindrops: John Button— A Labor life, Sydney: Allen & Unwin, 1999

(with C. O'Faircheallaigh & J. Wanna) *Public Sector Management in Australia*, 2nd edn, Melbourne: Macmillan, 1999

'Disentangling Ministerial Responsibility', *Australian Journal of Public Administration*, vol. 58, no. 1, 1999, pp. 62–4

(with G. Davis, E. Crasswell & S. Eggins), 'What Drives Machinery of Government Changes? Australia, Britain, Canada, 1950–98', *Public Administration*, vol. 77, Spring 1999, pp. 7–50

(with T. Wood) 'Departmental Secretaries: Profile of a changing profession', *Australian Journal of Public Administration*, vol. 58, no. 2, 1999, pp. 21–32; reprinted in *Management in Government*, vol. 32, no. 2, July–September 2000, pp. 41–59

'In Hot Pursuit of a Departmental Secretary', *Canberra Bulletin of Public Administration*, vol. 93, October 1999, pp. 4–8

2000

(edited with M. Keating & J. Wanna), *Institutions on the Edge: Capacities for governance*, Sydney: Allen & Unwin, 2000

'Australia', in G. Peters, V. Wright & R.A.W. Rhodes (eds), *Administering the Summit*, London: Macmillan, 2000, pp. 59–78

'Introduction: In search of governance', in G. Davis & M. Keating (eds), *The Future of Australian Governance: Policy options*, Sydney: Allen & Unwin, 2000, pp. 1–7

'Introduction: The institutions of governance', in M. Keating, J. Wanna & P. Weller (eds), *Institutions on the Edge: Capacity for governance*, Sydney: Allen & Unwin, 2000, pp. 1–9

(with M. Keating) 'Cabinet Government: An institution under pressure', in M. Keating, J. Wanna & P. Weller (eds), *Institutions on the Edge: Capacity for governance*, Sydney: Allen & Unwin, 2000, pp. 45–73

(with L. Young) 'Political Parties and the Party System: Challenges for effective governing', in M. Keating, J. Wanna & P. Weller (eds), *Institutions on the Edge: Capacity for governance*, Sydney: Allen & Unwin 2000, pp. 156–77

'Political Science Professor in Cabinet: Review article, of Neal Blewett, *A Cabinet Diary*', *Australian Journal of Political Science*, vol. 35, no. 1, 2000

2001

Australia's Mandarins: The frank and the fearless?, Sydney: Allen & Unwin, 2001

(with J. Scott, R. Laurie & B. Stevens) *The Engine Room of Government: The Queensland Premier's Department 1859–2001*, St Lucia, Qld: University of Queensland Press, 2001

(edited with R.A.W. Rhodes) *The Changing World of Top Officials: Mandarins or valets?*, Buckingham: Open University Press, 2001
(edited with G. Davis) *Are You Being Served? State, citizens and governance*, Sydney: Allen & Unwin, 2001
(with B. Stevens) 'Partner or Rival? Caucus and Cabinet', in S. McIntyre & J. Faulkner (eds), *True Believers: The story of the federal parliamentary Labor Party*, Sydney: Allen & Unwin, 2001, pp. 173–83
'Ministerial Codes, Cabinet Rules and the Power of Prime Ministers', in J. Fleming & I. Holland (eds), *Motivating Ministers to Morality*, Farnham, England: Ashgate, 2001, pp. 49–60
(with M. Keating) 'Rethinking Government's Roles and Operations', in G. Davis & P. Weller (eds), *Are You Being Served? State, citizens and governance*, Sydney: Allen & Unwin, 2001, pp. 73–97
'The Summit of their Discontents: Crisis or mere transition?' in G. Davis & P. Weller (eds), *Are You Being Served? State, citizens and governance*, Sydney: Allen & Unwin, 2001, pp. 196–204
(with J. Fleming) '"The Ballot is the Thing": The Labor campaign in 1901', in M. Simms, *1901: The forgotten election*, St Lucia, Qld: University of Queensland Press, 2001, pp. 117–34
(with R.A.W. Rhodes) 'Enter Centre Stage: The departmental secretaries', in R.A.W. Rhodes & P. Weller (eds), *The Changing World of Top Officials: Mandarins or valets?*, Buckingham: Open University Press, 2001, pp. 1–10
(with L. Young) 'Australia: Mandarins or lemons?', in R.A.W. Rhodes & P. Weller (eds), *The Changing World of Top Officials: Mandarins or valets?*, Buckingham: Open University Press, 2001, pp. 152–88
(with R.A.W. Rhodes) 'Antipodean Exceptionalism, European Traditionalism', in R.A.W. Rhodes & P. Weller, *The Changing World of Top Officials: Mandarins or valets?*, Buckingham: Open University Press, 2001

2002

Don't Tell the Prime Minister, Melbourne: Scribe Books, 2002
'Australia's Experience of Good Governance', *Damrong Rajanuphab Journal*, vol. 2, no. 6, 2002 (2545), pp. 67–81 (in Thai)
'Parliament and Cabinet: The institutions of governance', in E. van Acker & G. Curran (eds), *Business, Government and Globalisation*, Melbourne: Longman, 2002, pp. 1–72
'Governing Australia', in P. Duncan & R. Maddock (eds), *Aspire Australia*, Melbourne: The Business Council of Australia, 2002, pp. 79–88

2003

(guest editor with M. Bevir & R.A.W. Rhodes) *Public Administration*, special edn, 'Traditions of Governance: History and diversity', vol. 81, no. 1, 2003
(with J. Wanna) 'Traditions of Australian Governance', *Public Administration*, special edn, 'Traditions of Governance: History and diversity', vol. 81, no.1, 2003, pp. 63–94

(with M. Bevir & R.A.W. Rhodes) 'Traditions of Governance: Interpreting the changing role of the public sector', *Public Administration*, special edn, 'Traditions of Governance: History and diversity', vol. 81, no. 1, 2003, pp. 1–19

(with M. Bevir & R.A.W. Rhodes) 'Comparative Governance: Prospects and lessons', *Public Administration*, special edn, 'Traditions of Governance: History and diversity', vol. 81, no.1, 2003, pp. 191–210

'Cabinet Government: An elusive ideal?', *Public Administration*, vol. 81, no. 4, 2003, pp. 701–22; republished with 'Afterword' in R.A.W. Rhodes (ed.), *Public Administration: 25 years of analysis and debate*, Wiley-Blackwell, 2011, pp. 99–119

(with J. Fleming) 'The Commonwealth', in C. Sharman & J. Moon (eds), *Australian Government and Politics: The Commonwealth, the states and the territories*, Melbourne: Cambridge University Press, 2003, pp. 12–40

(with Xu Y.), 'International Civil Servants and Multilateral Negotiations', in R.P. Buckley (ed.), *The WTO and the Doha Round: The changing face of world trade*, London, England: Kluwer Law International, 2003, pp. 89–114

'The Australian Public Service: Still anonymous, neutral and a career service?', in K. Walsh (ed.), *Papers on Parliament: Bicameralism and accountability*, no. 40, Canberra: The Senate, December 2003, pp. 79–94

(with R.A.W. Rhodes) 'Localism and Exceptionalism: Comparing public sector reforms in European and Westminster systems', in T. Butcher & A. Massey (eds), *Modernising Civil Services*, Cheltenham, England: Edward Elgar, 2003, pp. 16–36

2004

(with Xu Y.) *The Governance of World Trade: International Civil Servants in the GATT/WTO*, Cheltenham, England: Edward Elgar, 2004

'Parliamentary Democracy in Australia', *Parliamentary Affairs*, vol. 57, no. 3, July 2004, pp. 630–45

'The Truth, not the Whole Truth and Nothing like the Truth', in Livio Dobrez (ed.), *Lying*, Melbourne: Australian Scholarly Publishing, 2004, pp. 145–53

'Parliament and Cabinet: The Centre of Government', in G. Curran & E. van Acker (ed.), *Governing Business and Globalisation*, 2nd edn, Melbourne: Pearson Education, 2004, pp. 60–71

2005

(edited with H. Patapan & J. Wanna) *Westminster Legacies: Democracy and responsible government in Asia and the Pacific*, Sydney: UNSW Press, 2005

'Investigating Power at the Centre of Government: Surveying research on the Australian executive', *Australian Journal of Public Administration*, vol. 64, no. 1, March 2005, pp. 35–42

'Parliamentary Accountability for non-Statutory Executive Power: Impossible dream or realistic aspiration?' *Public Law Review*, vol. 16, no. 4, 2005, pp. 314–24

(with R.A.W. Rhodes) 'Westminster Transplanted and Westminster Impacted: Exploring political change', in H. Patapan, J. Wanna & P. Weller (eds), *Westminster Legacies:*

Democracy and responsible government in Asia and the Pacific, Sydney: UNSW Press, 2005, pp. 1–12
(with B. Sharma) 'Transplanting Westminster to Nepal: The stuff of dreams dashed', in H. Patapan, J. Wanna & P. Weller (eds), *Westminster Legacies: Democracy and responsible government in Asia and the Pacific*, Sydney: UNSW Press, 2005, pp. 63–80
(with B. Stevens), 'On the Steps of History,' in S. Nolan (ed.), *The Dismissal: Where were you on November 11 1975?*, Melbourne: Melbourne University Press, 1975, pp. 69–75

2006

'The Australian Senate: House of review, obstruction or rubber stamp?', *Social Alternatives*, vol. 25, no. 3, 2006, pp. 13–18
'Ministers, Prime Ministers and Mandarins: Politics as a job', in T. Arklay, J. Nethercote & J. Wanna (eds), *Australian Political Lives: Chronicling political careers and administrative histories*, Canberra: ANU E-Press, 2006, pp. 55–9

2007

Cabinet Government in Australia, Sydney: UNSW Press, 2007
(with Xu Y.) 'Globalising International Organisations', in G. Curran & E. van Acker (eds) *Globalising Government Business Relations*, Sydney: Pearson, 2007, pp. 43–65
'Cabinet', pp. 80–2; 'Ministerial Responsibility', p. 342; 'Prime Ministers', pp. 460–3; 'Westminster Systems', pp. 636–7, in B. Galligan & W. Roberts (eds), *The Oxford Companion to Australian Politics*, Melbourne: Oxford University Press, 2007

2008

(with Xu Y.) '"To Be but not to Be Seen", Exploring the Impact of International Civil Servants', *Public Administration*, vol. 86, no. 1, 2008, pp. 35–51
(with R.A.W. Rhodes & J. Wanna) 'Reinventing Westminster: How public executives reframe their world', *Policy and Politics*, vol. 36, no. 4, October 2008, pp. 461–80
(with B. Sharma & B. Stevens) 'Nepal: A revolution through the ballot box', *Australian Journal of International Affairs*, vol. 62, no. 4, 2008, pp. 513–28
'The Public Service', in R. Manne (ed.), *Dear Mr Rudd: Ideas for a better Australia*, Melbourne: Black Inc, 2008, pp. 72–85

2009

(with R.A.W. Rhodes & J. Wanna), *Westminster Compared*, Oxford University Press, 2009
(with Xu Y.) *Inside the World Bank: Exploding the myth of a monolithic bank*, New York, NY: Palgrave Macmillan, 2009
(with A. Tiernan), 'Un trop fort mouvement de balancier ou l'angoisse existentielle des hauts fonctionnaires australiens (A Pendulum Too Far? Angst and Australian senior officials)', *Télescope* (Quebec), vol. 15, no. 1, Hiver 2009, pp. 35–49
(with Xu Y.) 'Chrik Poortman: A World Bank professional', *Public Administration Review*, September/October 2009, pp. 868–75; republished in N. Riccucci (ed.), *Serving the Public Interest: Profiles of successful and innovative public servants*, M.E Sharpe, 2012

(with J. Sharman) 'Where is the Quality? Political science scholarship in Australia', *Australian Journal of Political Science*, vol. 44, no. 4, December 2009, pp. 597–612

(with Xu Y.), 'The World Bank: An institution with many faces', *Social Alternatives*, vol. 28, no. 2, pp. 18–22

'Cabinet Government: Australian style', in J. Wanna (ed.), *Critical Reflections in Australian Public Policy*, Canberra: ANU E-Press, 2009, pp. 73–83

'Universities and the Study of Politics', in R.A.W. Rhodes (ed.), *A History of the Study of Australian Politics in the Twentieth Century*, Houndmills, England: Palgrave Macmillan, 2009, pp. 19–32

2010

(with A. Tiernan) *Learning to Be a Minister: Heroic expectations, practical realities*, Melbourne: Melbourne University Press, 2010

(with Xu Y.) 'Agents of Influence: Country directors in the World Bank', *Public Administration*, vol. 88, no. 1, 2010, pp. 211–31

(with Xu Y.) 'Why International Organisations Matter', in G. Curran & E. van Acker (eds), *Business and the Politics of Globalisation: After the Global Financial Crisis*, Sydney: Pearson, 2010, pp. 22–42

2011

(guest editor), *Public Administration*, vol. 89, no. 1, special edn, 'From Local Government to Narratives: Essays in honour of R.A.W. Rhodes'

(with J. Scott & B. Stevens) *From Postbox to Powerhouse: A centenary history of the Department of the Prime Minister and Cabinet, 1911–2010*, Sydney: Allen & Unwin, 2011

(with J. Wanna) 'The Irrepressible Rod Rhodes: Contesting traditions, blurring genres', *Public Administration*, vol. 89, no. 1, 2011, pp. 1–14

(with P. Hamburger & B. Stevens) 'A Capacity for Central Coordination: The case of the Department of the Prime Minister and Cabinet', *Australian Journal of Public Administration*, vol. 70, no. 4, December 2011, pp. 377–90

2012

'Fight, Flee or Fulminate: Prime ministerial challengers, strategic choices and the rites of succession', *Political Quarterly*, vol. 83, no. 1, March 2012, pp. 152–62

(with P. Hamburger) 'Policy Advice and a Central Agency: The Department of the Prime Minister and Cabinet', *Australian Journal of Political Science*, vol. 47, no. 3, September 2012, pp. 363–76

(with P. Cowan) 'Political Science in Australia 2011: Grants and staffing', *Australian Journal of Political Science*, vol. 47, no. 2, June 2012, pp. 285–93

2013

'The Variability of Prime Ministers', in P. 't Hart & R.A.W. Rhodes (eds), *The Handbook of Political Leadership*, Oxford: Oxford University Press, 2013 (with J. Sharman), 'International Relations Research Performance among Australian Universities', *Australian Journal of International Affairs*, vol. 67, no. 1, 2013, pp. 111–17

REPORTS AND SUBMISSIONS TO GOVERNMENT OR OTHER BODIES

(with G.J. Terry), 'Treasury Control of Federal Government Expenditure in Australia', *Royal Commission on Australian Government Administration*, Appendix Volume 4, AGPS, 1976, pp. 136–52

(with G. Davis) 'Strategic Management in the Public Sector: The Coastal Zone Inquiry', report for the Resource Assessment Commission, 1993

(with J. Forster & J. Wanna), 'Efficiency Dividend Arrangements', discussion paper prepared for the House of Representatives committee on banking, finance and public administration, 1993

(with D. Ink, J. Heath & B. Boorwathana) 'Administrative Reform in Jilin Province', report of UN Experts Group to the Ministry of Personnel, People's Republic of China, April 1994

'Politicisation and the Nepalese Civil Service', report to the International Institute for Democracy and Electoral Assistance, Stockholm, February 1997

'Policy and Governance', paper for the Humanities and Social Sciences Summit, National Museum of Australia, 26 and 27 July 2001, Position Papers

(with A. Tiernan) 'Ministerial Staff: A need for accountability and transparency?', submission to the Senate Committee on Finance and Government Operations, May 2003, <www.aph.gov.au/binaries/senate/committee/fapa_ctte/completed_inquiries/2002-04/mops/submissions/sub04.doc>, accessed December 2013

(with S. Webbe) *A Public Interest Map: An independent review of Queensland Government Boards, Committees and Statutory Authorities, Part A Report*, Brisbane, 2008

(with S. Webbe) *Brokering Balance: A Public Interest Map for Queensland Government Bodies: Part B Report, An Independent Review of Queensland Government Boards, Committees and Statutory Authorities*, Brisbane: March 2009

(Member of Advisory Group), *Ahead of the Game: Blueprint for the reform of the Australian Government Administration*, Advisory Group on Reform of Australian Government Administration, March 2010

(with A. Tiernan & J. Menzies)' Memorandum to House of Lords Select Committee on the Constitution', reproduced in *The Cabinet Office and the Centre of Government: Report with evidence*, HL paper 30, January 2010, pp. 182–4

COMPETITIVE RESEARCH GRANTS

2013–15 A.R.C. Discovery, Prime Ministers: Explaining why some succeed and others fail, $269,392

2011–13 A.R.C. Discovery (with Xu Y.), Decision Making in International Organisations, $328,000

2009–10 A.R.C. Linkage (with J. Scott & B. Stevens), From Post Box to Policy Powerhouse: The centenary of the Department of the Prime Minister and Cabinet, $93,000

2007–10 A.R.C. Discovery (with J. Wanna & A. Tiernan), Mapping the Federal Government's Advisory Capacity

2005–07 A.R.C. Discovery (with Xu Y.), International Civil Servants and the World Bank, $165,000

2002–04 A.R.C. Discovery Grant (with J. Wanna, R.A.W. Rhodes & H. Patapan), Westminster Transplanted, Westminster Implanted, $138,000

2001–03 A.R.C. Large Grant, Cabinet Government in Australia 1901–2000, $105,000

1998–01 A.R.C. Large Grant (with M. Keating, G. Davis & J. Wanna), The Future of Australian Governance

1997–99 A.R.C. Large Grant, Departmental Secretaries: Influence and impact in Westminster systems, $141,000

1995–97 A.R.C. Large Grant, John Button and the Australian Labor Party, $105,000

1992–94 A.R.C. Large Grant (with G. Davis), Organising and Evaluating the Machinery of Government in Federations: Developing and testing criteria for assessing performance, $105,000

1990–92 A.R.C. Large Grant (with B. Head, Ci. O'Faircheallaigh, G. Davis & J. Wanna), Power and Policy in Brisbane, $91,000

1986–87 A.R.G.S. Grant, Malcolm Fraser: The portrait of a Prime Minister, $36,000

INDEX

Abbott, Tony 44, 46, 234
Academy of Social Sciences Fellowship 23
Adams, David 252
administration *see also* mandarins; public service
    bureaucratic leadership 206–7
    democratic participation 205–6
    historical evolution and theory 214–16
    leadership *see* leadership
    modern bureaucratic form 213
    politics-administration relationship 18–19, 211–12, 214
    'rational' 214
    reforms 218
    United States 216–17
Administrative Appeals Tribunal 84
administrative history 146, 147–52
    administrative biographies 150
    approaches 158
    coverage 147, 159
    defining 147–8
    future of 157–9
    historical administrative cases 149–50, 153
    institutional histories 149, 152–3, 155–6
    key scholars and works 151–2
    'modernist empiricist' approach 148
    'new institutionalism' 152–3
    Weller's contribution 146–7, 152–9
    writers 150–1
administrative review 83
Aitkin, Don 16
Aitkin, Jonathan 14
Akerloff, George 167
Albury Grammar 15
Ali, Tariq 14
Allen, Sir Douglas 75
Allison, Graeme 19
Andeweg, Rudy 4
Arbib, Mark 39
Are Organizations Immortal? 106
Armstrong, Sir William 75
asylum-seeker policy 48
Australia and majority government 233–5

Australian Dictionary of Biography 15
Australian Journal of Political Science 23, 258
Australian Journal of Public Administration 147, 148
Australian Labor Party (ALP) 17, 38, 233, 249
  culture 34
  leaders, choosing 49
  public trust 46
  rule changes 48–9
  scandals 46
Australian National University (ANU) 4, 16, 17, 252
  Department of Political Science 19
  Research School of Social Science (RSSS) 4, 16, 17–19
Australian Political Studies Association (APSA) 23
Australian Research Council (ARC) 23–4, 25
Australian Wheat Board (AWB) bribery scandal 37–8, 85
Australia's Mandarins 77, 88, 90, 157
Ayers, Tony 136

Bakvis, Herman 88
Baldwin, Stanley 61–2
Barnard, Lance 50
Barnett, Michael 168–9, 172, 189
Barratt, Paul 137
Beale, Roger 91
Beazley, Kim 37–8, 43
Beijing Consensus 241
Bennister, Mark 55, 67
Berlin, Isaiah 14
biography
  administrative *see* administrative history
  appraisal of Weller 137–41
  collective 134–7, 138
  contemporary trends 123–4
  continuity theorists 139–40
  court politics 139–40
  historical institutionalism and life history 124–6, 138
  'institutional stretch' thesis 139

institutional studies 131–4
international civil servants 170
linear view 138
normative theory 138, 139, 255
political, approach behind 124–6, 137–8
qualitative data 138
single actor studies 127
theory versus description 139
Weller's approach 123–4, 125–6, 128–40
Blair, Tony 49–50, 55, 69
Blanchett, Cate 39
Bland, Henry 80
Bolt, Robert
  A Man for all Seasons 255
Bowen, Chris 43
Bradbury, Jonathan 58
Brereton, Laurie 37
Brisbane 5, 22, 156, 248
British Establishment viii–xiv
British government
  ethnographic research 63–4, 174
  mandarins 75
Brown, Alan 80
Brown, Gordon 49–50, 69
Buller, James 58, 59
Bulpitt, James 57–9, 67
Bunting, John 80, 133, 134, 152, 157
Bureaucracy in a Democratic State 209
bureaucratic versus democratic authority 209–13
Bureaumetrics 104–5
Bush, President George W. 207
Butler, David vii, 17
Button, James 40, 82
Button, John 39, 126, 129–31, 154, 206

Cabinet Government in Australia 78
cabinet government 21, 22, 33, 78, 126, 129, 132, 139, 230, 237
cabinet structures 99
Caiden, Gerald 147, 151–2
Cameron, David 231–2
Can Ministers Cope? 19
Canada and majority government 236

INDEX

Canadian Centre for Management Development 102
Canadian Public Administration 99
Canberra 16–17
Canterbury Cathedral 12–13
carbon tax 43–4
Caro, Robert 20, 127, 249–50
Carr, Bob 47–8
Carr, E.H.
    What is History? 14
Carr, Kim 45
Caucus Minutes 17
Centre for Australian Public Sector Management (CAPSM) 22, 100
children overboard scandal 21, 79, 138, 206
China 241
Claude, Inis 166
Clegg, Nick 231–2
climate change 38, 41–2, 43–4
Codd, Mike 134, 136
Cold War 166, 241, 243
Collingwood, R.G. 26
Commonwealth Department of the Prime Minister and Cabinet 21, 76, 86, 89, 132–3, 155–7, 258
Commonwealth of Nations 229
Commonwealth Ombudsman 84
Comparing Westminster 228
constructivism 26, 59, 158, 167, 168–9, 175, 178, 183
Coombs, Herbert Cole 'Nugget' 80, 152, 249
Coombs Royal Commission 19, 155, 249, 257
core executive 54–5, 56
corporatisation 88
corrective services 23, 257
Costello, Peter 50, 255
court politics 65–7, 139–40
    advantages of approach 67–9
    convergence 65–9
    statecraft thesis 57–9
Cowling, Maurice 59, 60, 62, 67
Cox, Robert 166
Craik, Jenny 3–4
Crawford, John 80

Crean, Simon 37
Crikey 77
Crossman, Richard 19
Cutt, James 18

Davis, Glyn 4, 22, 145
democratic versus bureaucratic authority 209–13
Dodging Raindrops 129–31
Don't Tell the Prime Minister 21, 79, 138, 206
Dunkel, Arthur 171–2
Dunleavy, Pat 4
Dunstan, Don 84

Economic and Social Research Council (ERSC) 4
economics 166, 167
Edwards, Peter 152
Eisenhower, Dwight 127
emissions trading scheme (ETS) 38, 41, 57
The Engine Room of Government 156
ethnography, interpretative 62–5, 138, 174
    observation 64–5, 68
    storytelling 64–5
European Union (EU) 230–1, 232
Evans, Chris 45–6
Evans, Mark 35
Excellence in Research for Australia (ERA) 23–4
executive studies 4, 17–18, 19–22
    administrative power 18
    approaches 54–65
    British 54
    cabinet government 21
    convergence of approaches 65–7
    core 54–5, 56
    court politics 65–7
    departmental secretaries 21, 133–4
    developments 54–65
    interpretative ethnography 62–5, 138
    ministers 21
    New Political History 60–2
    positional power 54

prime ministers 20–1, 25, 33–52,
    55–7
  statecraft 57–9

Farage, Nigel 232
federal elections
  1974 18
  2007 37, 38
  2010 34, 43, 44, 45
  2013 41, 48, 44, 45–6, 47–8, 51
Federal Management Agency 207
Feeney, David 39
Finnemore, Martha 168–9, 172, 189
First Among Equals 20, 34–5, 144
Fitzgibbon, Joel 45
Foley, Michael 139
Food and Agriculture Organization 24,
  176, 191
Forde, Leneen 27
Fraser, Malcolm 18, 36, 139, 155, 253
  Weller's biography 20–1, 126,
    127–9, 146, 154, 206, 250
free press 240
Freedom of Information Act 83–4
From Postbox to Powerhouse 156, 157

'garbage-can' model of decision-making
  111–12, 178
Geertz, Clifford 63, 174
gender and politics 46
General agreement on Tariffs and Trade
  (GATT) 171–2, 183–4
  Uruguay round 171, 183
Gillard, Julia 34, 36, 37, 38, 39–40, 41,
  42, 43, 57, 69, 233
  achievements of government 44–5
  critique 44–6
  destabilisation campaign against
    44–5
  leadership challenges to 45
  negotiation skills 44
  relationship with Rudd 50–1
  successful challenge to leadership
    47
  2010 election 43
  vulnerability 43–4, 46
Global Financial Crisis (GFC) 37, 45

Global Policy 177
globalisation 241–5
Gorton, John 34, 133–4
Goss, Wayne 37
Grattan, Michelle 19, 135
Greens 43–4
Greenstein, Fred 127
Griffith University 5, 23–4, 27
  School of Politics and Public Policy
    22, 145, 205

Haas, Ernst 166
Hamburger, Peter 156
Harper, Stephen 236
Harris, Lachlan 48
Hawke, Allan 83
Hawke, Bob 34, 50, 100, 134
Hawker, Bruce 39, 51
Hawker, Geoff 18, 19
  Who's Master, Who's Servant? 153
Heath, Edward 75
Heclo, Hugh 19, 145, 183–4, 249, 253,
  259
Heffernan, Richard 55, 59
Hennessy, Peter 4, 75, 139, 145, 258
Herbert, Robert 156
Hewitt, Lenox 133–4, 157
high politics 54, 57–8, 60–1, 66, 166
historical perspective on politics 247–8
Hobart 15
Hockey, Joe 38
Hogg, Douglas 14
Hollingsworth, Peter 85
hollowed-out government 110
Holt, Harold 36
Howard, John 36, 38, 50, 55, 85, 86,
  134
Hughes, Billy 124, 132, 139

Independent 76
information asymmetry 167, 171
institutional histories 21, 177–8
International Atomic Energy Agency
  193–4
international civil servants 169–75
  action, in 191–7
  authority, types of 189

INDEX

balance of interests 190–1
competence 195
decision-making processes 191–2
delegation 186–7
future study 197–9
GATT 183–4
influence 188–9
international organisations (IOs) and 182–4
missions of organisations 193–4
organisational culture 196–7
organisational entrepreneurs 184–91
principal-agent analysis 185–8
relationships 192
structural influence 192–3
theories 182–3
topic of research 180–2
treaties 184
Weller's approach 184–5
International Monetary Fund (IMF) 24, 176, 188, 191
international organisations (IOs) 24, 165–78, 261
    bureaucracies, as 168, 172, 183
    'bureaucratic dysfunctions' 189
    constructivist approach 167, 168–9, 175
    decision-making 176, 178
    individual leadership 171
    institutionalist scholarship 177–8
    international civil servants 169–75, 180–99 *see also* international civil servants
    international public policy 176–8
    international relations studies 166–9
    interpretative ethnography 174
    interview evidence 173–5, 184
    microeconomics 166–7
    missions 193–5
    organisational competence 195
    organisational culture 196–7
    principal-agent framework 167–8, 169, 171, 172, 175, 185–8
    rational-choice scholarship 167, 178, 190
    regime theory 182

    security-oriented 171, 193–4
    sociology influence 168
    structure 192–3
    technical 194
    theories 182–4
    understanding 184–91
    Weller/Xu scholarship 169–76
International Organization 178
interpretative ethnography 62–5, 174
    observation 64–5, 68
    storytelling 64–5

Jackson, President Andrew 214
Jackson, Professor Keith 145
Jacobson, Harold 166
James, Toby 58
Job Network 88
Johnson, Lyndon 20, 127, 249–50
Jones, George 139

Kane, Dr Kay 5
Kane, John 5–6
Karl, Barry 217
Katrina disaster 207
Keating, Michael 88, 134, 136
Keating, Paul 34, 50, 134
Kelly, Sean 41
Kennedy, President John 14
Kent, Jacqueline 39, 46
Key, John 235
Kindleberger, Charles 167
King, Professor Anthony 3
King Richard III 12, 248, 254–5
King's School, Canterbury 12–13
kitchen cabinet 37
Krasner, Stephen 256
Kyoto protocol 39

La Trobe University 16
Labor History 16
Latham, Mark 37
Laurie, Ross 156
leadership 205–7
    authority 209–13
    bureaucratic 206–7
    challenges 207–9
    'change-agent' style 207

'continental' form of administration 213
democratic 207–9, 216–20
democratic leaders and bureaucracy, balance 220–2
effective 220
legitimacy 207–8
politics-administration distinction 213–15
leaks 43, 240
Learning to Be a Minister 108
Lindsay, Norman 248
Lindsay, Philip
King Richard III 12, 248
Little, Graham 139
Lloyd, Beverley 17
Loveday, Peter 16, 17, 2498–9
low politics 60, 166
Lowe, Rodney 257
Lowi, Theodore 217

McAllister, Ian 135
McClelland, Robert 45
machinery of government
Australia's states 105–6
comparative analysis 102–3, 227
composition of ministerial portfolios 109–10
costs of change 108
department and agency creation 106
drivers for change 108
game theory models 107
gaps in research 109–13
government, evolution of 110–11
historical context of Weller 103, 109
horizontal governance 110
literature analysis 103–9
managerialist reforms 100–2
1987 restructuring 100–2
organisation theory 106–7
patterns, interpretation of 103
portfolio growth 105–6
prime ministers and 99–100, 111–12
principal-agent theory 107
public service reforms 100–2, 218–19

restructuring and reform, distinction 112–13
study methods and focus 98
Weller's contributions 99–103, 113–14
Weller's perspective 103–9
Weller's research 97–9
McLaren, Robert 184
McMahon, Billy 125
Macquarie University 19
Major, John 258
majority government 34, 43, 231–6
Australia 233–5
Canada 236
New Zealand 235
United Kingdom 231–3
Making and Breaking Whitehall Departments: A guide to machinery of government changes 108
Malcolm Fraser PM 20–1, 126, 127–9, 146, 154
Malcolm X 14
'managerial politicisation' 86
mandarins 75
administrative leadership 206
advisers to government 82–6
Australia's modern 80–92
collegiality 90–2
decline in power 81, 83
definition 77
facilitator role 89–90
implementation of policy 86, 87–9
independence of advice 82–3
managerial reform 87
media scrutiny 81, 83
neutrality 82–3, 86
political advisers and 84–5
politicisation of 86
studies of 136
term, usage of 76
Weller's assessment of role 88–9
Manipulating the Machine 105
Mantel, Hilary
Wolf Hall 255
March, James 177–8, 190, 192
marketisation 219

INDEX

Markham, Clements
    Richard III: His Life and Character 12
Marsh, David 4
Martin, Allan 16, 248–9
Martin, Lisa 188
media cycle 36, 38, 85, 240
Meier, Kenneth 209
Melham, Daryl 38
Menzies, Robert 36, 133
meritocracy xii–xv
Michels, Robert 170
mining tax 44
ministerial shuffles 45–6, 107
modernist empiricism 25, 58–9, 98, 148
Moore-Wilton, Max 134
Moran, Terry 134
Moriarty, Abram 156
Muldoon Robert 252–3
Murdoch press 46

Nairn, Bede 249
Namier, Lewis 135
Nelson, Brendan 36
neo-liberalism 91, 128, 130, 172
Nethercote, John 81
Neustadt, Richard 19
    Presidential Power 250–1
'new institutionalism' 58, 59, 125, 152–3, 183
New Political History 60–2
New Public Management (NPM) 87, 110
New Zealand and majority government 235
normative theory 139, 189, 255
North American Free Trade Agreement (NAFTA) 231
North, Douglass 177–8, 192, 261
Northcote-Trevelyan Report 214, 215
Norton, Philip 4
not-for-profit organisations 88

Oakeshott, Michael 26, 252
O'Faircheallaigh, Ciaran 22
Officer of the Order of Australia 23
Olsen, Johan 177–8, 190, 192
Olson, Mancur 167

opinion polls 35, 41, 44, 46–8
organisation theory 106–7, 190, 205–6
organisational culture 190, 196–7
O'Toole, Laurence 209
Overeem, Patrick 215
Oxford Union 14
Oxford University
    Exeter College 13–14, 248
    historical studies 13–14, 25
Oxford University Fellowship of the White Boar 248

pairing 49–51 *see also* parties and leaders, relationship
Papers and Proceedings of the Tasmanian Historical Research Association 16
Parker, Professor Robert 17, 151
Parliament Factions and Parties 248–9
parliamentary scrutiny 81, 83–4
parties and leaders, relationship 35–6, 42, 49–52
Peacock, Andrew 36
Peters, B. Guy 4, 211
Pimlott, Ben 125
Podger, Andrew 82
policy-termination literature 106
political advisers 84–5
political capital 36
political dynamics 107
political science studies
    biography 61, 68 *see also* biography
    convergence 60
    economics, influence of 166, 167
    history, uses of 62, 254–5
    impact 256–8
    interpretative study of high politics 61
    national politics as core 260
    natural science, as 254
    task of 253
    Treasury 18, 155, 249
    usefulness 256–8
politics
    definitions 251–3
    partisan 220–1
    policy 220–1
    understanding 251–6

Politics (Australian Journal of Political Science) 23
The Politics of the Budgetary Process 104
Poortman, Chrik 170, 174–5
power
    biographical studies 127, 129, 132, 154, 250
    executive studies theory 54, 55–7
    resource dependence 54–5
prime ministers 20–1, 25, 33–52, 250, 255
    balance of pressures 111–12
    incumbency and vulnerability 33–52
    limits of power 33
    machinery of government 97–114
        see also machinery of government
    normative readings 255
    pairing 49–51
    pragmatism 255–6
    predominance approach 55–7
The Private Government of Public Money 183–4, 249
privatisation 88, 108
prosopography 134–7, 138
Public Administration 22, 170
public interest disclosure 84
public management approach 88
public policy
    administration *see* administration
    international 176–8
Public Policy in Australia 22, 259–60
Public Sector Management in Australia 22
public service
    challenges facing 79–80
    confidentiality 83–4
    control of 100
    leadership *see* leadership
    mandarins 75–92
    neutrality 82–3, 221
    'new public management' 100–2, 218–19
    outsourcing 88
    politicisation 206
    prime ministers and 100
Public Service Board 19
Pusey, Michael
    Economic Rationalism in Canberra 90

Queensland Corrective Services Commission 23, 257
Queensland's Department of Premier and Cabinet 21, 156–7, 257
Questions of Procedure for Ministers 258

Randall, Richard 80
Rawnsley, Andrew 68
Realpolitik 18, 20, 25, 53, 58, 60, 68–9, 140, 153
Reforming the Public Service: Lessons from recent experience 100
regime theory 182
Reid, Gordon 18
Rein, Thérèse 5
resources and power 55
Rhodes, R.A.W. (Rod) 3–4, 21, 22, 63, 138, 144, 145, 174
Richardson, Graham 90
Rimmer, Professor Gordon 15–16, 249
Riverina College of Advanced Education, Wagga Wagga 17
Rose, Michael 16
Rowse, Tim 152
Roxon, Nicola 35, 42, 45–6
Royal Commission into Australian Government Administration (Coombs Royal Commission) 19, 155, 249, 257
Rudd, Kevin 5, 34, 36, 37, 55, 57, 69, 134, 233–4, 255
    analysis of prime ministership 39
    challenges from 40–1, 44–5
    critiques 35, 37–8, 39–42
    decision-making 38, 40–1
    destabilisation campaign against Gillard 44
    emotional intelligence 39
    factional base 38, 39
    relationship with Gillard 50–1
    2007 election 38
    2013 election 41, 48, 51
    Weller's political biography of 5, 24–5, 126

Sayre, Wallace 215
Scott, Joanne 156

security issues 243–5
Seldon, Anthony 68
Selznick, Philip 205–6
    Leadership in Administration 206
Senate Estimate Committees 83
Sheddon, Frederick 80
Shergold, Peter 134
Shorten, Bill 49
Simeon, Richard 259
Sir Roland Wilson Oration 80
Skidelsky, Robert 125
Slipper, Peter 46
Smith, R.F.I. (Bob) 18, 19
Smith, Rick 91
social networking 240
sovereignty 180–1
Spann, R.N. 'Dick' 149
spin doctors 254–5
Stapledon Exhibition 13
statecraft 57–9
Stevens, Bronwyn 17, 156
Stone, Randall 188
Strachey, Lytton 127–8
Strangio, Paul 139
Strategic Priorities and Budget Committee 37
Svara, James 215
Swan, Wayne 37, 44

Tange, Arthur 80, 152
Tanner, Lindsay 37
Terry, Larry 206–7
Thatcher, Margaret 104, 212, 257
Thomson, Craig 46
Tiernan, Anne 135
trade-related intellectual property rights (TRIPS) 183
transnationalism 242
Treasury 18, 155, 249
Treasury Control in Australia 155
Turnbull, Malcolm 36, 41

United Kingdom and majority government 231–3
United Kingdom Independence Party (UKIP) 232–3
University of Essex 3

University of New South Wales (UNSW) 4
    Centre for Social Impact 77
University of Sydney 16
University of Tasmania 15, 249
University of York 3, 144, 145
    Machinery of Government Project 104

Walsh, Kerry-Anne
    The Stalking of Julia Gillard 40
Walter, James 49–50, 139
Wanna, John 3–4, 22
Watson, Chris 37
Weaver, Catherine
    Hypocrisy Trap 190
Weber, Max 168, 170, 189, 192
Weller, Irene 12
Weller, Pat (Patrick Moray) 76–9
    analysis of public sector management 77–8
    bibliography 264–78
    biographer, as 123–41 *see also* biography
    books influencing 248–51
    'The Craft of Governing' workshop 5
    early days 11–17
    executive studies 19–22, 144–5
    first solo research 16
    history, interest in 12–14, 25, 248–9
    institution building 22–4
    international organisations studies *see* international organisations
    machinery of government research *see* machinery of government
    major areas of research 5
    PhD 16, 249
    political interests 13–14, 16, 247–62
    politics, understanding 251–6
    starting out 17–19
    teaching 15
    themes in studies 25–7, 97, 206, 259–61
Weller, Robin 12
Weller, Stanley (Sam) 12
Westerman, Alan 80

Westminster systems 21, 33, 64, 85, 216, 256
  administration and 216
  cabinet government 237
  centralised government 236
  challenges from within 230–9
  challenges from without 239–45
  collapse of Empire, effect 229–30
  collective and individual responsibility 237–8
  comparative analysis 227–45
  electoral systems 238–9
  establishment of 228–9
  fixed election dates 238–9
  globalisation 241–5
  independent sovereign countries and 230–1
  machinery of government see machinery of government
  majority government 231–6
  mass communications challenge 240
  new world order 241
  party system 238–9
  practice outside UK 229
  security issues 243–5
  technological development 242
  veto actors 230, 234, 239
  waning of 229–30
Westphalian system 180–1
Wettenhall, Roger 151

Wheare, Sir Kenneth 13
Wheeler, Sir Frederick 18, 80
'Whitehall Project' 145–6
Whitlam, Gough 17, 50, 84
Whitlam government 20, 249
Wildavsky, Aaron 19, 104, 145, 152, 183–4, 249, 259
Williamson, Philip 61–2
Wilson, Sir Roland 80, 136
Wilson, Woodrow 213, 214, 216
Wolfowitz, Paul 174–5
World Bank 24, 165, 172–6, 184, 190, 191
  directors 175, 193
World Health Organization 24, 176, 191
  decentralisation 193
World Intellectual Property Organization (WIPO) 24, 167, 176, 191
World Trade Organization (WTO) 24, 165, 169–72, 187, 199
  bureaucrats in 170–1
World War II 12, 15
Wright, George 48

Xu, Yi-chong 24, 165–6, 169–76, 261

Yeend, Sir Geoffrey 18
Yes, Minister 185